BK   760.092   P692H
HOWARD PYLE : WRITER, ILLUSTRATOR, FOUNDER OF THE
        BRANDYWINE SCHOOL   /PITZ, HENR
1   1965   25.00   FV

3000 493107 30016
St. Louis Community College

P9-AOW-551

Howard Pyle

Howard Pyle

WRITER,
ILLUSTRATOR,
FOUNDER
OF THE
BRANDYWINE SCHOOL

BY HENRY C. PITZ

Bramhall House • New York

T O
MOLLY
who has been behind the scenes in so many books

The Wyeths: The Intimate Correspondence of N. C. Wyeth, pp. 152, 153, 156, 163, and 172, copyright 1971 and 1973 by Betsy James Wyeth.

Copyright © MCMLXV by Henry C. Pitz. All rights reserved. This edition is published by Bramhall House, a divsion of Clarkson N. Potter, Inc., distributed by Crown Publishers, Inc.

a b c d e f g h

Library of Congress Cataloging in Publication Data

Pitz, Henry Clarence, 1895–
    Howard Pyle—writer, illustrator, founder of the Brandywine school.

  Bibliography: p.
  1. Pyle, Howard, 1853–1911. I. Title.
ND237.P94P57   760'.092'4   74–77563

Contents

Foreword

Writing a book is a fairly reliable way of acquiring a long trail of obligations. The real sources of a book can stretch back through a lifetime. The first source for this book certainly reaches back to when I was about ten years old and my parents gave me copies of Howard Pyle's *The Merry Adventures of Robin Hood* and *Otto of the Silver Hand*. *The Story of King Arthur and His Knights* followed shortly after, and presently I was a Pyle addict, tracking down his titles in the local public libraries. I began to know Howard Pyle by word and picture.

Then there was a lapse as I became interested in other things. However, in my later teens I found myself enrolled in an art school in the classes of Thornton Oakley, a former Pyle student. Howard Pyle entered into his every criticism. In addition, thanks to the indulgent way art schools were run in those days, I often visited my friends at the Pennsylvania Academy of the Fine Arts and sat beside them as we listened to the weekly criticism of George Harding, another Pyle student. About two years later, beginning my career as a professional illustrator, I enrolled in the night class of Walter Everett, a third Pyle student. It was only a year or two after this, when I was a busy practicing illustrator, that I became acquainted with Harvey Dunn and laughingly told him of my record with Pyle-trained instructors. He invited me to drop into his Grand Central Art School class any time I was so inclined. This I did twice. One thing I learned from these four experiences—Pyle's students' versions of picturemaking were far from identical.

During my student days at what was then the Pennsylvania Museum School of Industrial Art, I became acquainted with the artists of the Wilmington enclave, almost all of whom were former Pyle students. And then, as I joined the professional ranks I came to know the numerous group of Philadelphia artists with the same background. I discovered that the so-called Pyle group certainly had close ties with one another and many common interests but it was composed of some greatly varied personalities. Acceptance as a friend by one of the group opened the way to acquaintance with all or almost all.

Then during the years I was working largely for the New York publishers, it was inevitable that I should cross the path of many more of the Pyle illustrators. So, just in the course of pursuing an art education and its subsequent profession, I listened to many scores of anecdotes, reminiscences, and comments illuminating one central figure. It would never have occurred to me to make notes of all these interesting conversations. It would never have occurred to me that someday I might write a book about Howard Pyle.

Almost all of those illustrators, painters, editors, friends, and others who knew that amazingly gifted man are gone. They filled my mind with a wealth of material, some of it remembered. I can only list their names: George Harding, Thornton Oakley, Walter Everett, Harvey Dunn, N. C. Wyeth, Frank Schoonover, Stanley M. Arthurs, Herbert Moore, Violet Oakley, Jessie Wilcox Smith, Margaretta Hinchman, Elizabeth Shippen Green, Henry J. Soulen, Emlen McConnell, Edward Wilson, Blossom Farley, Joseph Chapin, Thomas Wells, Wuanita Smith, Katherine Wireman, Clyde DeLand, Olive Rush, Harry E. Townsend, Sarah Stillwell Weber, Anna Whelan Betts, Ethel Franklin Betts Bains, Gayle Hoskins, Remington Schuyler, William Aylward, W. H. Koerner, Arthur Becher, Gertrude Brincklé, Elenore Plaisted Abbott, Percy V. E. Ivory.

I would particularly like to mention Gertrude Brincklé, the family friend and Mr. Pyle's secretary for so many years, N. C. Wyeth, Frank Schoonover, Stanley Arthurs, and George Harding. I learned so much from them.

Central to all research upon Howard Pyle is the Delaware Museum of Art, with its incomparable collection of his work, documents, memorabilia, and its informed staff. The recent far-reaching Howard Pyle exhibition in its galleries, organized by its acting director Rowland Elzea, was the most comprehensive ever assembled. Mr. Elzea has given untiring help, particularly in the assembling of pictorial material. I have had help from Mrs. Elizabeth Hawks and all of the staff.

Mr. Howard Brokaw, a grandson of Howard Pyle, has allowed me free use of his collection, not only the illustrations and drawings but the letters, clippings, and other documentation relating to his grandfather.

Mrs. Willard Crichton, a daughter of Howard Pyle, has opened her memories to me and patiently answered my questions. Miss Constance Moore, a friend of the family and a director of the Wilmington Society of the Fine Arts for many years, and Miss Blanche Swain, also a family friend, have given me much information of the Pyle family life and their circle of friends.

Portions of the letters of N. C. Wyeth are selected from *The Wyeths: The Intimate Correspondence of N. C. Wyeth*, edited by Betsy James Wyeth and published by Gambit, Incorporated, Boston. They appear here by permission of Mrs. Wyeth and the publishers.

Kind permission to reproduce from original illustrations and drawings has been granted by the Delaware Museum of Art; The Boston Public Library; The Alumni Memorial Hall collection of the University of Michigan's Museum of Art; by Mr. Howell Heaney of the Rare Book Department of the Free Library of Philadelphia; The Brown County Library, Green Bay, Wisconsin; The Laurel Public Library, Laurel, Delaware; The Minnesota Historical Society, St. Paul, Minnesota, for *The Battle of Nashville* mural in the Minnesota State Capitol; Mr. Seymour Adelman; Mr. Howard Brokaw; Mr. Andrew Wyeth; Dr. Howard McCracken; Mr. Douglas Allen; Mr. Sewell Biggs; Mr. Robert Dodge, and Mrs. Philip D. Laird.

Harper and Row, Publishers, have been generous with help and permissions, and Mr. Frederic Ray, art editor of *American History Illustrated*, has given kind assistance. In addition have been the many kind letters and verbal messages from many admirers of Howard Pyle's works.

Chestnut Hill, Philadelphia

Howard Pyle

Chapter 1

BEGINNINGS

Howard Pyle was born on March 5, 1853, into a long Quaker heritage. That heritage was one of the most important factors in his life. The region where he was born—Wilmington, Delaware, and the Brandywine Valley behind it—was the country of his ancestors. His forebears had been in that region since the days of the early settlers: Quakers from England who had sought out the fertile farmlands of southeastern Pennsylvania and the northern rim of Delaware. His parents, William Pyle and Margaret Churchman Painter, sprang from prolific families that had generated a spreading network of grandparents, aunts, uncles, and cousins of all degrees. Howard Pyle was born with roots and attachments to his native region that formed the backbone of his life.

The home of his childhood was on the old Kennett Pike (now Pennsylvania Avenue) leading into Wilmington. It stood on ample grounds with fields surrounding it, several miles from the center of the growing city. There was a grassy bank and a wide lawn out to a grove of trees that partly screened the house from the carriages and heavy farm wagons that moved on the turnpike. There was a garden in the back, crowded with flower beds, bushes, and fruit trees, and ringed with cinder paths that led to arbors, a greenhouse, a wooden summerhouse, and a large rock outcropping overhung with vines and shade trees. The garden was the delight of his childhood and one of his fondest memories in later years. It came to life often in many of his pictures and stories.

It was in this garden that the youngster had his first impulse to create. Pyle has told of it:

> There was a great rock by the garden wall where there were ferns and ivy. I remember one time—I think it was spring-time, and I know that the afternoon sun was bright and warm—I was inspired to write a poem. My mother gave me some gilt-edged paper and a lead pencil, and I went out to this rock where I might be alone with my inspiration and purpose. It was not until I had wet my pencil point in my mouth and was ready to begin my composition that I realized that I was not able to read or write. I shall never forget how helpless and impotent I felt.*

Like the garden, the old house was another memory he cherished all his life and it, too, insinuated itself into his pictures. It was a fieldstone farmhouse in three sections, the oldest dating from about 1740, the second from the time of the Revolution, and the third, a new addition built by Howard's father at the time of the Civil War. It was a simple house with beamed ceilings, plain plastered walls, deep window embrasures, and large fireplaces. One could touch the ceilings with upstretched arm, and the floors were still the original wide, thick boards worn thin by years of passing feet. This was the setting, and it accords well with his historical pictures of an earlier America. The sights and sounds stored up through a lifetime shaped a career he could not even dream of yet.

It was a house with books. Dickens and Thackeray, Shakespeare and Milton, *Slovenly Peter* and *The Wonder Book*, *Grimms' Fairy Tales* and *Robin Hood*. *Slovenly Peter* was an early favorite, one his mother read to him along with *Tanglewood Tales*, *A Midsummer Night's Dream*, and others. The ambitious and devoted mother was delighted with her eager and thoughtful firstborn. She was a reader and thinker; she had had ambitions for a literary or artistic career which were now transferred to her children. As the two younger sons and the daughter developed, she pinned her hopes more and more upon Howard—he obviously had brilliant promise. Margaret Pyle was a strong, determined personality and she was the major influence shaping her son's early years.

Later, in the years of his fame, Pyle wrote of his early reading days.

> My mother was very fond of pictures in books. A number of prints hung on the walls of our house: there were engravings of Landseer and Holman Hunt's pictures, and there was a colored engraving of Murillo's *Madonna* standing balanced on the crescent moon and there was pretty smiling Beatrice Cenci, and several others that were thought to be good pictures in those days. But we—my mother and I—liked the pictures in the books the best of all. I may say to you in confidence that even to this very day I still like the pictures you can find in books better than wall pictures. . . .
>
> I can remember many and many an hour in which I lay stretched out before the fire upon the rug in the snug, warm little library, whilst the hickory logs snapped and crackled in the fireplace, and the firelight twinkled on the andirons, and the snow, maybe, was softly falling outside, covering all the far-away fields with a blanket of white—many and many an hour do I remember lying thus turning over leaf after leaf of those English papers, or of that dear old volume of *The Newcomes* (the one with the fables on the title page) or of *The Old Curiosity Shop* where you may see the picture of Master Humphrey with the dream people flying about his head. So looking at the pictures, my mother, busy with the work on her lap, would tell me the story that belonged to each.
>
> Thus it was that my mother taught me to like books and pictures, and I cannot remember the time when I did not like them; so at that time, perhaps, was the beginning of that taste that led me to do the work that I am now doing.*

*Howard Pyle, "When I Was a Little Boy," *Woman's Home Companion*, April 1912, p. 5.

This calls up a compelling picture of the seemingly idle days of childhood, while unconsciously he was filling heart and memory with the seed material for a whole lifetime of creation. But there were more than days with books and pictures. As he grew older he could range farther than the home acres. He could tramp through the fields and woodland patches behind their place and not only watch the procession of farm carts and wagons from the roadside but follow them as well. Best were the four-horse teams with the huge high-wheeled Conestoga wagons from the Pennsylvania German country, with their slapping, brass-decorated harness and loads of lime, grain, or wood. The upper portion of the Brandywine gorge was not too far away for small legs, and it was here with the clustered mills at the bottom that many of the great wagons took their supplies. Small boys could watch the loading and unloading, peer through open doors at the great millstones and even, from a distance on the hill, look down at the wooden sheds of the fearsome gunpowder mills.

Midway in Pyle's childhood, a major change came about in his family's life. The Pyle leather business fell upon bad times, and the fine country house and its acreage were beyond their now restricted means. It was sold and they moved to a smaller house in the city. It was painful for all to leave the spacious, rambling farmhouse but there were compensations. Most of the Pyle relatives and friends lived in the city and some of them were only a few steps away. Mrs. Pyle, who liked an active social and intellectual life, was now more in touch with her own kind and she was happy that Howard could be sent to a good school close-by. He could walk to the Friends' School which sat across from the old Meeting House on West Street.

His parents had expected him to be a prize scholar, but they were disappointed. He had the potential but not the interest. He did well sporadically but not consistently. His textbooks and notebooks were filled with drawings, and he read steadily and widely but showed little interest in stereotyped lessons. His parents, thinking a change of school might help, enrolled him in a small private school—Clark and Taylor's—but it made no difference. For the first time, however, he was thrown into the company of large numbers of children his own age and was participating in group sports, testing his capacity to get along with others. He was physically active, his strong growing body was the equal of any his age, and he was now used to roaming the city and its fringes as he had roamed the country. He couldn't resist the lure of the docks and wharves. The big transatlantic steamers went to Philadelphia several miles away on the broad Delaware, but there was a short channel to the Delaware from the junction of the Brandywine and Christiana (at the south point of Wilmington) that was deep enough for smaller vessels. Steam had largely taken over but there were still a goodly number of sailing craft of many sizes—lumber schooners from Maine, sugar and molasses boats from the Caribbean, oyster boats from Delaware Bay, and occasionally a square-rigger. These fascinated him most, and he began to know hull lines, the setting of the masts and rigging details, deck gear—all the visual and functional ship-knowledge that he would use so abundantly in his pictures in later years.

There were other attractions. It was always worth stopping at one of the blacksmith's shops to watch the forges blown hot from the big bellows, see the cherry-red metal hammered into precise shapes, and listen to hot metal sizzle and spurt when plunged into the water tub. There were carriage and wagon shops with wheelwrights shaving down the sturdy spokes with drawknives and fitting them into the wooden hubs, wagonwrights fastening the side panels of a delivery wagon, and painters with long-haired striping brushes weaving an arabesque of fine loops on the shafts and panels of an expensive carriage. The fire stations were especially enticing, with their glittering equipment and harness suspended over empty shafts, waiting for an alarm to sound. The trained horses would trot automatically into their places, the harness would drop and be fastened, and the great bells would sound as the pumpers and ladder trucks clattered out. Market days were special, too, with farm wagons arriving at daybreak, heaped-up stalls, and busy crowds. Down by the Philadelphia, Wilmington, and Baltimore tracks were the switch engines, the freight cars, and the rushing express trains.

The town was a treasury of wonders for a lively, inquiring mind, even the quiet, tree-lined streets of Howard's new neighborhood. There were a goodly number of Colonial structures still standing among the later Federal, Greek Revival, and early Victorian houses. Most of them were brick, presenting immaculate, staid fronts to the street, but behind there were almost always long yards with trees, garden beds, and clipped grass. It was a community of people from basically the same stock. To the eye it was a placid neighborhood, but below the surface was a concern with and apprehension of oncoming war; then later, the fever of war's arrival.

Geographically, the hills of Wilmington and its backcountry of the Brandywine Valley are a thrust of Pennsylvania into the general flatness of Delaware. The hills move in from the north and west in a diminishing way and end abruptly on the banks of the Christiana River. To the south delta land reaches to the tip of the peninsula, the so-called Eastern Shore. Socially and politically, at the time of Howard's boyhood the banks of the Christiana marked another division. Although Delaware was a slave state, albeit a halfhearted one, the confrontation of North and South took place, not on Delaware's artificially placed and curved northern boundary, but at the Christiana. The dominant element in Wilmington and the Brandywine country was Quaker and abolitionist. From their rooftops on the hills they could look down the vista of sloping streets to the flat plantationlike farms that were still largely worked by slaves. The owners of that land were mostly of a different faith and a somewhat different way of life. There was a conflict of mores and ideology but there was also friendliness, social relations, and even intermarriage. The two ways of life and thought were, nevertheless, brought into sharper contrast by such face-to-face proximity.

Young Howard grew up in that atmosphere of differences and confrontations. His parents and Quaker grandparents, numerous aunts and uncles, the large tribe of cousins, were a dense antislavery hedge between him and the enemy. He inherited his boyish abolitionist ideas. When news of the shelling of Sumter came up from the South, the time of commitment had arrived. For a small boy war was a time of pageantry and dramatic excitement. Soon there were troop trains from the North, packed with blue-jacketed recruits, stopping for food and drink at the wooden railroad station near the foot of Market Street. This was the gay time—like a party. Then came a different time when the trains came up from the South with the sick and the wounded. Some were the enemy—they were the ragged ones, sometimes in gray. When they spoke, it was English but with a different inflection. Sometimes they were hard to understand, but they weren't terrifying. All the wounded were carried up the streets to the jerry-built hospitals and, on summer days, small boys were allowed to march beside the stretchers and fan the hot faces.

The war lasted a long time—time enough for boys to do a lot of growing up. War was something different from what was expected. An artist and writer-to-be was packed with impressions—there were many things that could never be forgotten.

The misery and ugliness of the war could have been foreseen, but the visual reportage of it was not. The American audience had been awakening to the lure of the printed picture for several decades before the war, but slowly; now, suddenly they could not get their fill of war pictures. The newspapers and the weekly and monthly magazines were determined to satisfy this demand and did so quite successfully. The two largest and most aggressive publications in the field, *Frank Leslie's Illustrated Newspaper* and *Harper's Weekly*, were poised to record the first shot. Frank Leslie had his ranking staff artist William

Waud standing by the Confederate cannons pointed at Fort Sumter, and *Harper's* had commissioned on-the-spot drawings from several of the fort's officers. Both publications had artists attached to the Union armies during the war.

Obviously the pictures always lagged behind the news, although everything possible was done to speed the transition between the drawing and its reproduction. Usually drawings done in the field were too hasty and incomplete in detail to be engraved on the block. The drawing was conveyed by train to the publication offices in New York and then placed in the hands of one of the most gifted and experienced staff artists for additions and completion. This completed drawing was transferred to a boxwood block and engraved. To cut down the time of engraving, the block was sometimes sawn carefully into two or four sections. Each section was turned over to a different engraver and when all sections were properly engraved they were bolted together and printed. The artist-correspondents in the field experienced the bitter realities of warfare but the stay-at-home staff artists who finished the sketches did not, and they tended toward overdramatization. There was a good deal of unnecessary sword waving, theatrical gesture, and heroic posing in the earlier pictures, but they crept closer to reality as the war dragged on. Victorian habit and sentimentality gave way slowly and grudgingly, but the wartime proliferation of pictorial journalism gradually created a more critical audience, and a more gifted group of artists went into the field.

The youngster Howard, with his omnivorous appetite for pictures, swallowed everything, but comparisons were undoubtedly forming in his mind. He was probably

Ladies at a Picnic. Drawing by Felix O. C. Darley. FROM THE PAUL LEROY GRIGANT COLLECTION, THE UNIVERSITY OF MICHIGAN MUSEUM OF ART.

Illustration for a book cover, by Felix O. C. Darley.

becoming conscious of names and beginning to have preferences. He may have detected the name of Winslow Homer, not dreaming that one day he would know him and be his friend. He was certainly conscious of Felix Octavius Darley whose many prestigious volumes sat on so many of Wilmington's parlor tables and whose residence in nearby Claymont made him the only nationally known artist in the Wilmington area.

But the early pictorial fare that seemed to appeal most and that left a decided imprint on his own mature work was British. The British had developed the family magazine and the children's paper far beyond American efforts, and their illustration was greatly superior in quality and abundance. *Punch* and the *Illustrated London News*, without equivalents in America, were regular visitors to the Pyle household. Family and children's papers such as *Once a Week, Good Words, The Churchman's Family Magazine, The Sunday Magazine,* and *Cornhill* also found their way onto Howard's lap.

The British editors had such a notable body of accomplished illustrators to call upon during the middle years of the century that it was one of the rich periods of illustration. Usually called "The Illustrators of the Sixties," they flowed on into the later years of the century and it was upon this rich material that young Pyle's mind feasted. This was almost entirely a black-and-white-picture world, with every artist's drawing passing under the wood-engraver's burin before it found the printing press.

Pyle's taste was formed by such splendid draftsmen as Arthur Boyd Houghton, Charles Keene, and Frederick Sandys, by landscape illustrators who included J. W. North and Berket Foster, and by humorous artists such as John Leech and John Tenniel. Many of his favorite picturemakers were among those who later became part of the famous Pre-Raphaelite group, men like Dante Gabriel Rossetti, Ford Madox Brown, Holman

Book illustration by J. Mahoney.

Illustration by Sir Frederick Leighton.

Hunt, John Millais, and Edward Burne-Jones. Later he came upon the prints of such old German masters as Dürer, Burgkmair, Beham, Cranach, and others—which exerted such influence upon him that the quill pen illustrations of his professional years were largely founded upon their stylized engravings and woodcuts.

He had little opportunity to see paintings in those earlier years, only an occasional old portrait or landscape. The wall pictures he saw were more likely to be Currier and Ives lithographs or steel engravings of Renaissance masters. He became used to associating pictures with an accompanying text because so much of his pictorial fare came from books or magazines. The dialogue between the literary and the pictorial was ingrained from the beginning.

As he grew into his teens, the qualities shaping his future began to show more sharply: an incessant zest for drawing, a great love of fantasy and the heroic, sharp observation of the things about him, and unmistakable indications of the growth of an inner life.

Book illustration by Arthur Boyd Houghton.

Illustration by John Leech.

St. Cecillia, by Dante Gabriel Rossetti.

Der Ritter vom Turm. Old German woodcut, 1493.

Betrothal of Archduke Philip and Johanna of Castile, by Albrecht Dürer.

St. Anthony and St. Paul, by Albrecht Dürer.

Old German woodcuts also fascinated Howard Pyle in his youth, particularly the cuts and engravings of Albrecht Dürer. They formed the basis for his later bold, decorative style of pen drawing, as in his illustrations for *Otto of the Silver Hand* and the King Arthur books.

Illustration for *Otto of the Silver Hand*. Charles Scribner's Sons, 1888.

King Arthur findeth ẙ old woman in ẙ hut:

Illustration for *The Story of King Arthur and His Knights. St. Nicholas,* November 1902 to October 1903.

These two book illustrations, drawn by Howard Pyle in his later, professional years show the marked influence of his early accquaintance with the works of Albrecht Dürer and other German engravers of the sixteenth century.

Chapter 2

THE GROWING YEARS

School year followed school year at Clarkson Taylor's, but Howard Pyle the student was little changed, at least in the classroom. A good deal of the time he was present in body but not in mind. He lived for his solitary hours.

His parents could not banish concern from their minds. There was no question about their son's sharp intelligence or his pronounced talents, but they could not help thinking in terms of conventional learning, and in that area his record was unremarkable. There was no willingness to study. They always circled back to the thought that a few years of college would lay a foundation for any career, even writing or art. But his scholastic record was too poor to permit college entrance so a home study course was mapped out to repair the deficiencies. Home study, centering upon Latin and mathematics, began with amiability and good resolutions but tapered off into the old habits of sketching, reading, or daydreaming.

His parents yielded to the inevitable. The alternative was art school. A foreign art education was impossible because of lack of funds, and there was no art school or even private class of any repute in Wilmington. In Philadelphia, however, scarcely a forty-minute train ride away, was the oldest art school in the country, the Pennsylvania Academy of the Fine Arts. Whether because of cost or for other reasons, the famous academy was not chosen, but a small private school instead, presided over by an Antwerp-trained artist, Mr. Van der Weilen. So, at about sixteen, young Howard became a regular commuter to Philadelphia.

He immediately applied himself with complete absorption. This was a world in which he felt at home. He drudged away at charcoal renderings of simple plaster casts, then more intricate ones, then groups of still-life objects, and finally the posed model. There were hours of anatomical instruction. We know little of the school routine except what Pyle said in later years when, having rebelled against the limitations of his early training and worked out his own creative solutions, he could criticize the Van der Weilen methods in the light of experience. It was a copyist's training, a curriculum in pictorial imitation. The students were taught to observe exactly and report exactly with charcoal or brush. There was no attempt to stimulate either imagination or individuality. Technique was taught but not creation.

For a time Howard was well content to study and master technique, to train his eye to measure distances. And after a while, he was to discover that he was becoming the most accomplished student in the school: certainly we know of no other Van der Weilen student who became famous. But after three years of this routine he appears to have decided that he had come to the limits of what Van der Weilen had to give, and he returned home.

Back in his improvised studio at home he had to consider what the next step might be. Even while studying with Van der Weilen, Howard had worked in his father's leather business, which had not been doing well for a number of years. Now he gave most of his time to it, saving evenings and weekends for the studio. He felt he was drifting and was uncertain of his talents. He wrote little stories and usually tore them up in dissatisfaction. The sketches he made to illustrate them seemed inadequate. He escaped into the pleasant youthful activities of the Wilmington younger set.

His young friends, largely of Quaker background, were enjoying the growing relaxation of the older, rigid Quaker tenets. Very few wore Quaker dress, and all loved to party, giving rise to a round of picnics, dances, choral singing, charades, amateur plays, hayrides, skating parties, and sleigh rides. Howard had a good tenor voice and histrionic ability and was soon a popular member of Wilmington's younger set. In other ways he had already felt the easing of Quaker restraints. When he was about seven, his parents, who had become interested in the teaching of the mystic Swedenborg and had attended the Swedenborgian church, were read out of Meeting. After that the family attended the Swedenborgian church regularly. At first, the change of faith had meant little to him, but now in his late teens he and his mother pored over the Swedenborg volumes, trying to understand their mystical and puzzling language. Often the older Quaker preachments had seemed to frown upon Pyle's yearnings to be an artist, but there was nothing of this in Swedenborg's teaching.

Meanwhile the Pyle household was broadening its reading and consequently its discussions. Belatedly Trollope was discovered and embraced; even Carlyle was accepted warily. The most explosive new name, however, was Darwin, who was read with mingled dread and admiration. He was shaking many old foundations and was often difficult to follow, but the implications of his discoveries had to be faced. His adherent Thomas Huxley had a more persuasive rhetoric that was easier to understand.

Another new name was having a growing influence. Howard had discovered William Dean Howells through reading his novels *Their Wedding Journey* and *A Chance Acquaintance*. Here was the forerunner of a growing number of American writers who were to scrutinize the superabundant material of their native land with new eyes and

An early pencil sketch from a model. DELAWARE ART MUSEUM.

Untitled silhouettes.
These early silhouettes of Pyle's show a sensitivity of form and an ability to express character by simple means.

project their reactions in straightforward, realistic prose. This touched a responsive chord in Pyle's nature. He was discovering that although from his earliest days he had stepped readily into the world of fantasy and fable, he had an increasing predilection for seeing life as it was, for clear-eyed reporting that usually evoked the term "realistic." He was discovering in himself two seemingly opposing tugs of nature. Here was an intimation of the dual demands that would permeate his creative years. At the time he tried to write some stories in the Howells manner, but threw them away.

He always turned to his mother for criticism. She felt, and he agreed, that his adult stories, while promising, were still immature, that his articles for adults were beginning to show a professional touch, and that his little verses and tales for children showed the greatest immediate promise. His illustrations for children also seemed promising. Both Howard and his mother carefully examined the current magazines, comparing their professional prose and pictures with Pyle's. Most of this was depressing, and most of the time Pyle was full of self-doubt. However, an occasional glint of happy phraseology or an ingratiating bit of drawing would bring back momentary hope.

At about the age of twenty he tried another avenue for using his gifts. There was a short notice in *Every Evening*, Wilmington's evening newspaper:

> Art Instruction: Mr. Howard Pyle, a young Wilmington artist has taken Room No. 8—Masonic Temple, where he will give lessons in drawing, sketching and painting in oils. Mr. Pyle studied for two years in the Philadelphia art school of Prof. Van der Weilen, and also in the school of anatomy, and is, we doubt not, capable of giving valuable instruction to students. A picture of his in the window of Ferris' jewelry store, at Fourth and Market Streets, of a view of the Brandywine is attracting the public attention.

This is the only record of his first attempt to teach—we may assume from the lack of any mention of it again that it was not successful.

There seemed to be a long season of doubt and self-questioning, but better times were on their way. For years he had heard of the annual roundup of wild ponies on the island of Chincoteague off the coast of Virginia. It was an event he had often wanted to witness and it seemed unique enough to be the basis for an illustrated article. In the spring of 1876, he journeyed down the Eastern Shore peninsula and stayed on Assateague Island, a long, sandy, inhabited island just to the north of Chincoteague. He walked and sketched the pony roundup on Chincoteague; he showed them swimming across the narrow waterway to Assateague, the ensuing sale and auction, and drew the interesting settlement on the island. It was a fresh experience and provided new material for his portfolio. Back in Wilmington he worked and reworked his drawings and put the same hopeful care into his writing. It was the most ambitious illustrated writing project he had undertaken.

At the same time, for relief, he dashed off two small projects. One was a droll idea about a magic pill that transformed an old fretful parson into a terrible boy. He wrote a few verses and added several drawings in outline and sent everything off to *Scribner's Monthly* that summer (1876). When a letter of acceptance and a check arrived soon after, his hopes shot up and he mailed his second small effort, a fairy tale for children, to *St. Nicholas*, the most enterprising children's magazine of the day. It seemed incredible when that, too, was accepted and a check enclosed. He went back to the Chincoteague article, determined to make it the finest thing he had done and sent it off to *Scribner's*; back came the third successive acceptance, with the proviso that his sketches be redrawn by a staff artist for proper reproduction.

He had swung from dejection to elation in a few weeks, and he began to plan a whole series of new projects. Then his father, who had been on a business trip to New York, stopped at the Scribner offices. There he was welcomed by Mr. Roswell Smith, one of the magazine's editors and a partner in the firm, who had some very complimentary things to say about the work of young Pyle. Mr. Smith said that American publishing faced a great future, it needed gifted writers and artists, and the young man should come to New York where he would be in contact with many publishers, artists, and writers. Mr. Pyle came away with the impression that Scribner's would provide enough work to keep his son busy.

The opportunity was truly golden. The parents knew that separation from their son was inevitable—there need only be found the ways and means. Money was still a problem—the family leather business was struggling to survive the panic years—and Howard would need help until he became self-supporting. Both mother and father realized that once he became successful, it was likely that New York would become their son's permanent home. But they consoled themselves with the thought that Wilmington was less than three hours away by train.

So, in mid-October of 1876, Howard rode north on the New York express.

Chapter 3

NEW YORK APPRENTICESHIP

When Howard Pyle bade good-bye to his parents at Wilmington's Pennsylvania Railroad Station, he was facing the unknown. At twenty-three he was no youngster, but he had led a somewhat circumscribed life. He had never lived away from home, not even in the art student days in Philadelphia. His had not been a remote, sheltered life—he was one of a large family with a sister, brothers, and numerous cousins, and he had the usual neighbor playmates, children's games, school experiences, as well as an innate love of the sea and the countryside—but his absorption in books and picturemaking had set him apart from his companions. In short, he had his own strong inner life.

He was used to the interest and praise of his family and circle of friends, but what of the standards of New York, where the talent of the country was assembling? He was hardly prepared for the reality of New York: it was a recklessly expanding city that had practically submerged the old; an overnight metropolis jammed with the hopeful, the greedy, and the ambitious from all the states in the Union and every country in Europe. He was an unheeded atom in a multitude of pushing strangers.

Fortunately, he had some letters of introduction and addresses in his pocket, and he was counting on the editors at Scribner's and *St. Nicholas* to remember his work and his name. He had no difficulty finding comfortable lodgings with the Misses Marshall, former neighbors of his mother. The house was on East Forty-eighth Street, then considered to be far uptown, and certainly a distance from the publishers' offices, which were mostly clustered in the neighborhood of Union Square. Although the city's first elevated line ran down to the Battery and two others were being built, the only nearby transportation consisted of horsecars, which went down Broadway. In good weather Pyle preferred walking to save money.

As soon as he was settled, he went downtown to make himself known at Scribner's and *St. Nicholas*. He was sharply disappointed at Scribner's, but it is likely that he expected too much. Years later he scribbled this note in his scrapbook: "Mr. Smith, then President of Scribner's Monthly Co., told my father that I should come to N.Y. I took him at his word and went there, expecting to find employment with Scribner's. Fortunately for me, I found that I had to make my own way and that it was not [to be] made for me by Scribner's."

Certainly Roswell Smith was neither uninterested nor unkind. He had no immediate work suitable for young Howard, but he talked with him at length and, discovering that he had a good tenor voice and could read music, he offered him a paid position in his church choir. The young man refused, for his conscience forbade him to accept money for a church activity. Smith did promise, however, to offer him some small illustrating commissions from time to time, and he kept his promise.

The interview with Mary Mapes Dodge, the editor of *St. Nicholas* magazine, was more immediately helpful. The magazine was by far the most important of the periodicals for children, and it was growing rapidly. Mrs. Dodge recognized a promising if raw talent, saw that the young man was fertile in ideas, and encouraged him to make sketches with some attached texts and submit them to her. He left with revived spirits and went back to his lodging and set to work.

His many letters to his mother show that he was working doggedly. They describe a constant flow of themes that he struggled to express in acceptable prose with accompanying pen drawings that he labored over, trying to render them in a way that would reproduce clearly. His letters alternate between hopeful enthusiasm and discouragement, but from time to time he lists small sales, and he did not have to ask for help from home. If we are tempted to picture a lonely young man, spending long hours working in a small bedroom, we would be building up an exaggerated picture. The young man was separated from his home and familiar background, but he was making a good many new friends. His personality attracted people, and he was proving this daily in a new and strange setting. Even his solitary work hours in the lodging house had moments of relief as noted in a scrapbook years later:

> I occupied a small hall bedroom in 48th Street, then far uptown in New York. The people with whom I lived were old maids helping in a girl's school. I would sit in my room all day writing or drawing: would send what I had written to my mother, who would copy and correct it. Then I would draw the illustrations and sell the material to St. Nicholas.
>
> One day I remember looking up at the transom and seeing several girls' faces looking down at me as I sat at my work. The faces disappeared with much suppressed laughter.

Mr. Roswell Smith, who had so disappointed Pyle initially, proved a real friend. He read the young man's tentative writings and criticized them, instructing his art editor, Mr. Drake, to use Pyle's drawings where possible. Smith also invited the youth to his house for conversation and meals. Pyle described a dinner in another letter to his family dated 17 November 1876:

I went up to dinner at half-past five but unfortunately leaving my visiting cards at home, I had a desperate race around to obtain some more, and at last had to write them myself. One might as well make a call without shoes and stockings as without visiting cards in New York. I was dreadfully afraid I would be late, but arrived just in time. Although it was a family dinner, yet they had five courses and two desserts, but I got through without drinking the water out of the finger bowl because there wasn't any lemon in it, or cutting the butter with my table knife, because they didn't have any.

There was a Miss Smith who was obviously interested in him. She tried to induce him to join her church and arranged a horseback ride in Central Park with Pyle and another friend. He managed to evade both plans. His social opportunities multiplied to such an extent that Drake, who was Scribner's art director and who watched his efforts with paternal interest, felt he had to lay it on the line: "If you are going to have to try to make an artist sufficiently good to illustrate exclusively for us, you'll have to give up society entirely for the present, and devote your whole attention to study."*

Attending some evening drawing classes brought him in contact with other struggling artists, and he came to know some of the young professional illustrators and writers that he would see in publishers' offices. A good many evenings were spent at the theatre. He had developed a taste for the theatre back in Wilmington, but there the plays were intermittent and often indifferently produced. Wilmington was still very much of a Quaker town where the stage had few enthusiastic followers. But New York was the theatrical center of the country with a dazzling variety of new and old plays to offer and the best talent to produce them. Wallach's Theatre was his favorite—shabby, crowded, and poorly ventilated, but with an excellent stock company that had a wide repertoire of old classics as well as new and experimental plays. It was an extravagance but it fed his imagination. He tried to get a free pass through his newspaper friends but was told they were given only to the critics. Then he approached a few theatre managers, apparently with some success.

In spite of the long hours over his drawing board, he spent a good deal of time on the streets. He came to know the city quite well, from the tip of the Battery north to the region of open lots and shanty settlements where the streets were paved with Belgian blocks and the gas lamps were reaching out. There were the wonders of the rising piers of the Brooklyn Bridge, just being built; the miles of docks, wharves, and warehouses lining the Hudson and East rivers; the ships from all over the world—new swank steamers and coastal schooners with their long bowsprits jutting overhead above the waterfront streets. There were the ferry rides across to Brooklyn or the New Jersey shore or down the harbor to Staten Island.

He was seeing a wide variety of racial and ethnic groups for the first time. Immigrants were flooding in from all the countries of Europe, some with their belongings on their backs on their way West, and others heading for the foreign enclaves that crowded the city. Almost half the city's population was foreign born. Signs in foreign languages were common in certain neighborhoods and small ethnic restaurants offered new and strange foods at remarkably cheap prices.

He often returned to the newly opened Metropolitan Museum on Fourteenth Street with its collection of Audubon engravings, Kensett's Hudson Valley landscapes, plaster casts of Greek and Roman statues, and odds and ends of porcelain, glass, and metal antiquities. He had become acquainted with the work of some contemporary American artists during his student days in Philadelphia, but now there was more of their work to be seen at the National Academy of Design and at the private galleries.

*Quoted in Howard Pyle's letter to his mother dated November 24, 1876.

As the year crept toward the Christmas season, his mood became more and more despondent. Mary Mapes Dodge was dissatisfied with the way his drawings were being reproduced and sent him to an engraving house to watch the process and get some advice about preparing his work. Drake advised him to join a model class to improve his drawing. Both these suggestions were intended to be helpful and sprang from a real concern and interest in his development, but Pyle misread their intentions and felt they indicated grave doubts of his ability. Discouraged, he thought that there might be more hope in his writing. The winter was turning bitter and his room was cold. And undoubtedly homesickness was creeping in.

He writes to his mother in the winter of 1876:

> Thee strongly advised me in thy letter to stick to illustrating as my particular branch. I think thee is mistaken and that by all means a literary life is the proper one for me. Thee has not much confidence in my ability as a writer, nor have I much in myself, for I have not really turned my attention to it until the past six months. But one thing I can say and that is that where there are hundreds—thousands—of artists who can do infinitely better and more creditable work than I can and succeed in their profession while the market is overstocked with pictures, I have not met anyone as young in years and letters as I am who has succeeded better or even as well as I have.

As the new year opened, the feeling that he had lost favor with the magazines gave way to a realization of the true state of affairs, that temporarily he had overstocked *St. Nicholas* and *Scribner's* with his kind of thing and that it was unrealistic to place all his hopes on just two sources. He went back to picturemaking to provide himself with samples to show other editors. He was feeling more secure about his drawing at this time, for his latest experience in the model classes of the Art Students League had begun to open his eyes to the kind of drawing that suited his talent and his purpose. The drill of accurately copying a model had had its place in early training, but was now a hampering practice. His goal was not to copy but to *interpret* and *imagine*. His role was to quicken into visual life a scrap of text, his own or that of others. The posed model could only be helpful as a point of reference. It had to be modified, enhanced, transformed to create a personality existing in a world of the imagination. This concept, just perceived, was to become the keystone of his own practice and the core of his teaching.

With new drawings in his portfolio, his round of visits to different art editors was encouraging. His reception at Harper was particularly warm. Charles Parsons, the Harper art editor, was an exceptional man who was becoming a famous figure in American publishing history. He liked the bright young artist and his promising work.

The door to opportunity was now opening for young Pyle although he was not immediately aware of it. Parsons encouraged him to submit pictorial ideas and some were accepted; presently, he began to feel part of the Harper group and had the assurance of an adequate income. Being part of the Harper group was an education in itself. The House of Harper was the largest publication house in the country. Besides their *Monthly* and *Weekly* (both illustrated) they had their *Young People,* for children, and later *Harper's Bazaar.* In addition they were one of the country's largest book publishers. To be connected with this large enterprise presented many possibilities.

In two old buildings on Franklin Square were housed the personnel and machinery for complete production of both books and magazines. An alert and inquiring mind like Pyle's could follow the journey of a manuscript or a drawing from submission to its ultimate appearance in a magazine or bound book.

Charles Parsons, with his shrewd flair for picking talent, had assembled a prize group of artists on his staff. There was little precedent for this kind of organization. American periodical and book publishing was developing so rapidly that management had to expect

Illustration by Winslow Homer.

The Gosling States His Opinion of the Cock, illustration for "The Crafty Fox." *St. Nicholas*, February 1877.

Swinging on a Birch Tree, illustration by Winslow Homer.

constant change and be able to improvise—Parsons had the clearheaded and opportunistic qualities necessary. He was an artist by training and an accomplished watercolorist but he was also a practical organizer with a persuasive personality. He had to pick artists of excellence but of a new and special kind. There was no place for the moody and temperamental. He needed resourceful and prolific talents, who could execute projects rapidly and who could communicate pictorially to a large audience. The American illustrator-artist was in the process of becoming, and Parsons was helping to shape him. Parsons was described by Pyle in a letter to his mother dated February 28, 1878, as ". . . distinctly American in appearance . . . not the lanky, cadaverous American cast, though. He has a bald forehead, and gray hair which he brushes back, a gray beard, and wears glasses. He is kind, cordial, and in every way encouraging. . . . He is a gentleman, and a gentleman of refined tastes."

The team of talents that he had gathered about him was headed by the senior artist, Charles Stanley Reinhart, who was fresh from the European art schools. He was a facile, figurative draftsman with a fluent and sensitive pen line. In a group of artists avid to learn from each other, he was envied for his easy authority with crowded and complex compositions. Pyle studied them closely and liked to see them develop from the first sketch, for although he felt secure with one- and two-figure compositions, the spatial and gesture relationships between larger groups was a taxing and unresolved problem. This was just one of the opportunities offered by the Harper fellowship that could not have been matched by any art school in the land.

Although Edwin A. Abbey was young, almost exactly the same age as Pyle, he was placed next in ability to Reinhart. Everybody considered him a prodigy. He was a Philadelphian who had studied at the Pennsylvania Academy of the Fine Arts at the same time that Pyle was being drilled by Van der Weilen, but they had never met. Abbey's first illustrations for the Harper magazines were rather homespun and amateurish but in an amazingly short space of time he had established a personal pen style of engaging gesture and supple elegance. Along with the others, young Pyle greatly admired, and envied, his work. For a short time Pyle imitated Abbey, and the results can be traced in a few of his early illustrations. The two became fast friends and Pyle, in a letter to his mother in November 1898,* has left a description of Abbey:

> I like him very much. He has one of those pleasant faces that always makes a man feel better for looking at it. And then he is such a chipper, jocund little fellow, with a merry twinkle of his eyes and a laugh that means business. His very eyeglasses have a certain humorous character of their own. As for his going to Europe, I only wish that *Harper's* would send me—to Antwerp.

Another member of the group who became a lifelong friend was Arthur B. Frost. He, too, was greatly talented but at the opposite pole from Abbey. He was not elegant but homespun. He had a rollicking and disarming sense of humor; he never attempted the pretentious. He was completely the American artist, looking at backcountry farm life, the small town, the upstart middle class, roadsides, sports, and occasionally the new rich, with slyly amused eyes, and reporting it in a forthright but supple line that stopped this side of elegance. His masterpiece was the set of drawings he made for Joel Chandler Harris's *Uncle Remus*.

There were others whom Parsons relied upon, among them, W. T. Smedley, Frank Vincent Du Mond, J. W. Alexander, Thomas Nast, and A. R. Waud. Du Mond had large expansive pictorial dreams in his head and the magazine art room was just a way station on his journey. He was to become famous both as mural decorator and teacher.

*Reprinted in Charles W. Abbott's *Howard Pyle, A Chronicle*, New York: Harper and Bros., 1925.

Illustration by Edwin A. Abbey for *Hamlet,* for *Harper's Monthly.*

Alexander, too, was on his way to a famous painting career by way of Paris. Waud had been with Harper for many years—during the Civil War as an artist-correspondent in the field. Pyle had pored over his battle pictures as a boy. The most famous of the Harper artists was the grand old man Thomas Nast, whose bitter cartoons had broken the back of the corrupt Tweed Gang and sent its members to jail or exile. Nast worked in his Morristown home but his visits were an event for the admiring staff.

Pyle liked to linger in the cluttered art room, which was alternately quiet with concentrated figures bent over drawing boards or raucous with ebullient and inventive spirits released from picturemaking. It was rapid education to watch the experts build from a blank sheet of paper to a finished picture. And just overhead up a dusty flight of stairs was the engraver's room where the finished drawings were translated into engraved wood blocks that would print the impressions to be seen by tens of thousands. Here was where the fate of each drawing was decided. It was difficult for the artists to accept the fact that their drawings were just a step in a sequence of operations, that the wood engraving represented what the public would see. There were engravers of amazing skill and others less so—a block could be a telling and faithful rendition of the original drawing but it could also be botched.

Pen drawing of Edwin A. Abbey.

Pen illustration by Arthur B. Frost.

Political cartoon by Thomas Nast.

The wood-engravers' room was usually quiet, for engraving was a highly specialized skill that required great concentration. The engravers bent over their benches, eyeshades over their brows, their boxwood blocks adjusted by one hand, while the short-shanked steel gravers in the other hand nicked and cut their arabesques of delicate lines. One inaccurate stroke in an important area of a design and the artist's intention was modified if not spoiled. It was no wonder that the artists often regarded the engravers as natural enemies; yet it was politic to cultivate them for their friendship induced greater care. There was always competition to have one's drawing engraved by one of the top craftsmen.

Actually the hard feeling between the two groups was mutual. The engravers rightfully pointed out that many artists had little or no awareness of the possibilities and limitations of wood engraving and that they produced drawings or paintings that were impossible to translate accurately into a wood engraving. The block, almost always of the close end-grain of boxwood, was rendered into a proper printing surface by cutting with the triangular sharp point of the steel graver. These cuts were usually nicks or threadlike lines, and the completed block was a complex network of interweaving nicks and channels. When a block was inked, only the parts untouched by the graver, the original surface, received the ink—the portions removed by the tools remained white. In practice, a drawing made with sharp black pen strokes was the easiest to engrave—just the portions that had received no stroke were removed. But in tonal pictures, produced by mixing various tones of gray in watercolor or oil, translation onto the block required the greatest skill. Each tone had to be simulated by cutting with delicate threadlike lines so as to leave threadlike spaces between to receive the ink. This could not be a strict facsimile, it had to be a translation, a simulation of effect. A network of black and white spaces had to represent as nearly as possible the flat tone of paint. The best engravers demonstrated astonishing skill and discernment in achieving this.

At the time of Pyle's apprenticeship that skill was at its height. About a half century earlier the standard of American engraving had been quite low, often crude, but the influx of European engravers, largely British, had improved the profession greatly and by the late 1860s and early 1870s American engraving could match any in the world. Pyle was seeing American engraving at its best, for it was generally acknowledged that Harper had the best team in the country. The House of Harper boasted of this, although at the same time they complained of the cost—it cost them about five hundred dollars to engrave an average full-page block.

When Pyle walked across the upper-story bridge that spanned the two Harper buildings, he entered the printing department where the giant Hoe presses spun out their long webs of imprinted paper. Like most Harper equipment, the Hoe presses were the finest that could be had, amazingly fast and efficient. Here was the last stage of text and picture, printed upon paper, cut, folded, and bound in the binding machines, all ready to be sent across the country. Pyle could study every stage of the journey and soon came to realize through how many skilled hands an artist's picture passed before it reached the readers.

In the little library room or "morgue" stacked with all kinds of scrap and clippings, he consulted the earlier files of the *Monthly* and *Weekly*. This gave him perspective upon the changing styles of pictorial art, its content, and the format that supported it. It was borne in upon him that the American publication world was one of rapid change. Many of the mid-Victorian pictorial clichés had disappeared or were changing. The stiffness and self-consciousness were disappearing from the figures. They were moving much more naturally—muscles and bones were beginning to assert their existence under the pressed trousers and full skirts. The rendering was less formulated; the artists were better. He could see how competition in the field had stiffened and he could begin to sense the enormous capacity for growth that lay ahead.

He had now learned the details of getting an artist's picture into a form that could be duplicated endlessly, and he could now appreciate that in all the complex stages of periodical publication the one bottleneck that militated against speedy publication was the translation of the drawing onto a printable surface. A full-page illustration would normally require a week to engrave on the block. The only way to shorten the time was to carefully cut the block in quarters and assign each quarter to a different engraver. The four engravers had to have similar styles and skills. Where the quarters met, the engravers left a strip of about one-eighth or three-sixteenths of an inch untouched. When the engravers had finished their work, bolts were run through the sections, and the sections brought together into a close fit. Then the master engraver tooled across the unfinished strips where the sections joined and so justified and brought together the lines on either side of the joint. This was the scheme used on many of the Civil War pictures, when impatient readers were hungry to see pictures of the latest battles, but it was a troublesome method that required a superior staff. Even as Pyle acquainted himself with the mechanics of reproduction, many minds and hands were at work upon possible solutions and coming close to success. In less than four years the New York *Daily Graphic* would publish its first crude halftone picture entitled "Shantytown," a mechanical solution for a printable tonal plate. It would take more time to perfect the method, but the era of the wood engraver was coming to an end.

From all the study and the close association with workers in all branches of periodical publication, Pyle developed confidence and a feeling of belonging. An expression of his new confidence was his joining with two young fellow artists, Durand and LeGendre, in renting a large and comfortable studio in a more convenient location. There he threw himself into making a painstaking series of gouache drawings for his portfolio.

Another result of his new experiences was an enhanced perception of the power of the American periodical press and the part that the artist might play in it. He was now conscious of the vast United States, from coast to coast and border to border, blanketed each week and month by a drift of printed text and picture. He sensed the hunger behind this new demand. Never before had it been possible for an artist to reach so many eyes so rapidly. That was a great power that must be used wisely and beautifully—it was a great responsibility that called for the highest abilities. Pyle also began to feel that the American artist must find his own authentic speech and not merely repeat European formulas. These were thoughts that he would sharpen and preach about as he grew older. They would be expressed in his own pictures and in his teaching.

Chapter 4

THE YOUNG PROFESSIONAL

Young Pyle's new confidence and determination began to show results. The working group at Harper's were his new friends and they all seemed to feel that his future would be a bright one. It heartened him to discover that even the editor in chief of the *Monthly*, Henry Mills Alden, was accessible and interested in him. In a letter to his mother dated 28 February 1878, he tells of Alden:

> . . . a strikingly handsome man of about fifty. He has an unkempt look though, his hair and beard are shaggy and look constantly tousled. He has very regular features and deep brown eyes deep set under rather heavy brows. He speaks very little, and when he does talk he contorts his face as though the act of talking was a painful labor and effort with him. Last time I was down there he rather surprised me by coming into the art rooms and joining Mr. Parsons in talking with me for nearly half an hour about American art and artists and what not. Rather a complimentary thing for a poor devil of an artist like me.*

*Reprinted in Abbott, *Howard Pyle*, p. 51.

Parsons was buying enough "idea sketches" from Pyle to take care of the young man's financial needs but always the sketches were developed and brought up to a finished and reproducible state by one of the regular staff members. Pyle was deeply disturbed by this and rebellious. He felt humiliated that he could point to none of the magazine's reproductions and say it was entirely his. Finally he faced the problem and acted. It is best described in his own words, written years later:

> I took one day to Harpers an idea-sketch which I had called "A Wreck in the Offing." It represented an alarm brought into the Life Saving Station, a man bursting open the door, with the cold rain and snow rushing in after him, and shouting and pointing out into the darkness, the others rising from the table where they were sitting at a game of cards.
>
> I begged Mr. Parsons to allow me to make the picture instead of handing it over to Mr. Abbey or to Mr. Reinhart or to Mr. Frost, or some other of the young Olympians to elaborate into a real picture. With some hesitating reluctance he told me I might try, and that, in the event of my failure, Harpers would pay me ten dollars, I think it was, or fifteen for the idea. I believe I worked upon it somewhat over six weeks, and I might indeed have been working upon it today (finding it impossible to satisfy myself with it) had I not, what with the cost of my models and the expense of living in New York, reduced myself to my last five cent piece in the world. Then it was that my fate or my poverty, or whatever you may choose to call it, forced me to take the drawing down to Harpers, instead of drawing it over as I should have liked to have done.
>
> I think it was not until I stood in the awful presence of the art editor himself that I realized how this might be the turning point of my life—that I realized how great was to be the result of his decision on my future endeavor. I think I have never passed such a moment of intense trepidation—a moment of such confused and terrible blending of hope and despair at the same time. I recall just how the art editor looked at me over his spectacles, and to my perturbed mind it seemed that he was weighing in his mind (for he was a very tender man) how best he might break the news to me of my unsuccess. The rebound was almost too great when he told me Mr. Harper had liked the drawing very much and that they were going to use it in the Weekly. But when he said they were not only going to use it, but were going to make of it a double-page cut, my exaltation was so great that it seemed to me that I knew not where I was standing or what had happened to me. As I went away I walked on air . . .

This was an important turning point, a victory. At last he had passed from apprentice to professional. It banished the last doubt about the direction of his life work. The first sketch of *A Wreck in the Offing* was not preserved, nor were any of his previously accepted sketches, so there is no possibility of comparison with the finished blocks. We must assume that the first sketches showed some faults of execution or perhaps an overall look of not being quite professional enough, and that Parsons was only too happy to arrive at the point when he could entrust the young artist with the task of completion.

A Wreck in the Offing offers us a point of high achievement by a young artist of twenty-four. Its drama is visible at a glance, its powerful pattern of artificial light immediately captures the eye and holds it. It is a complicated composition, a taxing problem for any artist. The aroused group about the table is admirably handled, both as a group united by a shared emotion and as individuals. Then, as our eye follows the line of their tense faces to the right, we arrive at the single figure in the doorway, and our climax is somewhat blunted by the less accomplished rendition of this key figure. The composition is a notable effort and hints at great things to come but they have not yet arrived.

It is interesting to place this noteworthy picture beside the only other set of pictures that had been published up to this point without being reworked by other hands, namely, the group of black silhouettes drawn by Pyle for his story "Papa Hoorn's Tulip," which appeared in the January 1877 issue of *Scribner's Monthly*. Here are two utterly dissimilar pictorial offerings, important in that they express, even at this early age, the duality of his talents. *A Wreck* is drama realistically presented; the silhouettes are decorative conventions that, in spite of their simple and restricted means, reveal unmistakable personalities, sensitive but precise forms with overall charm. It is difficult to find common denominators in these two creations that would indicate them to be the work of one man. But this duality was to express itself in many ways during a productive lifetime.

The young artist had reason to be proud and happy and he wrote a gleeful letter home. When a proof was pulled from the block he posted it off to his mother and was rather taken aback by her matter-of-fact acceptance of his triumph and her dry words of criticism. By this time he, too, was critical of the wood engraver's interpretation of his picture and this was to become a recurring complaint during the remaining years of the wood engraver's ascendancy. Pyle was learning that the trite, leveling technique of the average engraver was particularly blighting on the work of those artists who displayed marked individuality and a pronounced style. But his general outlook was much more cheerful and he could write: "Work is beginning to roll in upon me at last. . . . My work is beginning to pay better, too, and I think before long I shall be able to pay off my debts to father *in toto*. I have just finished a picture for *Harper's Monthly*. . . . It was quite a success and they are going to put it into the hands of the best engraver in New York City, Mr. Smithwick."

He was now moving into a heavily productive period, an indication of the years to come. Likewise, his circle of friends and acquaintances was growing and all his hours were crowded and stimulating. He was still attending the night class at the Art Students League and it was filled with lively talents. His life was very different from the old days in Wilmington, but he was growing and his horizons were expanding.

One important new friend was William Chase, who had returned in triumph from study in Munich and whose reputation was rapidly expanding in America. His studio was a showpiece, with great tapestries, carved baroque furniture, Renaissance frames, and above all, his own paintings with their spontaneous and dexterous brushwork. He had personal charm—he was a natural showman—and had already attracted a company of admirers, imitators, and collectors. Soon his reputation as a teacher would match that as an artist. He and his work must have been a new experience for Pyle. Although they saw a good deal of each other as long as Pyle remained in New York, there is no indication that the young illustrator was influenced in any way by the dashing technique of Chase.

At this point Pyle was painting in gouache, but it would be only a few years before he would be practicing a facile oil technique; yet that facility was never extended to the point of display or to the sensuous enjoyment of the power of the brush. There was something in Pyle, a Puritan or Quaker check, that kept him from succumbing to the intoxication of paint.

Chase seemed the natural leader of the group that gathered once a week at the Art Students League and then repaired to a hotel around the corner for beer and pretzels. Walter Shirlaw, Charles Reinhart, and Pyle were regulars, along with Julian Weir, Frederick Church, John Mitchell, and Rufus Zogbaum. It was not long before they were discussing the advisability of forming an Art Students' Club and renting a room. Among the varied plans, Pyle reported to his mother, " 'Yes,' puts in the practical Church, 'and a dumbwaiter to send up beer and Welsh rabbits from a beer salon below, for there must be a beer salon below.' "

Mrs. Pyle seems to have expressed some concern about these plans but her son explained that the beer was to wash down the dry pretzels and lubricate the throat for conversation. He said, "We assemble there to imbibe inspiration, the beer and pretzels are secondary."

He enjoyed being more and more a part of the art life of the city and was proud to be one of a group asked to choose the ten most outstanding American artists in New York.

He reported that the ten ". . . will in all probability be Ward, the sculptor, possibly Church, the landscape artist, Chase, Shirlaw, Weir, George Inness, Swain Gifford, Louis Tiffany, Winslow Homer, John La Farge, possibly Abbey, or if he goes abroad, Reinhart. The outside honorary members will probably be Eikins [sic] of Philadelphia, Hunt of Boston, Boughton and Hennessey of England, with Abbey if he goes there, Bridgman of Paris, and Duveneck of Munich. . . ."

Many of these men were now his friends and it stimulated the young illustrator to be so close to the gifted talents he admired. He did many of the things they did, taking time to slip away from his drawing board to visit the increasing number of picture and sculpture exhibitions. His friends Abbey and Reinhart were exhibiting in the shows of the young American Water Color Society, and he was able to compare the rising vigor of the native aquarellists painting their own brilliant sunlight and varied backgrounds against the pale limpid washes of the English tradition. The bite and breadth of a Winslow Homer was an intimation of the coming power of the American school. Other friends like Chase, Inness, and Shirlaw were showing at the National Academy, with the advance guard of the Paris- and Munich-trained Americans. Many of these men were in a period of transition. Trained in European methods and schooled to see with European eyes, they were now awakening to both the wonder and difference in the seasons, particularly the brilliant autumns and the beauty of American snow. Our artists were gathering themselves for the making of a great American pageant, one of the world's great schools of landscape painting.

The discussions among these volatile young artists confirmed Pyle in his own native instincts. He was in accord with their missionary zeal to ignite the pictorial mind of America, to found a great native school of painting that would deal with the marvelous wealth of material offered by their own country. This was a conviction that he was to reiterate both in his pictures and teachings through his lifetime.

Meanwhile he had work at hand. Harpers was keeping him busy and making use of his growing competence. He could now afford better quarters and after shopping around he found an excellent large room at 788 Broadway, at the corner of Tenth Street. It had a fine north light and two side windows overlooking Broadway. At twenty-three dollars a month it was within reach of his pocketbook—and steam heat and running water were included, with an extra allowance for repainting and small repairs. It was within a quarter hour's walk of Harper's and two blocks from Scribner's.

His double-page showpiece, *A Wreck in the Offing,* had done a great deal for his reputation and his greatest desire now was to surpass that effort. So he schooled himself to draw and redraw, often discarding the work of days in an effort to reach the level of his own ideal. He had received a few letters from readers, and for the first time he felt close to a public that heretofore had seemed remote and without personality. He no longer felt he was working for the editors alone. He realized that the pages of *Harper's Weekly* and *Monthly* were show windows to the literate American public, and he pinned his greatest hopes there, although in odd moments of time he was still submitting work to *Scribner's Magazine* and *St. Nicholas.* In fact he had written home for the old family copy of Percy's *Reliques,* with its story of Robin Hood, from which he hoped to rewrite some of the tales and make pictures for them in his spare time. That early idea had to wait about six years for fulfillment.

Editor Parsons asked him to submit a sketch for a possible double-page spread in the Christmas 1878 issue of the *Weekly.* He began with high hopes and several ideas and finally settled upon the theme of *Christmas Morning in Old New York,* a prerevolutionary setting. The sketch was approved and he made all preparations to solve the multiple problems of a very complex composition. It was crowded with many figures of different types and conditions against a background of early architecture and accessories. He ran

Christmas Morning in Old New York, illustration for *Harper's Weekly*, December 25, 1880.

into many problems and slowly fought his way through them. Like *A Wreck*, it developed into a severe test of his staying powers. One difficulty was obtaining authentic costumes for his models. He searched all the available sources and finally found one that seemed to have possible material. But when it was delivered to his studio and he looked it over, he exploded. He described the sequel:

> . . . my disgust giving away to anger. I kicked the boot tops into one corner, the coat into another and the hat on top of the closet, in consequence of which I tore said hat. This morning the costumer—a big, flabby meek man, came to my studio. "How did you like dose soldier clothes?" he said. It was Sunday to be sure, but in spite of that I took him by the button hole and so restrained him while I reproached him bitterly. He took the costume and torn hat meekly away. In consequence of this I shall probably have to have a costume made.

This seems to have prompted the beginning of what became his large and valuable collection of authentic costumes comprised of both originals and copies from research. It was the beginning of years of research into the history of American costume, so that in time his knowledge of the subject was probably the most expert in the country and his hundreds of pictures of early American life carried a message of authentic historical fact to their large audiences.

Christmas Morning won some praise but it was not a triumph. It lacked the dramatic light and shadow pattern of the shipwreck picture. It was a collection of carefully drawn single figures rather than a crowd with bustle and purpose, and compared to the work that was being turned out by his colleagues Abbey, Frost, and Reinhart it was amateurish.

Sketch for "Among the Thousand Islands." *Scribner's Monthly*, April 1878.

Fortunately the original drawing has been preserved and we can see how the wood engraver was to blame for much of the stiffness of some of the figures. Compared to the work he would be doing in three or four more years, it shows how great an advance Pyle would make in that short time.

He was now deeply immersed in picturemaking, although he came back to writing occasionally when it dovetailed with the picturemaking. He still, for example, found time to write little tales accompanied by ingratiating pen drawings for Mrs. Dodge at *St. Nicholas*. And he wrote an article entitled "Among the Thousand Islands" and made some pictures for it. It was commissioned by Dr. Holland, the editor in chief of *Scribner's Monthly*, who had bought one of the islands. Pyle was paid one hundred dollars and expenses. His most important writing project in 1878 was a three-installment article with illustrations for *Harper's New Monthly*. It was called "A Peninsular Canaan" and dealt with a familiar part of the country—the Eastern Shore of Delaware, Maryland, and Virginia.

There was now no lack of opportunity to draw or write. Parsons offered him an extended trip to Texas to write and illustrate several articles. His reaction to this discloses some basic inclinations of his nature. At first he was enthusiastic and asked a salary of forty dollars a week plus expenses, which was granted. Then he demurred about doing both the writing and the pictures, so Harpers offered to send a writer with him. He drew back from this and finally refused the assignment altogether. His reasons reveal that he was not a born traveler, that he liked a comfortable, habitual life. "Here I enjoy myself," he said. "I have found at last congenial companions among the more considerable artists. There I shall have a hard life . . . and introductions to strangers, which I hate."

And yet he was indecisive about travel, particularly abroad. His attachment to his own land—its history, its wonder, its future—had often led him into disparagement of foreign influence. He was a missionary of Americanism, but under it all was a curiosity about Europe and a yearning to see it. Abbey, one of his new friends, was leaving for England and many times Pyle spoke regretfully of the parting and enviously of Abbey's opportunity. "I only wish Harpers would send me to Antwerp. Yes, Antwerp or Brussels is my latest fad."

With Abbey's leaving in 1878, the circle of friends began to break up. Reinhart left Harper and went off to Europe to paint. Frost moved back to Philadelphia. Some had married, or were moving to the country, others were simply losing the bounce of the very young and putting on dignity. There was a younger contingent of artists coming in but both the language and enthusiasms were changing. They considered Pyle—at twenty-six—as part of the older generation.

It was a time for taking stock. He could not doubt the record of his own success; he was quite a different artist from the anxious young man who had stepped off the ferry three years before. He reviewed his recent work: His latest short story in *Harper's New Monthly*, "The Last Revel in Printz Hall," he considered his best writing to date. The drawings for two recent articles, also in *Harper's New Monthly*, "The Old National Pike" and "Sea-Drift from a New England Port," also showed signs of growth. *Harper's* considered him a regular contributor of both pictures and text and so did *St. Nicholas*. He could probably renew relations with Scribner's and other publishers. Was Wilmington too remote from the publishing headquarters and would he vegetate there? His closest friend, Frost, was now working outside of Philadelphia with no feeling of inconvenience, and Wilmington was only the next express stop down the line. And Felix Darley, until his recent death, had worked for years from his Claymont studio, close to Wilmington. The Pyle family had been apprehensive about his becoming a permanent New Yorker—they would be overjoyed to have him back. And as for the proper atmosphere to write his proposed book on Robin Hood, the quieter pace of Wilmington was infinitely preferable.

The decision made itself. The Harper editors were understanding and felt no need of change in their relationships. He made a round of other visits and received many favorable replies. It was one of the most important decisions he ever made: it established the creative pattern of the rest of his life, and he never had reason to regret it.

The Swineherd Who Knew Curious Things, illustration for "Hans Gottenlieb the Fiddler," *St. Nicholas,* April 1877.

Chapter 5

PROMISE INTO FAME

The untried and apprehensive young man who had left for New York three years before, came back to Wilmington a confident and acknowledged professional. His friends had seen his illustrations in the magazines and read his articles and children's tales. He was a young celebrity in a town that was now calling itself a city. It was a community little accustomed to artists or writers. He was something of a hero to his own generation and an object of conversation to all. Some were surprised that he seemed to work long, regular hours and gave no sign of having picked up odd temperamental habits.

He had regrets, of course, particularly for the lively group of New York artist friends, but they had scattered and even if he had stayed he would have found them much diminished in numbers and less inclined to talk away the hours. Of his two closest friends, Abbey had decided to remain in England permanently, but Arthur Frost had moved to the outskirts of Philadelphia, which was within convenient reach of Wilmington. Frost was now Pyle's only close artist friend, the two often spending a day sketching along the Brandywine or in the surrounding hills, or meeting together in Philadelphia when one of the large painting shows was on. As Frost said, "Through the period of our intimacy nothing really happened—it was just a cordial, humdrum friendship." Some years later, when Frost moved to northern New Jersey, the two busy men kept in touch almost entirely by letter.

Wilmington and its valley were home to Pyle and his later life demonstrated his strong attachment to the town and its countryside. Only twice during the remainder of his life did he leave home territory for more than a few days. He never showed any inclination to visit the deep South or the far West. In Wilmington he settled down to his life's work.

There was ample studio space on the third floor of the Pyle home. His mother contributed odds and ends of family furniture and saw that the studio was kept clean. The inevitable easel and drawing table were added, with a cabinet for materials, and the artist was ready for work. The easel was little used in those early days, for Pyle was usually bent over his drawing board. At that time his principal mediums were pen and ink and watercolor, both transparent and opaque. The smell of oil and turpentine was not yet the familiar odor of the studio.

He soon found it was easier to plot his course away from the distractions of New York. He was beginning to come to terms with his own nature. His indecision as to whether to be an artist or a writer was solved by becoming both. He was discovering the pace at which to work and the need of transfers of interest to keep his creative enthusiasms at a high level. There were times when it seemed necessary to work upon two separate problems almost simultaneously. He had no testy temperament to cope with. Normally he could close his mind to the outside world and concentrate upon the picture or story before him. This power of concentration was a blessing, for it enabled him to deal with a versatility that often tugged him in several directions at the same time. He now accepted that versatility as an essential part of his nature and learned how to concentrate on one demand while holding another in temporary abeyance. Presently he schooled himself to the point where, under certain conditions, he could paint or draw and dictate a letter or story at the same time.

The Harper editors kept their promise and mailed him assignments from time to time. Although he was busy at his drawing board most of the time, he now had longer intervals for reading, mostly in the field of American history. He had developed an insatiable appetite for the complete story of his own country, and tracking down historical details for both his painting and his prose became part of the pattern of his life.

His accumulation of historical knowledge now played an important part in earning a living. Although the Harper editors were well aware of his reliability and accuracy with historical subjects, he decided not to depend upon the chance arrival of such manuscripts by other authors but to supply his own texts. He came across the journals of John and William Bartram, those two early Quaker naturalists, and read of their long wilderness journeys from Canada to the Gulf. He came up to Philadelphia and spent several days sketching the handsome cut-stone mansion of the Bartrams and its famous five-acre garden. The mansion was a gem of Colonial architecture, facing the lower reach of the Schuylkill River near Gray's Ferry. At the time of Pyle's visit, there was still countryside around the Bartram acres and the flats across the river were only beginning to be scarred by industry. Pyle developed eight illustrations from his sketches and wrote an article, "Bartram and His Garden," to accompany them. At that time the remarkable botanical discoveries of the Bartram father and son and the high regard in which they had been held by Benjamin Franklin and James Logan in the Colonies, and Carolus Linnaeus, Dr. H. Gronovius of Leyden, Sir Hans Sloane, and the Duchess of Portland in Europe, had been forgotten by many, so the Pyle article helped to revive a wave of appreciation.

Parsons and the other editors were delighted with both pictures and text and suggested that he treat other subjects in a similar manner. He chose a subject that he could complete while scarcely stirring from his third-floor studio, "Old-Time Life in a Quaker Town," an

Endicott and the English Flag, illustration for "An English Nation" by Thomas Wentworth Higginson. *Harper's Monthly*, April 1883. PRIVATE COLLECTION.

anecdotal tale of his hometown. Published in January of 1881, this too was a success, and now a pattern had been set that he would follow for quite a while. Actually he was accomplishing more than he had in New York, partly because of increased skills in both writing and picturemaking, partly because his purpose was now more sharply focused, and partly because distractions were fewer. But he was by no means leading a monastic life in his third-floor studio.

His old friends were happy to see him—some a little awed, all curious about a sudden celebrity in their midst. His circle came largely from the tight little society of affluent,

Drake's Attack upon San Domingo, illustration for "The Old English Seamen" by Thomas Wentworth Higginson. *Harper's Monthly,* January 1883.

middle-class Wilmington, still largely of Quaker and early settler background, with a sprinkling of Southern names and a few foreign ones. This was a small world that seemed adamant and fortresslike from without but which was stirring and seething within. The young were restless and often rebellious. No longer were the meetinghouse benches crowded on First Day. Quakerism had long passed its missionary stage; its middle stage of probity, prosperity, and decorum was fading as more and more Friends were seeking ritual in the Episcopal faith and sometimes the Roman Catholic, or hymn singing in the Baptist and Methodist chapels. Pyle's own family worshipped in the

Swedenborgian church, although most of his aunts, uncles, and numerous cousins were still Friends. Almost all the younger generation had either modified the plain Quaker dress or abandoned it.

The Quaker aloofness from the arts had also changed greatly. While the printed word had always been highly esteemed, writing for frivolous purposes, such as light fiction, had been frowned upon. Now, however, the latest novels were an important topic of conversation, an artist was no longer suspect, and the barriers against music had broken down. Quaker voices were now singing cantatas and oratorios, even Gilbert and Sullivan. Tennyson, Browning, and Swinburne were being read, and reproductions of the Pre-Raphaelites were hanging in some Quaker parlors.

The young people had organized a lyceum, where they could sing, debate, produce little plays, and listen to visiting lecturers or performers. The same group met for tennis, skating, canoeing, winter sleigh rides, and summer picnics. It was one of these picnics that brought about a major change in young Howard's life. The lyceum group mixed choral singing with their picnicking, but their tenor section needed another reliable strong voice, and Pyle had had a local tenor reputation when he left for New York. He was invited to join and he was persuaded. The first rehearsal was held at the home of the Poole family, and he was early. The door was opened by Anne, the Poole's young daughter, and from then on Pyle became a regular visitor. Their engagement was announced only a few weeks later, in July of 1880.

Even as an inhabitant of seventh heaven, young Howard lost none of his practical common sense. He spent some time working out theoretical family budgets. He was by turns optimistic and pessimistic. July 29 he wrote to his fiancée, who was summering with her parents at Rehoboth on the Delaware coast just south of Cape Henlopen:

> That will make a hundred and thirty-five dollars worth of work since Monday at noon. I guess we ought to be able to live on that if I keep it up. . . . I want to write a letter to old Parsons and tell him of my future prospects. I would rather see him but that would take another day and—well I can't spare it just now. He ought to know, however, as he holds the loaf of bread from which we are to cut an occasional slice.*

He delayed the New York trip until August when he saw both Alden and Parsons. They both had the same story to tell him: "The House" was concerned and complaining about the rising costs of magazine production. Since Harry Harper was away in Europe, important decisions would have to await his return. But Parsons was more definite than Alden. He asked the bridegroom-to-be how much he felt he needed from Harper's each year to support a wife and Pyle replied, "Twenty-five hundred dollars a year." Parsons promised to bring that to Mr. Harper's attention upon his return, and added, undoubtedly to cheer up the young artist, that he thought it quite likely that things would work out satisfactorily.

Still, young Pyle was discouraged. He made another trip to New York about a month later, particularly to talk to Scribner's. He was not optimistic about this visit for he feared he might have fallen into disfavor because of his desertion to Harper. To his surprise and delight he was received with great friendliness. He mentioned to Johnson, the subeditor, and Drake, the art editor, his idea of a trip to Stroudsburg and the Delaware Water Gap in Pennsylvania to make sketches and gather material for an article. They were very much interested but unable to commit themselves in the absence of Gilder, the editor in chief. So although he felt more cheerful after his warm reception, he ended his next letter to Miss Poole with a few discouraged sentences:

*Reprinted in Abbott, *Howard Pyle*, p. 75.

I felt fairly sick when I saw some of the designs that Drake had in the art room. They lay all over mine with several yards to spare. H.P. will certainly have to work up if he means to keep with the crowd. I hate that fellow Blum's work but it is decidedly artistic in many ways. One can't form a just idea of it by seeing the engravings alone. Then there is a young fellow—a mere boy—doing landscapes, phew, mine are not a patch upon them.

He made the trip to the Delaware Water Gap and from it came the illustrated article "Autumn Sketches in the Pennsylvania Highlands," which appeared in *Harper's New Monthly Magazine* in December 1881. Harper's liked it so much they suggested that he spend some time in the Pennsylvania Dutch counties of Lancaster, York, and Berks and delve into old country customs that had changed so little over so many years in a new country. He was happy to be offered this new opportunity and yet he recoiled from the thought of traveling. He could travel in the imagination with exhilaration, but in reality, only with reluctance. Even the suggestion from editor Alden that he travel to New Brunswick for an article met with objections.

The story of his experiences with the Pennsylvania Germans as written in letters to his fiancée reveals an unconscious self-portrait. It was a new and strange experience ranging from initial distaste for a life and people so different from his own through stages of adjustment into final appreciation.

Some of the best examples follow:

November 16, 1880

. . . I went around to a Dunker minister to talk things over. The minister seemed quite an intelligent man, but said that one Jacob Pfantz, living near Ephrata, would be the one to give me the most information, since he was both very intelligent and very well-informed, beside being a man of such entire leisure that to give information and to toddle about the country with me would be a positive luxury to him. Said Pfantz is a Dunker and knows all about the interesting spots. I want to stay with him if I can while I am gathering my material.

November 17, 1880

. . .You see where I am (Ephrata) and the name spelled right thanks to being printed. But I am not going to stay here—oh no! I am going back to Lancaster tonight. And I am going to stay in Lancaster and am going to get one meal at least in Lancaster. The unpronounceable proprietor of this Mount Vernon House told me today that this was a Dutch house, kept in Dutch style, and that I must help myself accordingly, which I did, to fat pork, turnips, diminutive sweet-potatoes, dried peaches and an indescribable pie, but oh my!—never mind, I won't say anything about my poor stomach just here . . .

And now for my absolute news. I found the natives here as hard to open as an oyster without a knife. Your mother was quite right. They do not expand with the geniality one might expect from the bucolic German. On the contrary they shut with the most persistent tenacity. . . . Mr. Bare had given me a letter to John (not Jacob) Pfantz, whom he represented as a man of great intelligence and knowledge of the German Baptists. I found at home a pleasant-faced German woman and a man with a long beard and a pendulous wen on his cheek. John was in the work-house; she rang the bell and he came. He turned the letter over and over in his hands with a vague look on his face that gradually broke with some intelligence as he said that he remembered Dan Bare. He maundered on about his having books and things, but happened to forget what was in them. I confess I felt rather helpless when I considered this as a sample of extra-intelligence, but the pleasant-faced woman (his daughter) explained that the old man was getting childish—which made the old man mad.

I had to give it up, so I walked up the road a piece to where one of the Bishops of the church lives, but he was not in. His wife informed me that "he'll generally be here till [at] ten o'clock. I don't think he'll be gone till very long." I waited an hour for him but no signs of his approach appeared—still, his wife every now and then dropped in to tell me that "he's generally here till ten o'clock or a little after. I guess he'll found somebodies down to the drain to talks," or something of the kind. I left at eleven o'clock and went up to see another man in reference to the sisterhood, who referred me to another man who was not in town. So I went down to the Cloister to look at it. It was stunning. It would make an article of itself. I shall certainly devote most of mine to it.

Then I went down to see the Bishop but found him as oyster-like as all the rest. But by that time I had my knife, so to speak, patience. I talked to him patiently and persistently, and he finally opened up quite succulently, so to speak. He gave me whole gobs of information, told me of many books of reference and wound up by taking me over to the big meeting house in his queer, rickety little rig, opening the place and showing me through generally. Just think of it! If I had been here last week I could have seen a love-feast, but I missed that and there won't be another until next spring.

Then I went down again to unintelligently intelligent friend Pfantz, applying to him also the oyster-knife of patience, and he opened also in as great a degree as he was capable of doing, promising to show me through the Sisterhood Cloister tomorrow. . . .

November 18, 1880

. . . Ye Gods! What a time I have had! I came back and found my friend Pfantz waiting for me at the station according to promise—and very much good he did me. Item to be booked for future use: Never take a man to be a fool when he seems anxious to represent himself as being one. To use an expression of your mother's, "These people are smarter than they look." At least, that is what is beginning to dawn on me. When you begin to enquire of a Pennsylvania Dutchman about things with which he thinks you have no business and which concern him, his face assumes a stony "expressionless expression," so to speak, most exasperating and most helpless to an impatient nature. My aged friend Pfantz showed himself quite agile and intelligent this morning. He talked to me and gave me quite an amount of information.

He took me up to the Cloisters and pointed out the different buildings, giving quite a little lecture on them. He took me in and introduced me to the chief sister, pleading in the most engaging fashion for permission for me to sketch. He took me around and introduced me to the minister, also pleading with him and finally got full and limitless permission to make all the sketches I wanted.

I think I can say without vanity that I made a complete "mash" of the chief sister. I talked to her in the sweetest way I was capable of doing, and she answered me in English as broken as an ancient Italian china. She was a very fat, dumpy specimen of humanity about sixty years old. She showed me all about the chapel and the cookhouse at the rear where the soup is cooked for the love-feasts. She took me upstairs and downstairs, into crumbling cubbies and moulding pantries. We ascended grasping a rope in lieu of a bannister. She introduced me to the other sisters of which there were three, exhibiting my sketches and assumed complete ownership of yours truly. She showed me old spinning machines, reels, dilapidated chairs, clocks inhabited by earwigs and things, flat wooden legs for stretching stockings upon, wooden candle-sticks and Providence only knows what else.

The minister who lives near asked me to dinner and a right good plain dinner it was. He was another I took to be stupid at first, but who turned out to be quite an intelligent and not a badly informed man.

"Do you speak German?" said he.

"No, sir."

"Also not at all?"

"No, sir."

"Then I might scold you well without your knowing, ain't," said he. I think I must have stared at him with the most absurd blankness, so surprised was I at his joke. . . .

I have only one regret—I asked the old sister to sit for her portrait, but she declined. I begged, I implored, I argued with her for half an hour—but no go. She smiled, looked sheepish, and declined in the best Pennsylvania Dutch.

November 19, 1880

Bur-r-ruh! but it was cold today. I managed to potter along tolerably well in the morning, sitting in the sun and sketching the old buildings of the Cloister. But when I undertook in the afternoon to go around and get another view, sitting in the shade, I had to resign. I worked along for some time with stiff fingers and chilled bones, but when I got to painting and the water I was using froze in little cakes all over the picture, I absolutely could not go on.

. . . I went in to warm my hands and the strict head sister took them into her own puffy palms in the most motherly way, saying with a surprised air, "dey is golt," just as if it were a land of Egypt out in the shadow of the woodshed. I thought it a good time to bone her again about having her picture taken, but she still firmly declined in Pennsylvania Dutch. . . .

As I could do no more at the buildings I went over to see my ancient friend Pfantz. I showed him the sketch I had made and he was interested. Then I asked him to sit for his picture. Here his daughter put in her word, objecting most strongly. I think the old man rather liked the idea. He had the queerest old trowsers that might have been worn by Noah anterior to his cruise—yellow with age and patched with parti-colored remnants—oh! so picturesque! His daughter thought it would be ungodly to have his picture taken. I thought she meant ungodly for me to draw it. "I'll take the responsibility," I said. "You better be responsible for yourself," said she, "one soul ought to be enough for you." Then I quoted Scripture and she answered with twice as much. Then I appealed to the old man. "She will scold at me," said he, "and make it onpleasant." To make a long story short I finally prevailed, provided I would not sketch more than his head.

The old man followed me out of the house when I was done. "Vos you going to publish that in *Harper's Weekly*?" said he.

"*Harper's Monthly*, if you will let me. I hope you won't object?"

"Ho-no-no," said he—then after a pause, "but don't tell my daughter."

"Oh no."

Again he hesitated. "You'll put my name, won't you?"

"Why I don't know."

"I t'inks you petter—ain't my name's John B. Pfantz—John Bauer Pfantz—aigh? (with a rising inflection). And you might send me one of the papers—aigh?"*

These trips of Pyle in his early years, where he encountered strange customs, different personalities, and new backgrounds, were an important part of his education. He was adventurous in mind but not in body. He was not moved to meet strangers and yet, once confronted by the new and unaccustomed, his natural charm and goodwill won their way.

The editors liked the Pennsylvania German article and so did the readers nine years later when it was finally published, but for Pyle, seeing it in print only reminded him how much he had improved in the interval. The autumn and winter of 1880/81 was a crowded, productive, happy, and relaxed time, for the two trips to New York had produced abundant results and the young artist was free of financial worries. Both Harper's and Scribner's were sending him work, and every spare moment was devoted to the drawings and text for his Robin Hood project. At the same time Harper was launching a new magazine for children, *Harper's Young People*, and Pyle was becoming one of their favorite contributors. All things were going well for him.

Everything conspired to stimulate him to do his best in that spring and summer of 1881. On April 12, he and Anne Poole married each other in the Quaker way in the Poole home. A. B. Frost was the best man, and the assembled Pyle and Poole families radiated happiness and approval. The striking couple was popular and admired. Anne was a true beauty, a personality with winning ways, and Howard was tall, sturdy, and handsome, with blue eyes and strongly modeled features. His hair was thinning and he would be quite bald by his middle thirties. A radiant future was predicted for them.

The Poole house at 607 Washington Street was large and comfortable, and the Pooles

---

*Henry Pitz, *The Brandywine Tradition*, pp. 74–78.

Illustration for "The Early Quakers in England and Pennsylvania." *Harper's Monthly*, November 1882.

wanted the newlyweds to live with them for a while. A room was fitted up for Howard's studio. When the summer approached the young people were left alone in the big house, for the Pooles always spent long summers in their vacation cottage by the sea. Later their daughter joined them for some weeks, but since there was no studio space in the cottage, Pyle worked in the Washington Street studio and joined the family over the weekends.

Spending long summers at Rehoboth Beach became a regular part of the Pyle pattern of living until the late nineties when Chadds Ford was selected as a site for a summer school. The Poole cottage stood in some trees facing the sea, with a wide porch across the front, where one could lounge in wicker chairs and scan the beach. The town was then small and quiet, a place to relax. The strips of sandy beach were long and uncrowded. Pyle loved to walk them, particularly the several mile stretch to Cape Henlopen. The high dunes, the tidal pools and sandbars, the curling breakers and distant swells he knew by heart. He sketched them hundreds of times and they were the settings for many of his pirate pictures.

Illustration for *The Story of Siegfried,* by James Baldwin.
Charles Scribner's Sons, 1882.

Illustration for ''Not a Pin to Choose.'' *Harper's Young People,* June 1890.

Illustration for *Harper's Young People*.

There was a passageway yawning before him, illustration for "Not a Pin to Choose." *Harper's Young People*, June 1890.

Illustration for "The Salt of Life." *Harper's Young People*, January 1890.

Howard Pyle with his oldest daughter Phoebe, mid-1890s.

After a few years he was able to afford a beach cottage for his growing family—a son, Sellers, born in 1882 and a daughter, Phoebe, four years later. A small wooden studio was built behind the house in the trees, and now he could close the door upon a hard day's work and within a few steps be on the beach and into the water. The small children thrived there, their mother was with them in the open a great deal of the time and their father, hearing their excited voices, could be tempted to drop his brushes and join them. His work didn't suffer—on the contrary, he had never been more productive and so consistently at his best. All the outside chores were quietly handled by the redoubtable John Weller, not the least of whose offices was as all-round model, posing for everything from a pirate or backwoodsman to a Continental general.

Howard Pyle with his young family on the beach at Rehobeth, mid-1890s.

With a growing young family gathering about him, and particularly with the young children romping in the waves and on the sands of Rehoboth, Pyle bought a new plate camera and took dozens of photographs of those early wholesome, lively days. It is interesting to note that the camera was used entirely to record the life of the family. There were a few photographs of models in costume but they were of John Weller, the handyman, or a friend, or one of the family. Pyle was never known to have painted from a photograph of a model—the still image bridled his imagination.

Pyle was now working on a book project of his own—*Robin Hood*. Although he had contributed a few scattered illustrations for book publications, and those were mostly pictures that had been reproduced previously in magazines, his first commission to completely illustrate a book came from Dodd, Mead & Company in 1891, the year of his marriage. Indeed, he was asked to make color drawings for two small children's books, *Yankee Doodle*, and *The Lady of Shalott*. Both were early American experiments in color printing for children's books, an attempt to emulate the excellent flat color printing achieved by the great English color printer Edmund Evans. Evans's fine success in printing the color drawings of English artists like Walter Crane, Kate Greenaway, and Randolph Caldecott had created an appetite for this kind of picture in America. Unfortunately, this early Dodd, Mead experiment fell far short of the quality of Evans's work. Pyle was displeased with his work in both books. There is no record of how the original illustrations were prepared or what process was used by engravers and printers. This was a period in which rapid strides were being made toward solving the problem of mass color reproduction but success had not yet been achieved. It was a time of many theories, many tentative methods, many experiments. Pyle's drawings for these books were his contribution to one such experiment. He had some liking for his *Yankee Doodle* pictures, which had a somewhat quaint chapbook quality. He hated those for *The Lady of Shalott*. Although he worked on the drawings for both books simultaneously, they were not only completely different in subject matter but also in treatment. Probably the uncertain reproduction and poor printing of the *Yankee Doodle* pages only enhanced their homemade charm. *The Lady of Shalott*, designed in the rather florid Art Nouveau style enjoying popularity in England, was quite unlike any other color illustration that Pyle ever did, and despite his dislike, it is an interesting period piece with more vigor and invention than most British illustration of the time.

Illustration for *Yankee Doodle*. Dodd, Mead & Co., 1881.

The·ſtout·bout·between·Little·Iohn·&·
Arthvr·a·Bland:·

Illustration for *The Merry Adventures of Robin Hood*. Charles Scribner's Sons, 1883.

Between pressing commissions he worked on the manuscript and pen drawings for *Robin Hood.* The typewritten pages and drawings were piling up and the end was in sight. This was his first lengthy project either in words or pictures. With its completion, his work habits were established, and they persisted with few modifications until his last working days. For instance, once an initial composition had been satisfactorily stated upon canvas or illustration board, he usually liked to be read to while he developed his picture. In a letter written at this time he mentions his enjoyment at being read Darwin's *The Descent of Man.*

The year 1883 brought a number of projects to fruition. *The Merry Adventures of Robin Hood* was published by Charles Scribner's Sons in New York and by Sampson, Low, Marston, Searle and Rivington in England. That it was appearing simultaneously in England and America was a great satisfaction to Pyle, not only because the subject was from English folklore but because he had great admiration for English illustration and now his work would be in direct competition. When he read the favorable reviews, particularly William Morris's surprised admiration that anything so good should come out of America, he felt justifiable pride. The American reviews were equally laudatory.

Robin and the Tinker at the Blue Boar Inn, illustration for *The Merry Adventures of Robin Hood*. Charles Scribner's Sons, 1883.

Illustration for *The Merry Adventures of Robin Hood*. Charles Scribner's Sons, 1883.

Howard Pyle on the front porch of his new studio, built in 1900, at 1305 North Franklin Street, Wilmington.

It was, of course, Pyle's first book and he had used every resource to make it a notable contribution to art and literature, and success was sweet. He had gone to great lengths to supervise the design and production of it—paper, binding, printing, and format. This had increased production costs and the resulting higher publication price had a dampening effect upon the early sales. But it soon won its way into popularity; it became a children's classic and ninety years after publication it is still in print.

Another important project, his studio, was completed in the same year. In the few years since his return to Wilmington, he had been able to accumulate some savings and was able to purchase a lot on the edge of the growing city, on the west side of Franklin Street between Pennsylvania and Delaware avenues. With an architect he designed a studio building for the back of the lot, leaving a broad lawn in front. It was a pleasant structure of brick, with a wooden porch and gable end framed in wooden beams with plaster between, that faced the street. From the porch one went through the front door with its brass knocker into a squarish reception room, with a long built-in bench occupying one wall and a line of casement windows another. To the left one stepped into the large high studio with its corner fireplace and northern skylight. A small extension of the studio was off to the left, with a glass ceiling that admitted sunlight so that models could be painted in an outdoor light. There was also a small office, washroom, and narrow stairway leading to a second-story room over the reception hall.

Pyle had very decided ideas about all aspects of the new building, and the architect and builder faithfully carried them out. When Pyle told them that he wished the interior walls to be the color of a telegraph pole they lined them with soft-gray weathered shingles. Entering the studio from the low-ceilinged entrance hall, the overhead light poured down upon all upper surfaces, but the misty color of the walls seemed to enlarge the dimension of the room. This building, still standing, was where Pyle spent almost all his creative hours for about twenty-seven years, except for his summertime studios at Rehoboth and in the old mill at Chadds Ford. When first built it was within sight of cornfields; today the city has enfolded it and moved beyond. Outwardly it looks the same; inside the gray shingles have been painted and the walls have a dazzle that Pyle never knew. It is owned and used as a studio by a group of Wilmington painters.

The decade of the eighties was a time of crowding ideas and abundant production. Day after day found Pyle standing at his easel painting under the slanting light or standing at his podiumlike desk, where he preferred to write his manuscripts or draw his compositional sketches and pen-and-ink illustrations. He liked to stand while he worked, saying it was almost his only exercise. In later years he employed a secretary who, in the intervals between typing and other chores, would often read to him. There was a period when his sister Katharine worked in the studio extension.

The steady flow of illustrations for the weekly and monthly magazines continued through the eighties, but now added to it was an outpouring of books. The initial success of *The Merry Adventures of Robin Hood* in 1883 was followed two years later by *Within the Capes*, a completely different kind of book. It was a novel of adventure designed for an adult audience. A year later Pyle returned to the children's field with *Pepper & Salt, or Seasoning for Young Folk*, a richly illustrated collection of lighthearted tales and fables. Then, in 1888, three more books appeared within a few months of each other. *The Wonder Clock*, one of his masterpieces for children, was brought out simultaneously by Harper in New York and Osgood McIlvane & Company in London. It had an excellent reception and critics placed it on a par with *Robin Hood*. Following that came *The Rose of Paradise*, a pirate story. Ostensibly for adults, it also found a teen-age audience. At the end of the year, *Otto of the Silver Hand* was published by Scribner's in the United States and Sampson, Low, Marston, Searle and Rivington in England. It was and is one of Pyle's great children's books.

Thus six books, which Pyle both wrote and illustrated, appeared between 1883 and 1888, four of them children's books that have been acclaimed as masterpieces. All four are in print today. Three of the four were published simultaneously in England, attesting to the approval of that audience. The two adult adventure novels were good of their kind but less exceptional than the children's books.

Looking over this span of years crowded with work of high achievement, it is interesting to note that Pyle the illustrator of adult magazines was almost entirely concentrating on the American scene, but Pyle the writer and book illustrator had produced four children's books with European backgrounds, one adult book centered in the Mozambique Channel, and one partly in America and partly in the pirate waters of the Caribbean.

This was a time when he was becoming more and more conscious, even militantly conscious, of his innate Americanism. Europe's bland disregard of American art irked him. He was yearning for a redoubtable and expressive native art that would stun Europe by its vigor. He thought he saw the beginnings of it in American illustration, an art that expressed the people and brushed away the arbitrary distinction between illustration and painting. He knew that American illustration rivaled the best of Europe and often surpassed it in vigor, imagination, and volume. It delighted him to hear artists returning from the Paris ateliers say that the foreign students cared nothing for what they saw of American painting but eagerly looked forward to the latest illustrated American magazines.

The Chapman, illustration for "Chapman Heroes." *Harper's Monthly*, June 1890.
DELAWARE ART MUSEUM.

Illustration for "The Soldiering of Beniah Stidham." *St. Nicholas*, December 1892. COLLECTION OF ROBERT M. DODGE.

King Stork.

Illustration for "King Stork," *The Wonder Clock.* Harper and Brothers, 1888.

Many of Pyle's illustrated tales of this period, such as "King Stork," were first published in *Harper's Young People.*

The·Prince·aids·the·Old·Woman·

Illustration for *Pepper and Salt.* Harper and Brothers, 1886.

Claus·and·the·Master·of·Black·Arts·

Illustration for *Pepper and Salt.* Harper and Brothers, 1886.

Illustration for "King Stork," *The Wonder Clock.*
Harper and Brothers, 1888.

Thus the Princess cometh forth from the Castle at twelve o'clock at night.

Illustration for *The Wonder Clock.* Harper and Brothers, 1888.

The blacksmith takes ẏ dwarf's pine-cones.

Illustration for "The Best That Life Has to Give," *The Wonder Clock*. Harper and Brothers, 1888.

The Drummer catches ẏ one-eyed raven ∴

Illustration for "King Stork," *The Wonder Clock*. Harper and Brothers, 1888.

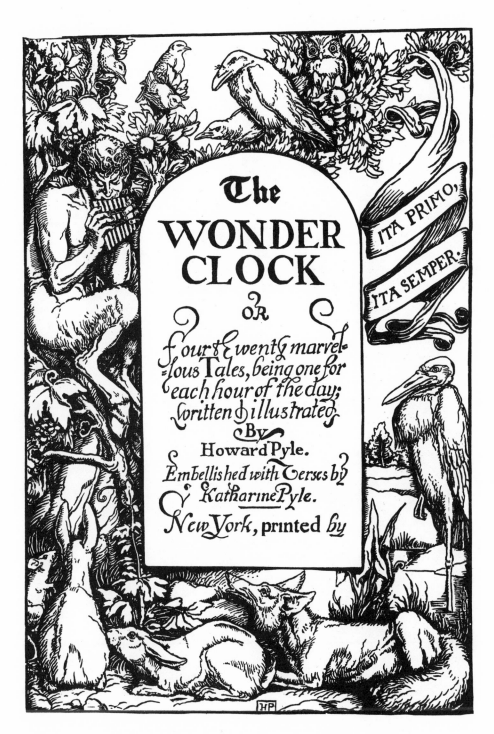

The
WONDER
CLOCK
OR
Four & Twenty marvel-
lous Tales, being one for
each hour of the day;
written & illustrated
By
Howard Pyle.
Embellished with Verses by
Katharine Pyle.
New York, printed by

ITA PRIMO,
ITA SEMPER.

Title page, *The Wonder Clock*. Harper and Brothers, 1888.

The poor, simple brother sitting under the pear-tree close to the bee-hives, rocking the little baby in his arms, illustration for *Otto of the Silver Hand.* Charles Scribner's Sons, 1888.

Illustration for *Otto of the Silver Hand*. Charles Scribner's Sons, 1888.

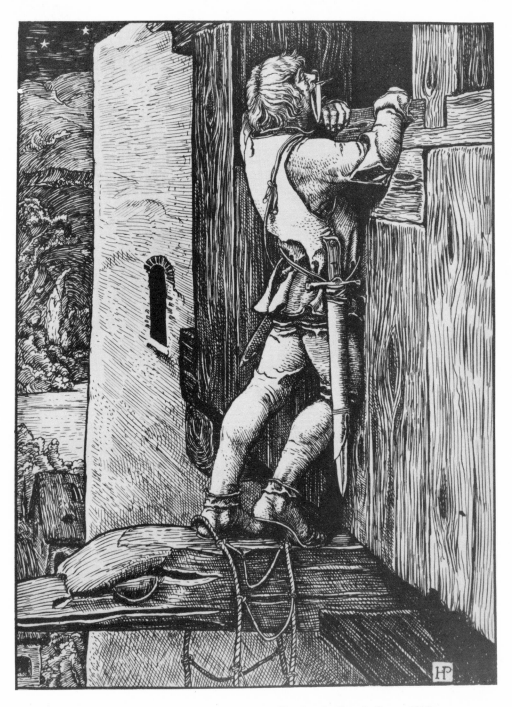

Illustration for *Otto of the Silver Hand*. Charles Scribner's Sons, 1888.

Pirates used to do that to their Captains now and again,
illustration for ''The Sea Robbers of New York,'' by
Thomas A. Janvier. *Harper's New Monthly Magazine,*
November 1894. COLLECTION OF HAROLD MCCRACKEN.

He had found the Captain agreeable and companionable,
illustration for ''The Sea Robbers of New York,'' by
Thomas A. Janvier. *Harper's New Monthly Magazine,*
November 1894. PRIVATE COLLECTION.

He was grateful to be included, with many other American draftsmen, in Joseph Pennell's monumental *Pen Drawings and Pen Draughtsmen* (1889) and to read the footnote in which Pennell said, after a careful study of the drawings and engravings shown at the Paris Exhibition of 1889, "American pen drawing, the Exhibition conclusively proves, is the best. . . ." A few years later he was pleased to be one of two Americans represented in Walter Crane's *The Decorative Illustration of Books*, although he had no admiration for Crane's tepid draftsmanship or his boneless maidens and expressionless youths. "Too many draperies, too many draperies," he said.

But the fascination of Europe was deeply imbedded in him. Although he sometimes rebelled against it, perhaps considering it a disloyalty to his Americanism, he could not erase those childhood hours spent poring over the old fables, folktales, and legends of Europe, nor his delight with reproductions of old pictures of sea monsters, ancient towns, great castles, men in armor, ancient ships, and strange animals. These were now a part of his pictorial vocabulary. On his library shelves were some of the European books he constantly consulted: old friends such as Joseph Strutts' *A Complete View of the Dress and Habits of the People of England*; the *Kultur Geschichtliches Bilderbuch* with its plates of Burgkmair, Dürer, Beham, and Cranach; the *Art Journal* of the fifties with its mid-Victorian wood and steel engravings; Paul Lecroix's *Moeurs, Usages et Costumes au Moyen Age* and *Le Militaire et Religieuse au Moyen Age*; and Meyrick's *Ancient Armour* in three volumes. There were many others and they were part of his past and continuing education. He could not close his mind to Vierge, Menzel, Keene, Dürer, the Pre-Raphaelites, or the Victorian engravers—they were advertised in many of his own pictures.

Morgan at Porto Bello, illustration for "Morgan," by Edmund C. Stedman. *Harper's Monthly*, 1888.
COLLECTION OF DOUGLAS ALLEN.

All the details and backgrounds for his many pictures that had foreign subjects were drawn from his imagination as reinforced by pictures and descriptions. He had never experienced the reality of them, had never traveled out of the country. There was a lurking fear that the reality would destroy the magic of the imagined scene. It never seems to have occurred to him that his imaginative involvement with the early history of his own country had been nourished, not crippled, by his acquaintance with his country's surviving monuments. His ambivalent plight is revealed in a letter to his old friend Edwin Austin Abbey who was now snugly ensconced in the village of Broadway in the Cotswolds.

> What jolly times you must have in your English life, with the right fellows you meet at your club and elsewhere! I wonder whether two lives could be more different than yours and mine: the one full of go, novelty and change; the other humdrum, mossy, and—no, I will not say dull or stagnant, for it suits me to perfection. Yes, it suits me so perfectly that I doubt whether I shall ever cross the ocean to see those things which seem so beautiful and dream-like in my imagination, and which if I saw might break the bubble of fancy and leave nothing behind but bitter soap-suds. I have always had the most intense longing to see some of those jolly bits which you are always throwing out as sops to us less fortunate mortals—by the bye, *do* you see them or do you only carry motives of them around in your "nut," the same as I do the old German castles?*

Abbey wrote a reply which, alas, was never mailed. It was a friendly, commonsense letter and might have brought some perspective to Pyle. Abbey in a slightly scolding way told him not to waste his time trying to imagine what had already been imagined, that a month's visit to some of the old German towns would open his eyes more than twenty years of pictures and descriptions. Pyle's fear of reality shattering imaginative conception versus his desire to witness the actual scene was never resolved—he was still looking for the answer in his last journey.

An additional reason for shrinking from travel abroad may be found in the heartbreaking experience he and his wife had during their first venture outside the country. Pyle, becoming more and more immersed in delineating in picture and prose the story of high-seas piracy, yearned to experience the tropical seas and their islands. He had used the beaches and dunes of Rehoboth and Cape Henlopen for many a buccaneer setting but he could only imagine the power of tropical sunlight, the color of the water, and the shapes and quality of the foliage.

He felt the need of experiencing these things and sketching them. So, in 1889, he and his wife sailed for Jamaica. Their two children—Sellers, age seven and Phoebe, three—were left with their grandmother in Wilmington. Anne was pregnant, but she accompanied Howard as he sketched and they both luxuriated in a pleasant and rewarding new experience until a delayed cablegram reached them—their young son had died suddenly. There was a desperate time of trying to find transportation back home and a wait of many days for a steamer sailing. They reached home long after the funeral.

The death of their firstborn in their absence left its mark upon them for the rest of their lives. Anne could never speak of the boy without tears, and Pyle was driven to write of death and the hereafter a number of times, particularly in the book *The Garden Behind the Moon*, which sprang directly from this brooding grief. Their third child, Theodore, was born that same year, 1889, and three boys and a girl followed.† The next decade saw a growing household of lively children. So, they picked up the threads of life again—Anne with the family, Howard in work. There was no slackening in the publishers' demands nor in his own inventive projects.

*Reprinted in E. V. Lucas, *Edwin A. Abbey*, New York: Scribner's, 1921.
†Howard, on Aug. 1, 1891; Eleanor on Feb. 10, 1894; Godfrey on Oct. 15, 1895; and Wilfrid on Oct. 29, 1897.

Chapter 6

CHILDREN'S BOOKS

With the publication of *The Merry Adventures of Robin Hood* in 1883, Howard Pyle established himself in the first rank of both writers and illustrators of children's books. There was no uphill struggle for recognition, it came in abundance with this first book and remained with him to the end of his days and beyond.

The book had been germinating in his head for years. It came straight from his early childhood; it merely waited for the necessary dual talents to ripen. When he wrote from New York to his mother telling of his plan to write and illustrate the book and asking her to send him the old family copy of Percy's *Reliques*, he only needed it as a general guide. He knew it quite by heart. But the sight and feel of the book brought back childhood horizons and established the youthful tone of what he would write and draw. It was a long and ambitious project and he didn't get very far into it during the time he was in New York, mostly because of a constant stream of commissions from Harper.

Once reestablished in his old home he had more time for a long-term project. It was not an uninterrupted project by any means but Pyle was now used to turning from assignment to assignment as part of the life-style of a busy illustrator-writer. The first installment appeared in *Harper's Young People* in January of 1883 and in book form a little later. The praise of the British edition particularly delighted Pyle, for the theme and background were completely British. He was not bothered by the criticism that he had never experienced the British countryside—he had evolved his own setting, a never-never land that suited an ageless folktale.

Although he had had relatively little practice in writing for children, mostly short tales for *St. Nicholas*, the prose of the new book had a pace and flavor of its own that was very congenial to young minds. He inserted a few archaic terms from time to time to nudge the mind backward in time, but he didn't overdo it. It was a natural, easy-paced prose that carried one along with jolly anticipation. Although a long book, it was not formidable. It could be taken in small or big bites. The end of each episode left a promise for the next.

The reading public and the critics immediately perceived that the text was not a mere convenience upon which to hang pictures nor were the pictures a subordinate embellishment of excellent narration. Both sprang from the same conception and were inseparable. The illustrations rounded out the characters. Backgrounds, costumes, and accessories implied a medieval atmosphere, albeit not a pedantically documented one. It was not an historian's report but an ageless folk theme reenacted for modern eyes. The decorative panels framing the full-page pictures are a most curious medley of Renaissance, baroque, and early Art Nouveau motifs. They take their playful place in somehow maintaining a medievallike climate although the grim purist might raise an eyebrow. They may have been given their form by an artist's happy whim. Certainly the prose-picture combination was a reiteration that a theme imbedded in the racial memory needs a new dress from time to time.

The success of *Robin Hood* opened the way to other books. Some of the books that followed were novellike tales of adventure written largely for older boys, but there was a group that had a kinship with *Robin Hood* in format and potential audience. In 1886 appeared *Pepper & Salt, or Seasoning for Young Folk,* sections of which had been presented to the readers of *Harper's Young People* since August of 1883, not long after the publication of *Robin Hood.* Pyle had been writing a series of tales in verse form for *Harper's Young People* with the intention of collecting them into a little giftbook. He had also been writing some folk stories for the same publication, and it was decided to combine the two groups in a larger format. This might suggest a kind of scrapbook collection but it was actually a most happy and unified collection, the kind that children delighted to dip into and taste bit by bit. The book, prose, verse, and picture, had an ingratiating, naive, and wholesome air in contrast with the generally prevailing Victorian stiffness and formality.

Two years later, in 1888, appeared *The Wonder Clock.* This should be linked with the *Robin Hood* and *Pepper & Salt* as a triumvirate of masterpieces. The three books are bound together by strong common excellences—the dominant hand is always visible but each has a personality of its own. All three are the happy triumphs of a rich creative period. In each case text, picture, and format design are in delightful accord. And through each runs the easy and ingratiating prose and verse of Pyle's youngish maturity, when his own childhood was not yet remote and his own young family was in the making.

We are tempted to think that the happy prose that runs through the three books was spontaneous and effortless. That is unlikely, for we have heard of discarded manuscripts and some of the early tales for *St. Nicholas* are not in the best vein; but essentially Pyle's folklore style needed only a little practice to become excellent of its kind. The simple, homely vocabulary, the blend of peasant shrewdness and racial wisdom, the ingenious styleless style, made their way easily into children's minds. It was such a readable style, prose for the lips as well as the eyes. Its foundations were laid in his very early years, when he was read to. A little later he was reading for himself and searching for new material. When he first began to think in terms of a writing career, folklore seemed the

Ye·song·of· ye·foolish· old·woman·

I saw an old woman go up a steep hill,
And she chuckled and laughed, as she went, with a will.
     And yet, as she went,
     Her body was bent,.
With a load as heavy as sins in lent.

"Oh! why do you chuckle, old woman;" says I,
As you climb up the hill-side so steep and so high?"
     "Because, don't you see,
     I'll presently be,
At the top of the hill. He! he!" says she.

I saw the old woman go downward again;
And she easily travelled, with never a pain;
     Yet she loudly cried,
     And gustily sighed,
And groaned, though the road was level and wide.

"Oh! why, my old woman," says I, "do you weep,
When you laughed, as you climbed up the hill-side so
     "High-ho! I am vexed,   steep?"
     Because I expects,"
Says she, "I shall ache in climbing the next.

H·Pyle.

Hope·in·Adversity.

Fear·in·Prosperity.

Page decoration and verse for *Pepper and Salt*, Harper and Brothers, 1888.

Pride in Distress.

M istress Polly Poppenjay,
Went to take a walk, one day.
On that morning she was dressed,
In her very sunday best;
Feathers, frills and ribbons gay;-
Proud was Mistress Poppenjay.

Mistress Polly Poppenjay,
Spoke to no one on her way;
Passed acquaintanes aside;
Held her head aloft with pride;
Did not see a puddle lay,
In front of Mistress Poppenjay.

Mistress Polly Poppenjay,
Harked to naught the folk could say.
Loud they cried, "Beware the puddle!"
Plump! She stepped into the middle.
And a pretty plight straightway,
Was poor Mistress Poppenjay.

Mistress Polly Poppenjay;
From your pickle others may
Learn to curb their pride a little;-
Learn to exercise their wit, till
They are sure no puddles may
Lie in front ; Miss Poppenjay.

Howard Pyle.

Illustration for "Pride in Distress." *Harper's Young People*, 1884.

A Tale ·of· a Tub·

1

You may bring to mind I've sung you a song,
    Of a man of Haarlem town.
I'll sing of another,—'twill not take long;
    Of equally great renown.

2

"I've read," said he, "there's a land afar,
    O'er the boundless rolling sea,
Where fat little pigs ready roasted are;
    Now, that is the land for me.

3

tart tree,
Where tarts may be plucked from the wild
    And puddings like pumpkins grow;
Where candies, like pebbles, lie by the sea,—
    Now, thither I'll straightway go."

4

Now, what do you think I've heard it said
    Was his boat, his oar, his sail?
A tub, a spoon, and a handkerchief red,
    For to breast both calm and gale.

5

So he sailed away, for a livelong day;
    And the sun was warm and mild,
And the small waves laughed as they seemed to play,
    And the sea-gulls clamored wild.

6

So he sailed away, for a livelong day;
    Till the wind began to roar,
And the waves rose high, and, to briefly say,
    He never was heard of more.

H. PYLE.

Illustration for "A Tale of a Tub." *Harper's Young People,* 1884.

The Swan carries the Prince over the hills and far away.

HP.

Illustration for "The Swan Maiden," *The Wonder Clock.* Harper and Brothers, 1888.

nearest reservoir of material and he read even more widely and delved into the history and background of this age-old subject. Folklore, particularly the European, was now in his blood. It had been assimilated, and it came from his pen, in prose and picture, as though from an original source.

Wonder Clock, with its subtitle *Four & Twenty Marvellous Tales, being one for each hour of the day*, was, like *Pepper & Salt*, a combination of prose and verse, but this time the verses with their pen decorations were the work of Howard's sister, Katharine Pyle. There was enough similarity of thought and execution between the two to make a book unified in appearance and literary flavor.

 he Fiddler gives the old wo = man all that he has in his purse . ❨ ❩:❨ ❩

Illustration for "The Staff and the Fiddle," *The Wonder Clock.* Harper and Brothers, 1888.

Stylistically, both in text and appearance, these three books stand together and some years later would be joined by another masterpiece group of books, the four-volume retelling of the King Arthur cycle. It must not be forgotten, however, that during the years that these books were being brought to completion, hundreds of other illustrations were being drawn or painted and articles and a variety of adult books written by Pyle as well.

One other book of folklike tales, *Twilight Tales*, was published in 1895, but it stands apart from the earlier triumvirate both in style and appearance. Using a lighter pen line, a

# The Prince comes to the old, three eyed Witch's house.

Illustration for "The Swan Maiden," *The Wonder Clock*. Harper and Brothers, 1888.

more modern touch creeps into the drawings and a somewhat more sophisticated tone into the prose. There is a wider range of source material, a great deal coming from the Eastern world, with an introduction that reveals Pyle as scholar and researcher. It is another excellent book but missing some of the intimacy and enfolding quality of the earlier three.

In the same year *The Garden Behind the Moon* was published. Although it may be classified as a long fairy tale, it is very different from the other books. It is not the retelling of an ancient tale or an improvisation upon one. It is an allegory and a fantasy

Sir Pellias encounters the Sorrowful Lady in Arroy

Full-page illustration for *The Story of King Arthur and His Knights*. Charles Scribner's Sons, 1903.

and because of the painful and saddening circumstances that prompted its creation there is no easy comparison of it with any other thing that Pyle wrote. The garden theme, welling up from Pyle's childhood memories of the home garden on the Kennett Pike, was a theme that he reiterated a goodly number of times in his pictures and here it became the background theme of an entire book. *The Garden Behind the Moon* became the dwelling place of children in the afterlife. Naturally sadness permeates the tale, a sadness restrained and misty. It could scarcely hope for a wide readership even though it contains some of Pyle's most moving word pictures.

When, almost two decades after the publication of *Robin Hood*, Pyle broached the idea to Scribner's of his interest in retelling and illustrating the story of the King Arthur legends, he compared it with the earlier book, suggesting a similar style with perhaps a more poetic and mature approach. Indeed, the project was the most taxing and monu-

The White Champion meets two Knights at the Mill.

Full-page illustration for *The Story of King Arthur and His Knights.* Charles Scribner's Sons, 1903.

mental that he had ever attempted. The four books, *The Story of King Arthur and His Knights, The Story of the Champions of the Round Table, The Story of Sir Launcelot and His Companions,* and *The Story of the Grail and the Passing of Arthur,* appeared at intervals between 1903 and 1910.

These dates coincide with the late and closing period of Pyle's active creative life. Work on the text and drawings for this monumental cycle was fitted into the intervals between his steady magazine commitments, other book illustrations, and several large mural commissions. The illustrations, executed in heavy ink line, show their debt to the *Robin Hood, Pepper & Salt, Wonder Clock* triumvirate, but have greater depth and power and a richer execution. They rose to the level of their epic subject and included many of Pyle's finest pictorial conceptions. Only in some of the last drawings are there signs of faltering and less convincing characterization.

The Story of
the
CHAMPIONS
of the
Round Table

Written and Illustrated
by
HOWARD PYLE.

NEW YORK

Title page for the *Story of the Champions of the Round Table*. Charles Scribner's Sons, 1905.

Sir Tristram leaps into y͏ᵉ Sea

Full-page illustration for *The Story of the Champions of the Round Table*. Charles Scribner's Sons, 1905.

The text also traces its line back to the earlier three books but that, too, with a change. Pyle was obviously working toward a more monumental prose that would nevertheless continue to impart a sense of intimacy to youthful minds. He made no particular attempt to imitate the Sir Thomas Malory prose, although it was the Malory version he had known from childhood days that was his principal source. But through his adult years he had explored other versions and the critical literature on the subject of the folktale, legend, and epic. We have no list of his studies in this direction but let us suggest that certain changes had taken place in his reaction to the folktale and the epic as he moved from youth to middle age. As the mature scholar added layers of learned information, he lost some of that innocence with which children view the world. It seems likely that the easy bounce of the *Robin Hood* prose was no longer natural to him and his investigation of sources other than Malory had given him new ideas of prose style.

There were some criticisms at the time of publication to the effect that he had not followed the simple and stately style of the Malory version. Some later criticisms pointed out that the Nordic influence of Malory seemed to have given way to a kind of Celtic mood and interpretation. Certainly the mood had changed, and stylistically, the sentences were longer and much more involved. An aura of mysticism, of magic behind the ordinary face of things, also crept in. More insistent are the word pictures used to induce mood while the cadence of words was more akin to a bardic rhythm, a cadence inducing a background of mystery and a link with a world behind the world of appearances. All this is Celtic.

We have no complete record of Pyle's sources but we have his own word that he had pored over "the most universally accepted sources." Almost certainly these must have led Pyle to the widespread roots of the Arthurian legend stretching through most of Europe, even south of the Alps. He must have encountered the varied accents of these sources as they passed through the German imagination of Wolfram von Eschenbach or appeared in the pages of *Perceval le Gallois*. And the Celtic traces discerned in his own version must have sprung from the *Mabinogion*, that collection of Welsh fables, five of which are concerned with Arthurian themes. Here was a glimpse into a remote pre-Christian world strangely different from the more orderly world of Malory. And the language rhythms were strange, too, dark, disordered, and shot with poetry. Matthew Arnold's description of these tales reveals their character:

> The medieval story-teller is pillaging an antiquity of which he does not fully possess the secret, he is like a peasant building his hut on the site of Halicarnassus or Ephesus; he builds, but what he builds is full of materials of which he knows not the history, or knows by a glimmering tradition, merely stones "not of this building," but of an older architecture, greater, cunninger, more majestical.*

These were some of the new vistas opened to Pyle by his mature research. The Arthurian cycles were infinitely more complex than anything disclosed by the family volume of Percy's *Reliques*. The strange provocative cadences of the *Mabinogion* revealed to him the opportunity to add his own harmonics to the Arthuriad, as so many had done before him. His labors in that direction were a triumph of prose and picture, attuned to a new, ripe twentieth-century audience.

It is scarcely possible to devise neat self-evident categories for Pyle's numerous and diversified books. The nine books here discussed can be placed under a myth–legend–fairy tale label for convenience. Eight of these books spring from the deeper roots of the race, the multiple tellings of ancient themes. The exception is *The Garden Behind the Moon*. Beyond these nine, the remaining books that may be classified as intended for children are fiction with an historical or adventure purpose.

The one fiction title that is closely allied to the eight legendary titles mentioned, both in writing and quality of illustration, is *Otto of the Silver Hand*. This story, laid in medieval Germany, is unique among all the other fiction titles. It is the first and best of three historical tales intended for children.

Like all Pyle's books in this category, it displays his wide and deep penetration into the intimate life of a period, an instinctive sense of its flavor, and a convincing grasp of the details of the time. The book, published in 1888, was a clean break with the still prevailing reluctance of writers to deal with brutality and evil in books for children. It was Pyle's first contribution to historical fiction for children, and it was a bold one. It appeared at a time when, with only the fewest exceptions, children's authors timidly

*In Vida D. Scudder, *Le Morte d'Arthur of Thomas Malory and Its Sources*. (New York: E. P. Dutton, 1921), p. 14.

Illustration for *Otto of the Silver Hand*. Charles Scribner's Sons, 1888.

Illustration for *Otto of the Silver Hand*. Charles Scribner's Sons, 1888.

circled away from the bitterness of life or threw a veil over it. Pyle's book was in no sense a defiant challenge to this convention. Against a background of medieval Germany, it straightforwardly and touchingly told a story of family hatred, of the mutilation of a young boy, Otto, and the consequences of this brutality. In no sense was it a tale from which a child would wince; it immediately enlisted deep interest and sympathy and its understanding compassion reached out to its new audience. The Middle Ages enfolds the characters into its bitterness and beauty. Pyle produced a deeply moving story without a hint of preachiness.

Illustrations completed the tone and effect of the story—in fact they initiated it. Almost inevitably a reader's first message from an illustrated book is a pictorial one. The strong, contrasting strokes of Pyle's pen, his network of dramatic darks, the simple, powerful, and yet poetic compositions, tend to prepare the reading eye and make it receptive to the prose. How well the pictures introduce the characters—they are already presences with a nature, a body, and a past history before we read a word. Dual talents such as Pyle's are scarce, and it is rarer still to find them so equal and balanced.

In the middle of the narrow way stood the motionless, steel-clad figure, illustration for *Otto of the Silver Hand*. Charles Scribner's Sons, 1888.

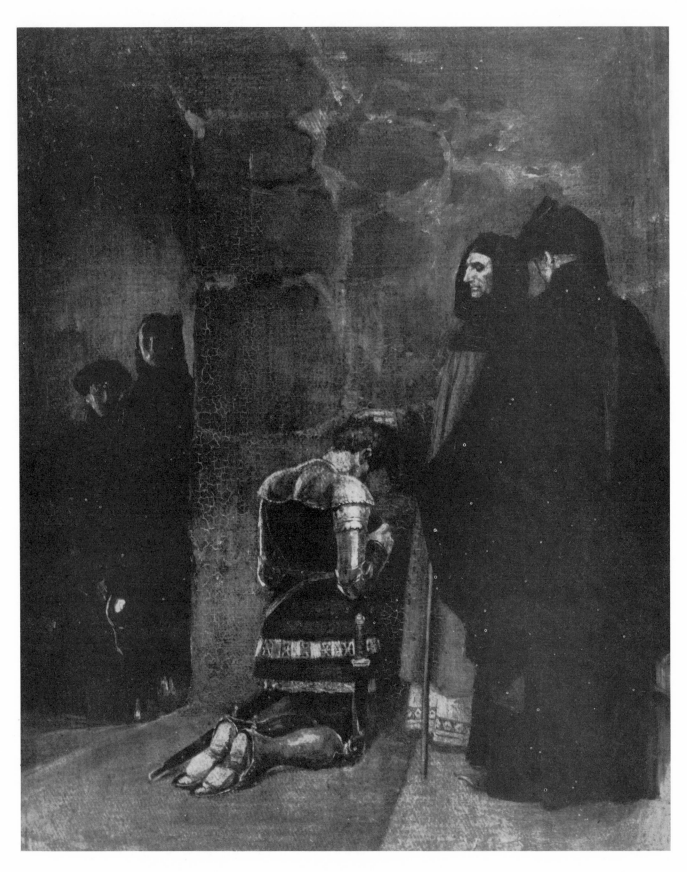

Illustration for *Men of Iron*. Harper and Brothers, 1891. FREE LIBRARY OF PHILADELPHIA.

There are three remaining books that can be considered to be for youthful readers. Two are historical adventure tales of novel length and the other a collection of four short stories. Physically these latter three do not resemble the others that have been discussed, largely because they are obviously intended for a somewhat older audience and are illustrated with tonal drawings instead of pen and ink. In fact, one of them might well appeal both to adolescent and adult. Each of the three takes place in a different spot geographically and in a different historical period. As might be expected, they coincide with Pyle's favorite geographical and historical areas—English medieval history, early American history, and the Spanish-American and pirate world of the Caribbean.

The earliest of the three, *Men of Iron,* published in 1892, is laid in fifteenth-century England. Its plot is simple and quite conventional: the development and final triumph of the boy Myles Falworth—his schooling into young manhood under the shadow of an injustice done to his family, and his heroic righting of an old wrong. The theme is an old one, but Pyle gave it new conviction with his evocation of the relentless schooling for knighthood. Pyle's historical sense was extensive and thorough, yet it never conveyed a sense of mere accumulated facts. The knowledge seems to have been relived in his imagination long before words were found. His detailed story of young Myles's grueling years as a squire and his sudden leap into knighthood conveys a strong image of late medieval life. That image, however, is not strengthened by Pyle's illustrations, largely because the method of reproduction had changed. The halftone method had now become a reliable and accepted process, and pen and ink was in diminishing demand. At any rate, the new process dictated different techniques of illustration, principally painting in oil or watercolor. The *Men of Iron* pictures were painted in oil and well painted but they lack the bite and power of the pen drawings for *Otto of the Silver Hand.* They are well composed, the forms are there, the figures characterized, but the method of reproduction has sapped the contrasts and encouraged the shapes to be factually accurate rather than imaginatively arresting. The eye travels over the gray panels without much temptation to linger and find long satisfactions.

Three years later, *The Story of Jack Ballister's Fortunes* appeared. In order to impart an early eighteenth-century flavor to the book, Pyle added a long explanatory subtitle to the title page: "Being the narrative of the adventures of a young gentleman of good family, who was kidnapped in the year 1719 and carried to the plantations of the continent of Virginia, where he fell in with that famous pirate Captain Edward Teach, or Blackbeard; of his escape from the pirates and the rescue of a young lady from out of their hands." That subtitle is, of course, a synopsis of the plot, again a fairly standard one, but Pyle brings it to life with constant action, good characterizations, and his always reliable power to evoke an authentic historical setting. The story has been criticized over the years for Pyle's propensity to pause and instruct or point a moral. Certainly such a galloping tale is scarcely a suitable vehicle for admonishing interludes, but they are easily skipped and ignored.

The last children's book, *Stolen Treasure,* was certainly an afterthought, made up of four pirate tales that had originally appeared in magazines about ten years before. This compilation appeared in 1907, the same year that marked the publication of *The Story of Sir Launcelot and His Companions,* the third in the Arthurian cycle. At that time Pyle was also working intermittently on the text and pictures of *The Story of the Grail and the Passing of Arthur,* the last book that he would write and illustrate.

It is interesting to note that of the thirteen children's books discussed in this chapter, seven had earlier publication in various magazines and another was excerpted. It is also noteworthy that eleven of the thirteen had simultaneous publication in England. England accepted Howard Pyle, word and picture.

Illustration for *Jack Ballister's Fortunes*. The Century Co., 1895.

A page from *Yankee Doodle, an Old Friend in a New Dress*. Dodd, Mead & Co., 1881. DELAWARE ART MUSEUM.

Illustration for *The Lady of Shalott*. Dodd, Mead & Co., 1882.

Washington's Retreat from Great Meadows, illustration from "Colonel Washington," by Woodrow Wilson. *Harper's Monthly*, March 1896. COLLECTION OF THE BOSTON PUBLIC LIBRARY.

Washington and Mary Philipse, illustration from "Colonel Washington," by Woodrow Wilson. *Harper's Monthly,* March 1896. COLLECTION OF THE BOSTON PUBLIC LIBRARY.

Washington and Steuben at Valley Forge, illustration from "General Washington," by Woodrow Wilson. *Harper's Monthly,* July 1896. COLLECTION OF THE BOSTON PUBLIC LIBRARY.

The Fight on Lexington Common, illustration from "The Story of the Revolution." *Scribner's Magazine*, January – December 1898.
DELAWARE ART MUSEUM.

Assassination of LaSalle, illustration from *The Works of Francis Parkman*, Vol. VI. Little, Brown & Co., 1897. COLLECTION OF THE LAUREL PUBLIC LIBRARY, LAUREL, DELAWARE.

The Fishing of Thor and Hymir, illustration from ''North Folk Legends of the Sea.'' *Harper's Monthly,* January 1902. DELAWARE ART MUSEUM.

Experimental sketch in ink and watercolor for *The Fishing of Thor and Hymir.* DELAWARE ART MUSEUM.

St. Brendan's Island, illustration from "North Folk Legends of the Sea." *Harper's Monthly,* January 1902. DELAWARE ART MUSEUM.

Sketch for *The Fairy Morgana,* illustration from "North Folk Legends of the Sea." *Harper's Monthly,* January 1902. DELAWARE ART MUSEUM.

Illustration from "The Pilgrimage of Truth." *Harper's Monthly*, December 1900. DELAWARE ART MUSEUM.

Illustration from "The Pilgrimage of Truth." *Harper's Monthly*, December 1900. DELAWARE ART MUSEUM.

Truth Before the King, illustration from "The Pilgrimage of Truth." *Harper's Monthly*, December 1900. DELAWARE ART MUSEUM.

First color painting of intended illustration for "The Pilgrimage of Truth." *Harper's Monthly*, December 1900. DELAWARE ART MUSEUM.

At the Gate of the Castle, illustration for *Harper's Monthly,* December 1903. DELAWARE
ART MUSEUM.

I Clutched at His Ankle, illustration from "Sinbad on Burrator." *Scribner's Magazine,* August 1902.
DELAWARE ART MUSEUM.

He came to her —in his helmet a fox brush, illustration for "The Fox Brush." *Harper's Monthly*, August 1903.
COLLECTION OF HOWARD BROKAW.

Blackbeard's Last Fight, illustration for *Jack Ballister's Fortunes.* The Century Co., 1895. DELAWARE ART MUSEUM.

The Pirates Fire upon the Fugitives, illustration for *Jack Ballister's Fortunes.* The Century Co., 1895.
PRIVATE COLLECTION.

Chapter 7

OTHER WRITING

Howard Pyle the writer evades neat cataloging. On all fronts we face his versatility. Reviewing the rich harvest of his children's books, we have seen how varied they are. The prose of *Robin Hood* is not that of the four Arthurian books; there is a wide difference between the telling of *Jack Ballister's Fortunes* and that of *The Garden Behind the Moon*. To some degree the differences can be attributed to an evolution of style, born of practice and experience, but this can be only partly true, for many times he practiced several styles almost simultaneously. In one richly productive period of about four years he wrote an adult adventure story and a pirate thriller, two children's books of folktales and verse, and his finest book of historical fiction for children. At the same time he was writing a handful of smaller pieces for the magazines: a number of historical articles like "The Early Quakers in England and Pennsylvania," and "Buccaneers and Marooners of the Spanish Main"; travel pieces like "A Peculiar People"; and short stories such as "Squire Tripp's Old Arm Chair." All these were sandwiched between his regular painting and drawing hours in the studio and often he was working on two writing projects at the same time. There were times when it appeared that his nature demanded two contrasting problems at the same time.

Etching, by Howard Pyle.

On the Way to Tyburn, illustration for "A Famous Chapbook Villain." *Harper's Monthly*, July 1890. PRIVATE COLLECTION.

Headpiece for "Through Inland Waters." *Harper's Monthly*, April 1896.

Illustration for *Hugh Wynne, Free Quaker,* by S. Weir Mitchell. The Century Co., New York, 1897.

Illustration for *Hugh Wynne, Free Quaker*, by S. Weir Mitchell. The Century Co., New York, 1897.

Pyle the reporter and journalist is usually brushed aside to make way for Pyle the author of notable children's books, and rightly so, for the journalistic pieces are of only passing interest. But they played their part in his education. They were a great help in launching his early career as both writer and artist—they gave him practice in the craft of words and the roving assignments that came a little later forced him out of his snug Wilmington ways at least briefly. Too, a number of his short pieces were vehicles for some of his best pictures, for example, *Travels of the Soul* for *Century Magazine*.

The adult books he wrote were interspersed with those for children. In order of publication they were, *The Rose of Paradise*, 1888; *The Buccaneers and Marooners of America*, 1891; *A Modern Aladdin*, 1892; *The Price of Blood*, 1896; *Rejected of Men*, 1903; and *The Ruby of Kishmoor*, 1908. *The Rose of Paradise* and *The Ruby of Kishmoor* are pirate fiction, and obviously piracy is the theme of *The Buccaneers and Marooners of America*, although that book was an abridged reprint of Esquemeling's *Buccaneers of America*, which was edited by Pyle and for which he wrote an introductory chapter. *A Modern Aladdin* and *The Price of Blood* were called "extravaganzas" by their author, and that is as good a term as may be found to indicate their mixture of fact and fantasy, of the mundane and the miraculous. Finally, *Rejected of Men*, a novel of Christ's life and death in modern New York, stands totally apart from all Pyle's other published works.

To return to the mostly anonymous critics of the time for opinions of Pyle's work, most were generous in their praise, some voiced qualified approval, and a few were sharply critical. Most of the adventure-pirate-extravaganza books were treated as adult fare by the critics although there were some who thought of them in terms of a younger audience. In any case, there was a pronounced tendency to compare Pyle's adventure books with those of Robert Louis Stevenson.

The first novel, *Within the Capes*, deftly uses the principle of contrast. The story begins in the Quaker atmosphere of a quiet Pennsylvania town and countryside, as old Captain Tom Granger tells of two youthful and explosive years of his life. Those two years are tightly packed with familiar ingredients—the sea, privateering in the War of 1812, shipwreck, desert islands, buried treasure, murder, false accusations, detective work, and a wedding. The breathless excitement of those two years is enhanced by the old sailor's artless, rambling sentences.

With the next book, *The Rose of Paradise*, Pyle plunged into the hot and bloody world of piracy and high-colored romance. The setting is the Mozambique Channel in the year 1720. The "rose" is a ruby of fabulous worth; there is capture by pirates and recovery of the jewel, so the plot moves in well-worn grooves, although with some quirks that tug at the boundaries of credulity. This again is an autobiographical narration but less successful than that of Captain Tom Granger, probably because it takes place more than a century earlier and both speech and spelling have an archaic form. At least two reviews greeted it as a boy's book and the same number compared it, not particularly unfavorably, with *Kidnapped* and *Treasure Island* by Robert Louis Stevenson.

Stevenson had his own say about the next book, *A Modern Aladdin*. He liked it, saying, "I thought Aladdin capital fun" and adding, "—but why, in fortune, did he pretend it was moral in the end. . . . 'Tis a trifle, but Pyle would do well to knock the passage out, and leave his bogey tale a bogey tale, and a good one at that." Seldom could a tale have been so improved by striking out three paragraphs. The old Aladdin theme was taken out of China and set going again in the France of Louis XV, which in itself tantalizes the expectations. Pyle's gift for introducing salient details added piquancy to an excursion into fantasy—there was a plethora of the incredible, the diabolical, and the frightening, and one willingly surrendered to it.

The Price of Blood, like *Aladdin*, is listed as an "extravaganza," in this case of life in New York in 1807. As the title suggests, the staid New York of the early nineteenth century is

The Rush from the N.Y. Stock Exchange, illustration for "A History of the Last Quarter Century," by E. Benjamin Andrews. *Scribner's Magazine*, June 1895.

Meeting of Greene and Gates, illustration for *The Story of the Revolution*, by Henry Cabot Lodge. *Scribner's Magazine*, January to December, 1898. DELAWARE ART MUSEUM.

Illustration for "How the Declaration was Received in the Old Thirteen," by Charles D. Deshler. *Harper's Monthly,* July 1892.

Illustration for "General Washington," by Woodrow Wilson. *Harper's New Monthly Magazine,* July 1896.

The Sacking of Panama, illustration for "Buccaneers and Marooners of the Spanish Main." *Harper's Monthly,* August 1887.
COLLECTION OF DOUGLAS ALLEN.

Illustration for "So It Is With Them All."
Harper's Young People, November 1892.

Illustration for *The Novels and Tales of Robert
Louis Stevenson.* Charles Scribner's Sons,
1895. DELAWARE ART MUSEUM.

The three fellows were brought aft, illustration for "The Rose of Paradise." *Harper's Weekly*, 1887. FREE LIBRARY OF PHILADELPHIA.

the background for an unrestrained thriller, furnished by Pyle's newly found fancy for strange and fearsome characters out of the mysterious East bent on incredible and murderous missions. This is Pyle letting go with a will, a melodramatic catharsis that may have purged him for more shapely things. No one could have guessed that the author of this thriller was even then working on *Rejected of Men*.

The last pirate book, *The Ruby of Kishmoor*, did not find a publisher until 1908, although it had been written years before. Here we again encounter the literary confrontation that had been used before and that related so closely to Pyle's own ambivalent nature—the prosaic Quaker youth plunged into experiences totally remote from his own life and nature. Pyle certainly read himself into these tales: How well he understood the restraint and decorum of an ancestral Quaker background and the imaginative thirst for high action and incredible experience.

Scanning his writing, in retrospect we can see patterns emerge. He had no inventive sense of plot or structure. He took old frameworks and fleshed them out. His characters were usually well drawn but of no great complexity. They performed with voice and muscle. They were suited to the boundaries of an adventure tale. In his writing, he remained the colorist and picturemaker, succeeding well with the settings and establishing a feeling of place.

He was a born romantic and all his books spring from that impulse, not excepting the strange and solitary *Rejected of Men*. But the bred-in-the-bone romantic was tantalized by a secondary craving for realism—he wanted to write like William Dean Howells. That made for a conflict but also for a blend—the passion for accurate observation and patient detail provided a background of substance for headlong action and incredible happenings. His realism was mostly tutored by his artist's eye; it concerned itself largely with the appearance of things, not with penetration. Both in his prose and his pictures romanticism and reality existed side by side, blending and implementing each other.

Illustration for "The Price of Blood." *Collier's Weekly,*
December 1898. DELAWARE ART MUSEUM.

Heading for "By Land and Sea." *Harper's
Monthly,* December 1895.

1

Headpiece 3 for "By Land and Sea." *Harper's Monthly*, December 1895.

The tide of historical-adventure-fantasy fiction—of which much of Pyle's writing for adults was a part—began to ebb through the early years of the twentieth century. A whole cluster of popular names was fading: Rider Haggard, Maurice Hewlett, Richard Harding Davis, Stanley Weyman, Winston Churchill, George Barr McCutcheon, Mary Johnson, S. Weir Mitchell, and many others. Pyle may have been conscious of the slackening of interest, of the fact that the vein had been overworked—at least temporarily—and of the growing power of a drive toward realism. But the romantic in him was not to be converted into a no-nonsense realist, merely modified a touch or two. Pyle was astute enough to applaud the worth of Howells's work and to value him as a forerunner and active advocate of the powerful realistic movement that was gathering its forces, but the younger talents like Hamlin Garland, Stephen Crane, Frank Norris, and Harold Frederic seemed to have been of little interest to him. The spirit of American self-awareness, the deep examination of its past and present that was showing itself in all areas of American life, created an ideal climate for Pyle's own talents, particularly his historical pictures. History provided him abundant opportunity, and his contribution was great. But his deep love of northern folklore, legend, and epic, which had found such splendid expression in so much of his writing and picturing for children, seemed untouched by the new quest for an American heroic tradition, for an American mythology.

Everywhere America's past was being reclaimed, nowhere more diligently than from the old ballads and frontier legends. The giants of the past were being brought back into the light, refashioned, amplified, exploited—Paul Bunyan and Daniel Boone, Mike Fink, Johnny Appleseed, Davy Crockett and John Henry, Pecos Bill and Whiskey Jack. They were a preposterous, comic, roystering race of newly discovered superheroes; they had to be taken with laughter. Europe's heroes were serious. Ours, as Max Eastman said, were "Cockalorum demigods," but they had frontier flavor and frontier humor. Perhaps this is why Pyle seems to have had no interest in them. In spite of his declared Americanism, there was nothing of the frontier American in him—he was more European than he realized.

In the Woodcarver's Shop, painting for "By Land and Sea." *Harper's Monthly*, December 1895.

Chapter 8

THE ART OF THE PEN

Pyle was a multiple person and an ambivalent artist. Opposites met in him, but in the main they excited and enriched both his pictorial and writing talents. Study of his varied pen styles reveals many of his deepest characteristics.

These styles formed themselves during his early years when he was contributing his adult pictures to *Harper's New Monthly*, *Harper's Weekly*, and *Scribner's* and his children's pictures to *St. Nicholas* and *Harper's Young People*. Obviously, these two audiences could scarcely be served by the same type of picture, but aside from that there was a need in him to explore two quite different pen techniques and to perfect the resulting types of pictorial effects. One type was deeply traditional, readily tracing its origins back to the Middle Ages. It was a deliberate, decorative, richly outlined art. The other was of its time, stemming from the Impressionist painters' explorations into the study of light and their attempt to seize and fix transitory natural effects.

In 1883 when Pyle's *Robin Hood* appeared, it revealed his decorative style to a wide audience. Pyle was thirty and on the threshold of artistic maturity. His impressionistic style had kept pace with the other, more traditional, style but had not yet reached the more

The·Mighty·Fight·betwixt:
Little John·and·the·Cook:

Illustration from *The Merry Adventures of Robin Hood*. Charles Scribner's Sons, 1883.

permanent form of book illustration. In fact, he would never use it as widely in that field. The *Robin Hood* drawings represented an important milestone in the development of his decorative style, but it had been in formation for years, reaching back to childhood and his first awareness of picture books and magazines. His impressionistic style had more recent roots, from the time of his apprenticeship in New York City.

The *Robin Hood* theme offered a splendid opportunity to put into concrete and continuous form the dreams and backgrounds that were such a part of his earlier years. The theme was English and medieval and that naturally set its stamp upon picture and text. While his audience was late Victorian, it was a restless and dissatisfied one, reaching for change; just as unconsciously Pyle's multiple talents were stirring with the same need for change. The old legend was part of his childhood, first read to him in his earliest years by his mother and then read and reread by him later. He knew it thoroughly in the somewhat stilted versions of Percy's *Reliques* and Ritson's *Robin Hood*. His mental picture of its characters and background was formed by the wood engravings of the English Victorian illustrators. The Little German Masters and particularly Albrecht Dürer were a somewhat later passion, as was an interest in some of the British illustration of his own day, which was tending toward a style that is now characterized as Early Art Nouveau.

All these elements were ingredients in Pyle's maturing decorative pen style. The pen was the chosen instrument not only because of its simple direct suitability for a young audience, but because it permitted a cheap and uncomplicated method of reproduction. The pen told its story in line—rich, positive but supple line with certain spaces enriched with ornament or details of texture. Little attempt was made to indicate light and shadow; each form was kept intact. Pyle's design instinct seldom faltered; he produced page after page of beautifully integrated pictorial patterns, supplemented by decorated initial letters, chapter headings, and tailpieces.

By the time of the publication of *Robin Hood* in 1883, his drawing had matured. The necessity of delineating the human form day after day was developing his confidence and certainty with a widening variety of poses. Most poses could be drawn from a well-stocked memory; only the more unusual and difficult required a model. In spite of their confining ink outline his figures moved and gestured with ease and informality—seldom were they frozen into inertness by his decorative method.

This was a period of rapid growth. The apprentice days were behind him, but he was still malleable, packed with multiple possibilities, teeming with energy, and driven by great ambition. In the hungry way that seems instinctive to almost every accomplished artist in his growing years, Pyle was searching the work of those talents he admired— probing and analyzing method, purpose, and emotional content for the secrets of successful expression. The picture mind and the literary mind commingled and fertilized each other. If we mention them separately, it is for convenience' sake and sometimes a necessity, but it can be misleading—both sprang from a deep common source.

Later, as he passed from book to book, he modified his style to accord with new material, demonstrating the flexibility of a method that could easily have become rigid and repetitious. The *Robin Hood* was followed by the naive humor and peasant flavor of *Pepper & Salt*, in turn followed by the enchantment of *The Wonder Clock*. The drawings for *Otto of the Silver Hand* were haunting and gripping. They made no concessions to the pattern of cozy charm and sprightliness that was generally expected of children's pictures of the time. And Pyle told the story just as directly, turning his back upon the clichés and sweetly doctored prose of the great bulk of late Victorian children's literature. The book marked a turn of taste and conception.

One decorated book stands apart from the rest. *Stops of Various Quills*, a slender book of poetry by his friend William Dean Howells, was a labor of love. The individual decorations were originally used for magazine publication, but both author and illustrator knew that book publication was in the future. There was great kinship between the men, and the same feeling infuses both text and picture. Outwardly, Pyle was using stock allegorical forms of the period, the same repetitive figures found in the decorations of Edwin Blashfield, Kenyon Cox, Will Low, and others—draped female characters symbolizing Justice, Peace, or a hundred other virtues; the cloaked figure of Death with his scythe; countless singing angels and brooding wise men or suppliant sinners. But Pyle's innate sturdiness and wholesomeness enabled him to escape the inherent sentimentality of this approach.

Illustrations for *Pepper and Salt*. Harper and Brothers, 1886.

Abbott Otto, of St. Michaelsburg, was a gentle, patient, pale-faced old man, illustration for *Otto of the Silver Hand*. Charles Scribner's Sons, 1888.

These illustrations, one from *Otto of the Silver Hand* and one from *The Wonder Clock*, clearly show the influence of Albrecht Dürer's work. Other *Wonder Clock* pictures, with a more humorous content, exhibit more certainly Pyle's individuality in adapting the medieval influence to his own purposes.

he Great Red Fox goeth to the store-house and helps himself to the good things. ❡

Illustration for "How Two Went into Partnership," *The Wonder Clock*. Harper and Brothers, 1888.

Illustration for *The Wonder Clock*. Harper and Brothers, 1888.

How Two went into Partnership.

Heading for *The Wonder Clock*. Harper and Brothers, 1888.

Peterkin, with ỹ help of the hare, carries off the Giant's goose.

Peterkin and the Little Gray Hare, illustration for *The Wonder Clock*. Harper and Brothers, 1888.

The poor man touches the door with ý stone.

Illustration for ''Which Is Best?,'' *The Wonder Clock.*
Harper and Brothers, 1888.

Illustration for *Otto of the Silver Hand.* Charles
Scribner's Sons, 1888.

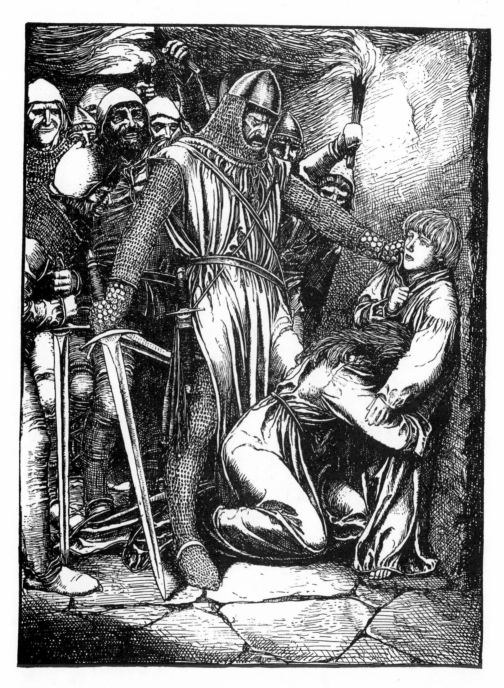

He strode forward into the room and laid his hand heavily on the boy's shoulder, illustration for
Otto of the Silver Hand. Charles Scribner's Sons, 1888.

In an instant he was flung back and down, illustration for *Otto of the Silver Hand.* Charles Scribner's Sons, 1888.

In a small format he projected a feeling of largeness, of convincing mood and honest emotion. It demonstrated that he could move from the particular to the general. *Stops of Various Quills*, published in 1895, has never attracted as much attention as Pyle's other decorative books, yet it had a unique flavor. Behind it were the splendid array of *Robin Hood, Pepper & Salt, The Wonder Clock,* and *Otto of the Silver Hand,* and ahead of it were the four King Arthur books. This collection of book decoration is unique, for each book shows an adaptation of what might have been a standard pictorial solution to the particular flavor of a different subject. Yet the differences spring from a basic, personal outlook—the Pyle touch is in every design.

The four volumes of the King Arthur series that followed *Stops of Various Quills* were Pyle's last, large decorative book efforts. The first, *The Story of King Arthur and His Knights,* was published in 1903. Although initially serialized in monthly installments in *St. Nicholas,* the book design had been in Pyle's mind from the first stroke. It was an instant artistic and literary success. In many ways the pictures were the richest and most full-bodied of any of the Pyle books. The characters were real personalities, but with extra dimensions. Arthur and his land were Pyle's own reconstructed dream.

The three other volumes, *The Story of the Champions of the Round Table, The Story of Sir Launcelot and His Companions,* and *The Story of the Grail and the Passing of Arthur,* followed at intervals of several years, the last in 1910. So the project, his most ambitious in decorative pen technique, saw its completion scarcely a year before his death, at a time when by far the greater part of Pyle's work and interest lay with his brushes and oil palette. In the last two books are signs of the waning of his decorative interest. The sense of fresh invention is gone, the designs are repetitive.

Heading for *The Story of King Arthur and His Knights. St. Nicholas,* November 1902 to October 1903.

King Leodegrance cometh to the assay of the Sword.

Illustration for *The Story of King Arthur and His Knights. St. Nicholas*, November 1902 to October 1903.

How Arthur drew forth ẙ Sword.

Illustration for *The Story of King Arthur and His Knights. St. Nicholas,* November 1902 to October 1903.

The Lady of the Lake sits by the Fountain in Arroy.

Illustration for *The Story of King Arthur and His Knights. St. Nicholas,* November 1902 to October 1903.

Illustration for *The Story of the Champions of the Round Table.* Charles Scribner's Sons, 1905.

Sir Lamorack herds the swine of Sir Nabon

Illustration for *The Story of the Champions of the Round Table*. Charles Scribner's Sons, 1905.

The Queen of Ireland seeks to slay Sir Tristram.

Illustration for *The Story of the Champions of the Round Table*. Charles Scribner's Sons, 1905.

ueen Morgana appears unto Sir Launcelot.

Illustration for *The Story of the Champions of the Round Table*. Charles Scribner's Sons, 1905.

Sir Launcelot of the Lake.

Illustration for *The Story of the Champions of the Round Table*. Charles Scribner's Sons, 1905.

The bold, linear, decorative method of pen drawing that had already reached a ripe period in *Robin Hood*, and which came to an end with the last of the King Arthur books, was balanced by an equally successful growth in a markedly different, impressionistic, method. The Spanish-born Parisian Daniel Vierge had been the god of the younger pen artists that Pyle had mingled with in New York, and the rage in Paris. Vierge's work was constantly appearing in the Parisian journals and his masterful illustrations for Cervante's *Don Quixote* and DeOuevedo-Villegas's *Pablo de Segovia* were widely imitated. Vierge had translated the technique of Impressionist painters into the unlikely medium of the pen line. The shimmering sunlight and transparent shadows, the envelopment of the human figure and other solids in atmosphere, the appetite for transitory effects, all this Vierge was able to duplicate in the tracery of a delicate steel nib.

Pen illustration by Daniel Vierge.

He had an accurate but imaginative eye for nature's forms, and a butterfly touch. In the shadowy patches he placed so knowingly, he used the age-old device of the crosshatch but in a very loose, open way so that the area seemed luminous with reflected lights. Since the French methods of reproduction permitted it, he often introduced a spot or two of gray or black wash. But he was always very sparing of darks, and he had a remarkable instinct for placing them in the most telling areas, leaving the greater part of his picture sparkling with the reflected light of the white, untouched paper. He translated the blinding sunlight of his native country by means of cunningly drawn black lines.

These were the pictures that educated a whole school of pen artists in Europe and America and particularly in America, where there was no special tradition in linear art. Most of the young talent that clustered about the big publishing houses in New York felt some attraction and kinship with Impressionism. Some imitated Vierge up to the limits of their abilities. The more accomplished artists used the Vierge influence as a way station on the journey toward an individual expression. Joseph Pennell and Ernest Peixotto retained the Vierge sparkle and the darting pen strokes in their mature work; others like Charles Reinhart and Frederic Remington picked up elements and assimilated them into the mainstream of their strong pictorial convictions. A generation later Joseph Clement Coll, one of America's greatest pen artists and a self-educated one, built an amazingly vibrant, imaginative, and dramatic technique inspired by the Vierge style. In a still later generation, Lyle Justis used that same inspiration to evolve his own notable calligraphic style.

It would be a distortion and oversimplification to imply that there were only two schools of pen expression and that Pyle's work fell rigidly within those boundaries. It was a period of abundant talents and much experimentation, and Pyle did his share of the

Pen illustration by Daniel Vierge.

The Challenge, unpublished ink drawing, 1903. COLLECTION OF ANDREW WYETH.

Pen drawing for "By Land and Sea." *Harper's Monthly*, December 1895.

latter. He did a goodly number of drawings that fell somewhere between the two schools and a number that resist classification. Like his fellow illustrators, he felt the impact of other influences, notably the work of the Englishman Charles Keene and the German Adolf Menzel, as well as the drawings of the English Pre-Raphaelites. All this reflected the natural creative appetite of a healthy, expanding talent reaching for sources of pictorial nourishment.

We can now scan the pageant of Pyle's pen art in either reproduction or original and it is a story of growth and expansion. It clearly shows two dominant styles: an urgent decorative sense that liked to deal in large impressive forms and to indulge in pattern, and an equally powerful urge to capture the fleeting effects of nature's light, to establish a sense of atmosphere and aerial recession, and to report the world with a realist's eye. The two points of view were not necessarily antagonistic: there were many points of reconciliation and Pyle did, at moments, explore them.

These two approaches to graphic expression grew and flourished side by side. Had they been presented to their audiences with different signatures, they would have been accepted as the work of two separate personalities.

It was not just two types of pen art that were flourishing side by side. From 1898, Pyle began using oils and wash constantly; his writing for both adult and young audiences was in full tide, and his teaching took up the fringe hours of the day. All these avenues of expression, remarkably diversified as they are, were the product of one mind and one hand and we must enlarge our vision to embrace his great versatility.

Pen drawing for "By Land and Sea."
Harper's Monthly, December 1895.

Pen drawing for *Harper's Young People.*

Pen drawing for *Harper's Young People.*

New York Colonial Privateers.
by Thomas A Janvier

Pen drawing for *Harper's Monthly,* February 1895.

Pen illustration for "By Land and Sea." *Harper's Monthly,* December 1895.

One reason for the final fading of his decorative pen style and his virtual abandonment of the pen was the rapid changes occurring in the publishing world. American technology had perfected the halftone and color reproduction processes, and the public was enamored of the results. The demand was for realistic pictures, fully modeled in color or black and white, and Pyle undoubtedly relished the opportunities offered by this trend. And we must remember that his last major concern was with mural decoration. There seemed to be a more hidden reason as well, an inner one dictated by his Quaker ancestry.

Those Quaker instincts of plainness, sobriety, and revolt against display refused to dovetail meekly with the exuberance and extravagance of his equally innate sense of decoration. There must have been times when one or the other was uppermost. Some of his students have told of his warnings against overpreoccupation with design. One of them, who taught for many years, was known for a repeated expression, "Decoration is an invention of the Devil."

In this regard, scanning the work of his former students through their professional years brings to light an intriguing fact. Among the men, almost all practiced a type of realistic painting more or less akin to that of the master's late period, but often infused with decorative qualities. Only Maxfield Parrish was an out-and-out decorator, and his style was largely formed before he came under Pyle's instruction. Henry Soulen's work had a strong decorative bent, and George Harding in his later years devoted himself entirely to mural decoration. But the work of the women students tells another story. Almost all their work shows a strong decorative awareness. Studying a hundred or more reproductions of their work we see immediately that they represent a school of their own, with strong common characteristics shining through the personal touches.

This can be said of such artists as Elizabeth Shippen Green, Charlotte Harding, Jessie Wilcox Smith, Sarah Stillwell Weber, Margaretta Hinchman, Wuanita Smith, Olive Rush, the Betts girls, Katherine Wireman, and Ida Dougherty. Violet Oakley, too, was preeminently the decorator throughout her long history of mural design.

All the above-mentioned women were Philadelphians and they became a rather closely knit group during most of their middle and sometimes later creative years. This undoubtedly contributed to their rather similar pictorial outlook, giving the effect of an *illustrative school*. For a decade and more theirs was a very important contribution to American illustration but it gradually faded as the taste of the times shifted. Only Jessie Wilcox Smith's work was popular well into her advanced years.

All of these women were fulsome in their praise of their master instructor and gratefully nostalgic about the months and years they had spent in his classes. In their reminiscences they frequently used the word *composition*, in the sense of design or decorative arrangement. And they all built their pictures upon a skeleton of line, creating shapes that were filled in or modeled with tone or color. Their work has a much more homogeneous look than that of the male students, and this may well be due to a factor in art education that is often overlooked. *Students educate each other.* Art teachers of long experience know that under certain conditions, aspirations latent in a group of students can be triggered, resulting in the students' striving and fumbling as a group toward their realization. The answers they work out as a team coalesce into a manner, a way of seeing, a school. This can happen regardless of sex, but in this case it was the women students who worked out a group style. Another commanding factor was that Pyle had so many gifts to bestow—his students took from him what they could assimilate and were often oblivious of the rest.

Chapter 9

PYLE, THE TEACHER

Although Howard Pyle never taught until the middle years of his life, intimations of a desire to do so appear much earlier. One of the roots of this desire lay in his rebellion against certain lacks in his own art training. His schooling under Mr. Van der Weilen, although good of its kind, was limiting.

It is true that day-after-day practice over a period of three years by a gifted young student was virtually certain to inculcate sharp observation of the human form, rapid evaluation of proportions, and a trained hand to record that knowledge. Pyle did learn to copy the posed model quite well, but in a way that tended to restrict his all-around pictorial powers. First, to ask models to pose for three hours a day or a series of days (as was customary), was to force them into a routine of stock, inert poses that could be borne for long periods of time. No matter how alert at the beginning, a model would shortly show dullness and fatigue in every contour. This kind of art course was often derisively referred to as "Training in Drawing Tired Models." Second, the unvarying northern light taught sameness—it provided no experience with the multiple effects of out-of-doors nor the mysteries of artificial light indoors. There was insufficient appeal in this for an

Rough sketch for *The Coming of Lancaster,* early 1908. This is a typical example of the quick pencil sketches that Pyle made as he searched for a definite composition.

Howard Pyle in his studio, circa 1900.

imaginative pictorial mind. It probably worked well enough for aspiring portrait painters but not for hopeful illustrators.

All that this training encouraged was a type of copying: there was no scope for compositional invention, no encouragement to draw upon the imagination. Only after a few months in New York, struggling with the impossible task of expecting a model to furnish all needed information about character and movement, did Pyle begin to depend more upon his inherent imagination and his growing store of pictorial memories. He started to reeducate himself in drawing and to think beyond the model.

Another thing that spurred him toward teaching was his growing concern with the standards of American illustration. He had a deep conviction that an illustrator should have an earnest sense of responsibility to his audience and that only the best talents should be recruited for that art. Those talents should have strong imaginative powers and the gift of immersing themselves in the drama and emotions they were trying to communicate. He believed the art schools of his time were ill equipped to nourish this kind of talent, and, as he reached his middle years, he felt within himself the power to answer that need.

At last Pyle decided to act upon his convictions. There was no established art school in Wilmington to which he could offer his services, but in nearby Philadelphia were four. Three were newcomers—the Philadelphia School of Industrial Art, then about twenty years old and established to prepare the artist and designer to enter the world of headlong industrialism; the School of Design for Women; and the Drexel Institute, another school that was formed to answer the needs of a technological civilization. The fourth was the prestigious Pennsylvania Academy of the Fine Arts, the oldest art school in the country, with a long list of famous former students.

It was natural that Pyle should offer his services to the academy. They were refused. The refusal was by letter, a document that has since disappeared. From the accounts of several of his students, the import of it was that since the academy was solely concerned with the fine arts, illustration was not within its province. That rebuff rankled and not least because one of the tenets of Pyle's faith was a conviction that *fine art* was a term of high attainment and illustration on its superior levels was just that. There was a sequel to this. Sometime afterward when Pyle's fame as a teacher had spread, he was invited to become a member of the academy faculty on his own terms. His comment was "He who will not when he may, when he will he shall have nay."

It was only a short time after the academy refused his suggestion that a teaching offer came, out of the blue, from the Drexel Institute of Art, Science and Industry. There seems to be no actual record of the approach but Clifford P. Graycon, director of the department of fine and applied arts at the time, said in a later letter dated September 1894:* "When Dr. James MacAlister [then president of the institute] asked if I could suggest anyone—I told him that we had one of the ablest illustrators in the country practically right in Philadelphia. Howard Pyle, living in Wilmington, would probably be interested in such a class."

Dr. MacAlister was suitably impressed when Pyle came up to Philadelphia to talk to him. MacAlister offered suitable terms, complete charge of a course in illustration, and generous classroom space and equipment. The institute had a new building with three floors of classrooms, galleries, and offices grouped around a central, skylighted courtyard well. An excellent classroom was set aside on the top floor and advertisements were inserted in the Philadelphia newspapers. The catalog of the department of fine and applied arts for the academic year 1894/95 stated:

ILLUSTRATION.

A course in Practical Illustration in Black and White under the direction of Mr. Pyle. The course will begin with a series of lectures illustrated before the class by Mr. Pyle. The lectures will be followed by systematic lessons in Composition and Practical Illustration, including Technique, Drawing from the Costumed Model, the Elaboration of Groups, Treatment of Historical and other subjects with reference to their use of illustrations. The student's work will be carefully examined and criticized by Mr. Pyle.

*Philadelphia, Penna. Records of the Drexel Institute of Art, Science and Industry.

The class met at 2:00 P.M. on Saturdays and was an instant success. Pyle's name attracted many more applicants than could be accepted, but since only advanced students were sought and an examination in drawing was mandatory the initial class was brought down to thirty-nine.

Whatever doubts Pyle may have felt upon facing his first audience were soon dispelled. His warmth, knowledge, and personal magnetism captured his students from the beginning. He was fluent, straightforward, and concerned. There was nothing of the pedant or remote schoolmaster about him. He felt completely at home with a cluster of students about him.

Some of his students showed an immediate and marked improvement, but Pyle had some lessons to learn too. There were problems of time and pacing to be solved. Meeting adequately the demands of thirty-nine students in the space of two hours is a matter for experts. The mathematics of such a situation could well frighten any beginning teacher— a possible three minutes for each student. Consider some of the normal incidents that can subtract precious seconds and minutes from the quota: all the little and big happenings that can delay the prompt opening of the criticism, then the preliminary remarks, the mere lifting of each picture from the pile and placing it on the easel, the retreat to viewing distance and the hurried look of appraisal as the seconds tick away, the necessity of forming judgments almost immediately, and finally the hurried words of analysis as the hand reaches for the next picture. It would be fatal for the critic to appear to be delivering snap judgments. On the face of it an impossible task, but it has been done by experts and Pyle speedily became one. But like other concerned critics in similar circumstances, he executed his virtuoso performance with increasing dissatisfaction and resentment. This was not the way to get close to the individual student and learn the workings of his mind and nature. The class must be reduced to teachable size.

Pyle soon learned another thing. He was delighted and exhilarated to discover a group of brilliant talents in the class, students who were to win names for themselves in a few years. These aroused the best in him and he saw their talents expand under his enthusiastic concern and wise analysis. There were others, of little discernible ability, but deeply eager and with some imaginative powers. They, too, touched him deeply and stimulated his best efforts to help them. But the largest group gradually emerged as a docile but inert mass, incapable of response and devoid of creative spark. After a winter and spring of futile effort he had to admit defeat in certain cases. He realized that for success he must look for certain innate qualities in his students.

As he became more acquainted with the ways of students, they learned to expect certain things from him. After some general remarks preceding the individual criticisms, they watched him lift the first picture to the easel and inevitably pause for scrutiny. Then, if his brow wrinkled and his hand crept slowly up to stroke his cheek and nose, his first words were likely to be "I feel in this . . ." and the student braced himself for a hard time. If he slowly nodded his head and the hand did not reach reflectively for the nose, he would be likely to say, "I like this and I'll tell you why." Then the student concerned could relax and look forward to words of praise.

Because of the limited opportunity for dialogue between teacher and student in the criticism class, Pyle encouraged the students to come to him during the drawing classes where there was more time or between classes. Much as he enjoyed a relaxing lunch he often sacrificed it on student problems. He learned to become more flexible in his criticisms. He began to examine the temptation that faces most teachers of becoming too doctrinaire, and to resist that other pedagogical temptation to dominate. He learned rather to explore and evoke.

Pyle was giving of himself in a prodigal way and even the most sluggish student was aware of this, but the master was making his own discovery—that his students were teaching him, broadening his understanding of human nature, and even widening his awareness of pictorial possibilities. There was growth on both sides and the atmosphere of accomplishment that permeated the Pyle class at Drexel spread rumors through the city and beyond.

When the next year's class opened its enrollment for the 1895/96 school term, the flood of applicants was larger than before. It was necessary to screen far more carefully, but still the numbers diluted the amount of individual instruction to a worrisome minimum and Pyle was far from happy. Apparently President MacAlister was also perturbed by conditions and important changes were planned for the following year. The class became a school and the announcement in the 1896 catalog read:

SCHOOL OF ILLUSTRATION

After two years of experiment in conducting a class in Illustration at the Drexel Institute, under the direction of Mr. Howard Pyle, the results have been such as to warrant the Institute in extending considerably the scope of this branch of its work in the Art Department. The work in Illustration has therefore been reorganized and will be carried on in two parallel lines of study and training.

Pyle was now committed to two full days of teaching. Instead of the Saturday afternoon class, he now came up on an early train on Mondays and Fridays. For an hour in the morning he was available to his students for consultation and special criticisms. From 10:00 A.M. until noon the model classes were in session, and the composition and practical illustration classes met in the afternoon. Evening model classes were abandoned after a year's trial.

Pyle was now in command of all classes, he was less hard pressed for time and had more opportunity to know his students on an individual basis. He felt he was coming closer to ideal teaching conditions, even though the new arrangements were lessening the creative hours in his own studio. Four times a week he rode the train back and forth, but this was usually worktime—poring over manuscripts or planning his next illustration. On winter days he rose in the dark and came home after sunset. He was still young enough to be spendthrift with his energy.

In the drawing and painting classes, his early training under Van der Weilen strongly conditioned his own teaching. He had learned the shortcomings of regarding the model with utterly literal eyes, devoid of imagination. He believed in developing a picture sense from the very beginning. He introduced his students to the posing model in this way: "Here is your model—make a picture of him! You will have to scrutinize him sharply to find his proportions, how his weight is supported, how each joint is functioning. Watch for the presence of the body under the clothes, how the folds and wrinkles tell the story. Look for the color and tone and texture of the garments. See how the light falls on the figure especially on the face. But above all, this is an opportunity to make a picture—a picture more than a copy!"

After two years of this kind of teaching he could see unmistakable results, and a growing outside audience could also. Not only was the repute of the course spreading by word of mouth, but the professional work of some of Pyle's first students was beginning to appear in the current magazines, newspapers, and books. Names like Maxfield Parrish, Violet Oakley, Walter Everett, Elizabeth Shippen Green, Clyde DeLand, Jessie Wilcox Smith, Charlotte Harding, and others were becoming familiar to American readers. Drexel was now the only institution in the country to have classes in illustration considered worthy of the name.

Pyle realized that the presence of highly gifted pupils in his class was his great good fortune and that he would not have been able to show such immediate conspicuous success without them. Maxfield Parrish had been the most obviously gifted star. His individual style was already discernible when he entered the class. He had had some training at the School of Industrial Art (now the Philadelphia College of Art) and had left behind a mural panel painted on a classroom wall. He had also studied at Haverford College and left behind a chemistry notebook filled with vagrant sketches, which is carefully preserved in the college library. He was no callow, groping youth but a maturing artist. Pyle felt that his arrival merited some special attention, so he introduced the newcomer to the others in a short, gracious speech, and Parrish, in his self-possessed way, replied in a few appropriate words. This was the kind of impromptu event that generated warmth and informality in the class.

As the pick of the first class were beginning to make their marks in the professional world, there were younger talents shaping up under Pyle's eyes. He felt a particularly fatherly concern for two of the most promising—Stanley Arthurs and Frank Schoonover. They were to be his friends and helpers to the end of his days. Arthurs was a Wilmington boy, and he rode back and forth on the same commuter train as his teacher. He became a trusted and dependable friend, and he and Frank Schoonover took over the hundred and one little chores of class life as informal monitors.

Young Schoonover had been preparing himself for the ministry when the full-page newspaper announcement of Pyle's illustration class caught his eye. Overnight his goal in life was changed. He was permitted in the class only as an auditor until his drawing ability was more adequate. He sat in the back row, looking over the heads of the more fortunate, and drank in every word. The next year he had joined the chosen circle and was making great strides.

Pyle needed someone to talk to informally on his teaching days, and the two boys filled that need. He often invited one or the other or both to have lunch with him, for that hour was not only a blessed respite in a long day's work but a chance to indulge his fondness for good food. He enjoyed introducing them to new dishes—Philadelphia pepper pot at the Hotel Bartram or Pennsylvania Dutch specialties at the Reading Terminal Farmer's Market.

One midday he invited Schoonover to come with him for lunch. On the walk up the street Schoonover detected irritation and resentment in the air. At the table the explosion came: "I can't stand those damned women in the front row who placidly knit while I try to strike sparks from an imagination they don't have." Infinitely patient when he found earnestness and response, he was angered by stupidity, disinterest, and laziness. He was now able to evaluate his students more knowingly and assess his own powers and limitations as a teacher. It was impossible for him to coddle the unworthy.

In spite of his discontent, one of his ideas was working out handsomely and pointed toward a successful teaching future. The idea of a summer school in the country had been in his mind for some time, so the Pyle custom of spending the summer vacation by the sea at Rehoboth changed to renting a house in Chadds Ford on the Brandywine. Chadds Ford was a small historic village in a cup of the Pennsylvania hills not more than a dozen miles from Pyle's studio door on Franklin Street. He had known it since early boyhood and loved every foot of its meadowland and rounded hills.

When Drexel raised a fund of a thousand dollars for him, the school came into being. The money was divided into ten one-hundred-dollar scholarships, to be awarded by Pyle to his best pupils. This covered board, lodging, instruction, everything except supplies and personal expenses. Pyle was to receive no remuneration. An old gristmill in the meadow across the road from the Pyles' rented house made an excellent studio and headquarters.

It was the summer of 1898, and that summer program as well as the summer classes of the following year were memorable ones in the minds of all those fortunate enough to attend. A prodigious amount of work was accomplished, most of it of high quality. Much of the work was done outdoors, both from the model and landscape, and the students, freed from the tyranny of conventional studio lighting, became accustomed to the infinite variations of shifting outdoor light. Their pictorial inventiveness was stimulated and they developed a confidence in their growing powers. Life in the open with time for games, walks, and swimming had much to do with the feeling of well-being and expanding horizons, and with this went the feeling of a snug purposeful unit very close to its master and his family.

At the end of the first summer sessions, Pyle reported to Dr. MacAlister in part:

> All the students have shown more advance in two months of summer study than they have in a year of ordinary instruction. This, of course, might have been largely due to the fact of the contact of the students with nature and of their free and wholesome life in the open air. Their labors were assiduous and unrelaxing, their recreation being only taken in the evenings. They prepared for work by eight o'clock in the morning, and they rarely concluded their labors until five or six in the afternoon. The result of this close application shows, I think, in our exhibition.
>
> In this outline of our summer work I make no mention of the brighter and happier coloring which your bounty brought so generously into these young lives. Apart from the great and abundant happiness they enjoyed, they were also able to earn considerable amounts of money from their art work.
>
> Another season I will volunteer, as I have during the past summer, to give my instruction gratuitously to a summer class.*

At the close of the next summer's session, his report read:

> Though the work done by the pupils during the past summer is perhaps not so great in number of examples finished for exhibition purposes, it is yet in many respects of the highest order achieved in our Institute. Each pupil has been working throughout the summer at a single composition made originally by the individual. These have been worked up into finished pictures in more or less full color. I had photographs taken of these examples of work and showed them to my friends Harper & Brothers. These publishers were so pleased with the work that they have expressed a willingness to publish all or nearly all of the drawings made by the summer school in *Harpers Weekly*, and also others done through the season under the auspices of the Class of Illustration at the Institute. . . . Besides these examples of full work, one of the pupils has made two illustrations for *McClures Magazine*, and others have illustrated books for Houghton Mifflin & Company and Dodd, Mead & Company. This has, of course, consumed a part of the summer, but my chief instruction has been directed to the perfection of our Institute work, and those people who have been delayed in the finishing thereof because of these important books undertaken are remaining here at their own expense to complete the Drexel Institute Class work.†

This report contains a description of what had become a regular practice of Pyle, one that was to continue until the end of his teaching days—the steady presentation of the work of his qualified students to New York editors, and a long list of works accepted by them. Over the years, student after student painlessly crossed the line into professionalism without the usual door-to-door canvass of editorial sanctums, portfolio under arm. There was no precedent for it; Pyle was doing something unique.

But this heartening proof of the professional acceptance of his early students, plus the remarkable spirit and success of his two summer sessions only made Pyle more aware of the difficulties and drawbacks of the winter sessions at the institute. Plans for an ideal school of his very own, based on the experience of the two successful summer sessions

*Philadelphia, Penna. Drexel Archives.
† Ibid.

Drawing for poster advertising *To Have and To Hold,* by Mary Johnston. Houghton Mifflin Co., 1900.
DELAWARE ART MUSEUM.

grew and grew in his mind until there remained no alternative but resignation. His letter
of withdrawal was dated February 14, 1900, and said in part:

> 1) My time is very valuable, and now that I find myself quite matured in my art
> knowledge, I think it both unwise and wrong to expend my time in general teaching.
> (2) The great majority of a class as large as that which I teach (35) at the Drexel Institute
> is hopelessly lacking in all possibility of artistic attainment. (3) There are only one or
> two who can really receive the instruction which I give (4) to impart this instruction to
> these two or three who can receive it appears to be unfair to the others who do not
> receive such particular instruction. (5) This apparent favoritism upon my part must
> inevitably tend to disrupt the Art School or to make the large majority discontented
> with the instruction which they receive in contrast with that which the few receive; nor
> is it possible to assure such discontented pupils that that which I give them is far more
> abundant and far more practical than that which they could receive from any other Art
> Institute . . . the fact remains in their minds that they are not given that which I give to
> other pupils and that apparently there is favoritism in the Class.*

His resignation was accepted with regret and some consternation. Except for Pyle's
classes, the institute's department of fine and applied arts had been shrinking for a
number of years. Its painting classes could not compete with those of the Pennsylvania
Academy of the Fine Arts, and its design course was severely challenged by those of the
Philadelphia School of Industrial Art. Presently the art department was phased out.

That plans for a new school had matured in his own mind is proved by a letter written
a few weeks before his resignation to J. Henry Harper, his publisher.

> It is a great disappointment to me that my teaching at the Drexel Institute has not
> done more than it has, and I have given the matter no small consideration. The first

*Reprinted in Abbott, *Howard Pyle,* pages 213–14.

thing, obviously, is to resign my position as teacher of the School of Illustration, for I cannot waste my time teaching mediocrity. . . . It now remains to turn my acquired knowledge of teaching to some real account. To this end the following plan has suggested itself to me.

That I build here in Wilmington a studio or set of studios adjoining my own studio; that I gather together in these studios some six or nine pupils, singling them out, not from Philadelphia alone, but from the larger schools in other cities, such as New York, Boston and Chicago.

I propose giving my instruction gratuitously, expecting the students to pay only a small rental to cover the interest on the money invested in the building. They would, besides, have to pay for their models and for heating the building in winter. Beyond this there would be no expense for instruction and I think that from seven to ten dollars a month (exclusive of the hire of models) would be all that they would be called upon to pay.

In the meanwhile I shall endeavor to throw in their way all the illustration of the first class I can obtain, thus endeavoring to instruct them first of all to make their art useful before turning it into the direction of color work. I also think that by doing such illustrative work they would not only be able to pay their expenses of studio rent but even provide their living expenses as well. . . .*

Shortly after this a more detailed letter was written to his friend Edward Penfield, art editor of Harper's:

My final aim in teaching will not be essentially the production of illustrators of books, but rather the production of painters of pictures. For I believe that the painters of true American Art are yet to be produced. Such men as Winslow Homer and Fuller in figure painting, and a group of landscape painters headed by George Inness as yet are almost the only occupants of the field. To this end I regard magazine and book illustration as a ground from which to produce painters.

My plan of teaching, as it grows in my mind, is something as follows: the students who come to me will be supposed to have studied drawing and painting as taught in the schools. My first object shall be to teach them to paint the draped and costumed model so that it shall possess the essentials of a practical picture. To teach this requires considerable knowledge not usually possessed by the artist-teachers in the schools, and this knowledge I feel myself competent to impart. I believe I am not devoid of a sense of color and I trust that I will be able so to instruct the pupil as to preserve whatever color talent he may possess.

My experience is that within a year of such teaching the pupil will be sufficiently grounded in a practical knowledge of painting to be able to embark upon illustrative work.

I shall make it a requisite that the pupil whom I choose shall possess—first of all, imagination; secondly, artistic ability; thirdly, color and drawing; and I shall probably not accept any who are deficient in any one of these three requisites. It is needless for me to say that my opinions as to the requisites of color and form may not be the same as those entertained by the art schools.

My instruction . . . would embrace not only daily criticism of the work done in class, but also instruction in composition, Facial and Figure Construction, Anatomy, Perspective, and Proportion. I shall give lectures perhaps twice a week in the evenings. . . .†

With the letter of resignation the die was cast, and plans and dreams had to be translated into realities. Immersed as he was in both writing and illustration, Pyle, it is clear, had dreams and hopes that were reaching for even more territory—nothing less than American art. American painting and American illustration he regarded as two facets of the same pictorial creativity. The differences were incidental and superficial; any seeming barrier between them was arbitrary and artificial. He hoped to demonstrate this in his future teaching.

*Reprinted in Abbott, *Howard Pyle*, p. 215.
† Ibid., pp. 216–217

The Fall of Montcalm, illustration for *The Works of Francis Parkman, Vol. XV.* Little, Brown and Co., 1896.
DELAWARE ART MUSEUM.

Chapter 10

THE STUDENT ENCLAVE

The formation of a new school required money, planning, and housing. Time was a precious element too, beset as Pyle was by an unending series of deadlines. But he had no regular classes to attend, and he could use that time to confer with architects and builders and later to supervise construction. He set aside a capital fund for building, which was something of a hardship, for although his income had risen steadily over the years and was a generous one by contemporary standards, his savings were not great.

Ground was broken in the summer of 1900 and the brick walls began to rise on the Franklin Street plot of ground where his studio stood. It was a long rectangular building, divided into three studio units. Each unit was self-contained with a separate entrance, a squarish skylighted studio, and a steep and narrow staircase leading to a small second-story room that could be used as a bedroom, but which more often became a dressing room for models or a catchall for the usual debris of an artist's life.

The entrance on the long side of the new building faced the brick path that led from the street to the door of the master's studio. A small square of courtyard was formed by the end wall of the students' building, the side walls of Pyle's studio, and the boundaries of the plot. Facing the angles of the two buildings was a larger plot of grass, shrubs, and trees where the students would often eat their lunches on pleasant days. Franklin Street was tree lined as were the neighboring streets, and the countryside was just beyond, for it was the very edge of town in those days. The neighbors watched the walls go up with great interest and some apprehension, dubious of permitting an enclave of young artists in their midst.

Pyle's first impatient class, mostly familiar recruits from his Drexel course, moved in to the smell of fresh paint and wet plaster. With them came odd bits of furniture and accessories brought from plundered attics or from the secondhand shops on lower Market Street. The bare look quickly gave way to comfortable clutter. Some of the students were making their first acquaintance with steam heat, a relatively new method of heating. Pyle, mindful of the cold drafts seeping down from his own skylight glass in winter, had made the architect frame each skylight with a line of steampipe. He was to boast that not even in the art schools of Philadelphia or New York was there such a comforting device.

How the students were apportioned among the studios at first is not certain. We know that Ethel Franklin Betts and Dorothy Warren were placed in the rear studio but no list exists and later memories were uncertain and sometimes contradictory. We know that, toward the latter part of the year, Frank Schoonover and Stanley Arthurs were installed in the rear studio (where they stayed for many years); Henry J. Peck, Clifford Ashley, Gordon M. McCouch, Ernest J. Cross, Arthur Becher, and William J. Aylward were in the central section; and Philip R. Goodwin, Samuel Palmer, James E. McBurney, and Francis Newton were in the unit nearest the street.

Pyle had little taste for the mechanics of even an ideal school. Organizational details were kept to a minimum and usually handled by others—volunteers Stanley Arthurs and Frank Schoonover, and a paid secretary, Anna Hoopes. There was no tuition, but the interest charges on his capital outlay were prorated among all. This charge varied slightly from year to year according to the number of students enrolled, but it was always a modest sum. In 1902, for instance, it was about $4.90 a month for each student. Model fees were also prorated and art supplies were sold at the school at dealer prices.

The incidental chores were performed by willing students: they cleaned up, readied a studio for compositional criticism, shoveled walks, and took charge of the supply closet. Walter Whitehead was placed in charge of the supply store to be succeeded by Thornton Oakley and Allen Tupper True. They were in charge of sales, inventory, and collection of monthly accounts. The average yearly supply expense for each artist was between forty and sixty dollars and total school expenses for a year were sometimes as low as $160. Most could manage this and their board and other expenses without strain, but a few had to watch every penny. Pyle knew the resources of each artist, and found small paying chores for those who were pinched. If their work had reached a superior level he managed to find illustrative commissions for them in the professional world.

Pyle's powers expanded under the new conditions. He was now master of his own colony, with the burden of complete responsibility, but the rewards of complete command. He became a kindly and considerate though exacting despot. His innate power to kindle creative fire in others, to win loyalty and confidence, was at its peak.

Both in the classroom and before his easel he was an actor, a dramatist. His histrionic ability was not melodramatic display or a contrived act. It was the natural surfacing of deep imaginative currents, called into spontaneous play by emotional concern. It was all the more impressive for the quiet command of the man, for his lack of pretense. The outer man, calm and poised, brisk but not bustling, radiating an air of great competence, impressed all as a prime and worthy exponent of a long Quaker ancestry. Facing eager students or a pictorial concept, he could dredge persuasion and eloquence from the depths either in paint or words. He had the power to stir and electrify and in these prime middle years he had behind him great accomplishment and experience.

The studio building for students at 1305 North Franklin Street, 1912. In the picture are, from left to right, Helen Hoskins, Gayle Hoskins, and Dolly Strayer.

In many ways these were his best years. He had gathered together the kind of students he had always wanted, and they were directly under his eye in familiar and beloved surroundings. It was a snug arrangement and he had a weakness for snugness. His days followed a pattern. After a leisurely breakfast in the big house at 907 Delaware Avenue, he would stroll up the maple-shaded street, planning the day ahead. There were observant days and absentminded days, depending on his mood and the problems of the moment. There were days when, closing the studio door behind him, he would find himself saying to his secretary with a start, "Good heavens, I'm afraid I walked past Mrs.——, without greeting her. She'll think I am the rudest man in Wilmington!"

His students were expected to be at work by eight o'clock and he often stopped off briefly to give a few words of advice and encouragement before opening his own studio door. His secretary would have his mail opened; he would dictate answers and then put on his painting smock and face the easel. There might be an unfinished picture resting there. A spray of retouching varnish would restore the dried-in areas to brilliancy and he was ready for the morning-after appraisal. He knew only too well the treacheries of that glow generated by the creative excitement of a day's painting and the flattering light of yester evening.

Howard Pyle at his studio easel, 1898.

Perhaps all was well, and brushes and palette could be picked up in high hopes of a triumphant continuation. Perhaps the morning light reported doubts and dissatisfactions, and areas had to be touched up or completely repainted. These appraisals and decisions had been experienced and solved hundreds of times before and would continue until the end but occasionally it ended in utter frustration. One of Thornton Oakley's favorite anecdotes in later years was his story of knocking upon Pyle's studio door, hearing a muffled voice within, and taking it to mean permission to enter, walked in to see his teacher stamping on a botched canvas and cursing.

Pyle had abundant technical facility, much of it hard won, and he could not resist taking pleasure in his competence and dexterity, yet he felt the need to disparage it. It seemed like a kind of ostentation that grated on the plain Quaker in him. He seldom talked about technique to his students, lest they should fall in love with their own skills. He talked to them of the transforming power of the imagination, of immersion in the emotions of their pictorial themes and the necessity of feeling a oneness with the world of their subject. This was his innermost craving: the identification of the inner light of the Quaker and Swedenborgian with the inner light of the artist.

There is really no sign in any of his work of dash and dexterity for its own sake, although it might be argued that a flick of it now and then might have added spice to his solid food. He was not a showy painter, and his brushwork was without bravura. He painted rapidly, knowingly, and with great ease. He preferred small or medium-sized brushes and painted relatively thinly. He seldom used impasto—palette knives were for scraping out, not piling on, pigment.

He could paint steadily for hours, occasionally retreating from the easel to squint and appraise the allover effect, then advancing to add a stroke or two. Quite often he would ask his secretary to read aloud as he painted—perhaps from Thackeray, Swedenborg, Howells, or Conrad. There were even times when he dictated letters or a story from the easel.

If he was heedless of the clock, the factory whistles from the lower town and the banks of the Christiana would bring him out of the world of the imagination into the realities of the brick pavements of Delaware Avenue and a hot lunch at home. Sometimes he stopped in one or more of the studio units for a few words.

He liked a leisurely lunch and "forty winks" too, but about an hour later he would repeat the well-known walk under overarching maple trees. Sometimes, in good weather, a few laggard students sprawling on the grass before the studio building would evaporate at his approach. Another four or more hours before the easel, watching a picture take form, and then relaxation as the skylight darkened. Some musing on the day's work and, if the scrutiny was heartening, a visit with the students, for he liked to carry good spirits with him. If the day's work had not been satisfying, he might make his brooding way past their studio doors.

The pupils, for their part, would gradually relax with the fading light, scrape their palettes and wash the brushes, scrub their hands and screw back the caps on their paint tubes. The end of a hard day's work often brought a sudden slump in spirit, sometimes a temporary collapse of hopes not helped by having a boardinghouse meal to look forward to. They craved a lift from outside, a reassurance that the drudgeries of an artist's apprenticeship could pave the way to triumphs. Pyle sensed this and knew that he was the answer to it.

The students waited for the telltale thud of his closing door, the return slap of the knocker, and then the footsteps. Sometimes they passed by and faded down the walk; usually they mounted the outer step and came inside. Pyle often entered with a book in his hand, for he frequently read a favorite book for a few minutes at the end of a day's work. At this time he was deep in the works of Swedenborg, particularly *Divine Providence* and *Arcana Coelestia*. The latter he wrestled with sentence by sentence, probing for its deepest meanings. It tantalized his imagination and impelled trains of thought that cried for communication with other minds.

So Swedenborg was often present at these close-of-day interludes. But there was no programming of these meetings—they were informal and impromptu discussions. The unexpected often came up and topics frequently ranged far from the realm of picturemaking. These sessions were a time of give-and-take, an unplanned exchange springing from the mood of the moment. They were certainly as important to Pyle as they were to the students. He needed to talk out his thoughts, for he seemed to have no circle of friends in the area who were of the same inquiring mind. The students, too, needed to express themselves in words and welcomed the warm feeling of joint exploration.

Pyle carried the same warm feeling home to the wife and children he had seen so little of during the daylight hours. After a leisurely dinner and some time with the children, he would often return to work again, but usually in the family circle, with the children until they were put to bed and then with his wife who often read aloud as he worked. Much of his writing was done in the evenings and perhaps a pen drawing making an average day of ten, eleven, or twelve hours of teaching, writing, and picturemaking.

That was the general pattern of his days and as the fame of the school spread, more and more of his time and energy was absorbed by his students. Scarcely a day passed without an application for his classes, either by letter or in person. Would-be students arrived on his doorstep unannounced. Parcels of drawings appeared in the mail. The glow of success was tempered by a certain amount of annoyance.

We have the statement from a former student that twelve were admitted to the classes during the first year from upward of five hundred applicants and, in 1903, there was room for only three from almost three hundred aspirants. The applications came from all parts of the country, ranging from hopeful youngsters in their middle teens to practicing painters and illustrators, but mostly from students in the large and small art schools of the country. Pyle could have found many more gifted students but physical space imposed strict limitations and experience had taught him that numbers diluted his message and sapped his energy. He was at his best and most contented when he had a family-sized group.

Pyle developed an uncanny instinct for judging student potential. Over the years he made only a few unfulfilled judgments. The quality called *talent* was only one gift he looked for. He looked deeply for character, purpose, general intelligence, ambition, imagination, and health. He read the submitted drawings, not for skill, finish, or surface display but for an inner purpose, for imagination and a hint of individuality. His attitude toward this problem was tersely expressed in two sentences of a letter he wrote an applicant: "When you apply for membership to the school, don't send me, 'samples,' of your work, send examples! There are no samples of art."

If the examples met Pyle's searching standards there could be a personal interview. Again his instinct came into play and he could read beneath appearance and manner. Again his judgment was seldom at fault.

No more intimate account of such an interview could be given than Newell Convers Wyeth's story of the late October day in 1902 when as a hopeful youth of twenty, he faced the master for the first time.

> My most vivid recollection of Howard Pyle was gained during the first five minutes I knew him. He stood with his back to the blazing and crackling logs in his studio fireplace, his legs spaced apart, his arms akimbo. His towering figure seemed to lift to greater heights with the swiftly ascending smoke and sparks from the hearth behind him.
>
> . . . I was young, ambitious and impressionable. For years, it seemed, I had dreamed of this meeting. Success in winning this master's interest and sympathy to the cause of my own artistic advancement seemed so much to ask, so remote, such a vain hope. But here I was at last, seated before him in the very room in which were born so many of the pictures I had breathlessly admired from boyhood. Paintings and drawings that had long since become a living and indispensable part of my own life.
>
> And as Howard Pyle stood there, talking gently but with unmistakable emphasis, his large and genial countenance hypnotized me. The mobile mask of his face became more than individual. My rapid reflections were swept beyond the actual man. It was bewildering. I heard every modulation of his voice and I took note of every word. Occasionally I would answer a question. I remember this clearly. But a searching beyond his countenance persisted.
>
> The soft top-light from the glass roof high above us poured down like a magical and illuminated mist over his magnificent head . . . the entire countenance became majestically severe, forceful, unrelenting. The recollection of the masks of Beethoven, Washington, Goethe, Keats, passed in swift succession before my vision, and in a sudden grasp of the truth I realized that the artist's face before me was actually a living compromise of the men of history and romance which he had so magically and dramatically perpetuated on canvas.*

*Reprinted in Henry Pitz, *The Brandywine Tradition* (Boston: Houghton Mifflin, 1969), pp. 127–28.

Although the majority of applicants were obviously unqualified, there were many with conspicuous abilities that still could not be accommodated, and it touched Pyle's heart to say no so many times. Even so, he accepted more than he had planned—newcomers came crowding in and studio space was becoming cramped. Besides Wyeth, some of Pyle's most famous students were enrolled—Harvey Dunn, George Harding, Allen True, Percy Ivory, Thornton Oakley, Harry F. Townsend, Walter Whitehead, and Sidney M. Chase among them. The older students, mostly from the Drexel classes, were now a closely knit group and well accustomed to Pyle's ways and he to theirs. As the newcomers joined, one by one they had to adjust to a strange new background. There was an abundance of friendliness but there was always a trial period of quiet scrutiny and evaluation. Without any guidelines, the students managed to group themselves in approximate accordance with ability and seniority. One student described the three student units this way: "One was for the babies, another given to the middle age students, and another studio, the third, was given to two very august grandees or graduates, Arthurs and Schoonover."

But the arrangements shifted with growth and attainment. Some moved out of the "babies" unit in a short time, like Wyeth who was transferred to studio two in a few months and then to the "grandee" group in studio three about a year later. A very few never moved from studio one. On the first day, the newcomer would experience an explanatory and heartening conference with the master; then there would be an introduction to the monitors, Arthurs and Schoonover, who would acquaint him with his colleagues in unit one and set him to work, usually drawing or painting from a model.

Thornton Oakley has left an account of his first day's work:

> I had been endeavoring with oils and brush and palette to suggest on canvas the spirit of the model that had been posed before us. It was my first handling of the medium—as it was, I believe, of other raw recruits who formed the class, and my efforts, I full well know, were terrifying to behold. When H. P. stood before my easel, he was silent for many a minute. At length he spoke. "Oakley," he said, choosing his words with care, "either you are color blind, or else you are a genius."*

The pattern of the school was now set. The more advanced students worked on individual projects, usually finished illustrations that could be shown to art editors as demonstrations of professional ability, or, in some cases, illustrations that had been commissioned for books or magazine publication. The beginners' group worked day after day drawing or painting from the model, aiming to make a picture of it, not a copy. They also had periods of drawing heads and figures from their imaginations, trying to realize a certain characterization each time. And they had time to make charcoal sketches for imagined compositions. The middle group, too, worked from the model but spent more time on independent compositions. Two mandatory classes were the famous Monday evening criticism class, when all who were eligible handed in original compositions, and the Saturday evening class, when all, including H. P. himself, drew pictures for a chosen theme entirely from their imaginations. Except for occasional outdoor sketching trips in good weather, this was the pattern of the school. The administrative mechanism was hardly apparent: there were no class rolls, no attendance records, no tuition, no marks or grades, no formal graduations. In later years, there were no records to consult. Questions about what had occurred and when had to be answered from personal memories, sometimes uncertain.

Even with records and paper work reduced to negligible amounts, there were other

*Richard Wayne Lykes, "Howard Pyle—Teacher of Illustration" (Paper delivered at the University of Pennsylvania).

day-to-day problems. A group of highly gifted, ambitious, and competitive young men and women, united in purpose but varied in talent and temperament, was volatile material. It sometimes demanded a series of small, nagging decisions for Pyle, but he managed well with his usual concern, dignity, and aplomb. After all, he was in supreme command and his edicts were law. There were a few cases when students were peremptorily banished. Pyle's sense of humor rescued some occasions from acrimony but it had its limitations. One of his more accomplished students and a general favorite, Gordon McCouch, working over a charcoal drawing of a model and becoming bored, obeyed a whim of the moment. In a corner of his sheet he made a careful, minutely detailed drawing of a bottle fly. It amused many of his fellows and they praised him for his skill. Presently the master entered and moved from easel to easel, criticizing and sometimes demonstrating. Pausing before McCouch's drawing he waved a hand to drive off the bothersome fly. It had no effect and he waved again with no result. He peered more closely and discovered he had been taken in. He froze in a cold rage. A laugh would have united all in a tide of friendly humor but his discomfort was only too evident. A day or two later McCouch's father received a letter asking him to withdraw his son from the school.

Although the little society of students was naturally competitive and a breeding place for ambivalent feelings of admiration and envy, it was also an unusually intelligent and responsible group linked by a common purpose, and by affection and respect for their teacher. A good many personal conflicts and dissensions were settled internally. Undoubtedly there were times when Pyle was aware of troubles but wisely allowed them to settle themselves. He knew, too, that there were explosives in young muscles and inventive minds and that even the long hard hours of creative work could not drain off all that caldron of energy.

The master himself was very inventive about extracurricular activities. The nearby Brandywine was the usual place for outings and picnics in the warm months and skating parties in winter. Hayrides and sleigh rides were popular. The students were full of party ideas. They were adept at improvising impromptu costumes from a storehouse of scraps and castoffs and they liked to draw and hand-letter invitations, attach them to twigs and toss them through open doors. There was a party every time a picture was sold or a publisher commissioned an illustration.

Practical jokes and impromptu capers seemed just part, albeit unscheduled, of the curriculum. Wyeth, Schoonover, and several other boys organized one successful episode. They dressed in lumbermen's shirts and high laced boots, borrowed a surveyor's transit and long tapes, and set up a mock surveying operation at one of Wilmington's busiest intersections. They speedily collected a crowd and created a traffic jam and then slipped away before the police detected the hoax.

Sometimes their parties were very important and elaborate, as when the class celebrated the master's fiftieth birthday with a sumptuous medieval banquet. A score of students based their costumes upon well-known characters from Pyle's books—Robin Hood, King Arthur, Little John: a noisy collection of brightly colored figures. The walls were decorated and a banquet table was filled with so-called medieval dishes and drinks. It was an evening of toasts, speeches, jokes, and ceremonies. When the guest of honor retired at eleven thirty, the students were still full of explosive energy. Wyeth has described what happened in a letter to his mother:

> Unbeknown to me how it started, there was a rush and a crash and two bodies of fellows clashed together, about nine on a side, each wielding a huge sword striking right and left. Every light was extinguished and one could see nothing but continual spatterings and sunbursts of sparks caused by the clashing steel. Becker's sword was wrenched from his hand and hurled through a window followed quickly by Ashley's.

This kept up for some twenty minutes until fellows dropped out from sheer exhaustion. They all dropped out but Pfeifer and I, and the battle-royal continued for five minutes under strenuous conditions. I had a broad sword and wielded it with all my might and he had a Cavalry sabre and did the same. Amid cheers and yelling we fought until by a lucky stroke I broke his sword at the hilt sending the blade with a br-r-r-r across the room. Thus ended the duel. I arose at 9:30 stiff as a board.*

At fifty Pyle was at his creative peak and staunch physically. His work hours were long and crowded, yet his energy seemed undiminished. He was riding on a high current of admiration and demand from his own circle, the publishers, and the reading public. His unflagging ambition led him into still more commitments.

Visitors were always welcomed to the classes and they came in numbers, largely to the Monday evening criticism talks that had become particularly famous. The visitors comprised artists, editors, and other art teachers and directors, and they often pressured Pyle to extend his teaching to other centers. Pyle was tempted. In 1904 he wrote to Joseph H. Chapin, art director of Scribner's:

> The year that has passed has convinced me that I really am of use to the younger artists through the advice and criticism which I give them, for it has been my happy lot to establish several young lives, and I think it likely that some of my pupils will reach unusual distinction in their profession. I am speaking very intimately to you when I say that I feel that this is due in some measure to my instruction—I am sure the ideals with which I have inspired them are both broad and large. It has occurred to me that I might broaden my work by extending it to New York, and I want to ask you as a special favor, to tell me very frankly what you think of such an idea.
>
> In general, my thought is, that I should come every two weeks upon Saturday, and should deliver lectures upon composition as I do here in Wilmington, and that I should take the opportunity of criticizing and advising with young artists concerning their pictures. It occurred to me that I might give an hour to such criticism and an hour to a composition lecture—the one, say, from four to five and the other from five to six. I should like to make such lectures free to all who care to attend, and to give my services without charge, though I think such a class should pay my traveling expenses, which would amount to not more than fifteen dollars for each trip from here to New York. New York.
>
> If such a plan is worthwhile, and if it could be put into operation, I would like it to be conducted under the auspices of the Art Students League.†

Chapin was delighted with the plan and found the board of the Art Students League equally delighted, so plans were soon worked out for biweekly visits by Pyle. The lectures went on during the winter months of 1904 and 1905 and into the following spring; but, on May 8, he wrote a deflated letter to Chapin: "I am about closing my series of lectures before the young artists of the Art Students League, and I think you will be interested to know that the effort was not a success—indeed, I think it has been a decided failure."‡

His disappointment was probably excessive, for there were many who attended the series who had only high praise for the experience. But Pyle had not prepared himself for the one- or two-time tasters, the curiosity seekers attracted by a famous name, or the foolishly hopeful who felt that a few words from the great man would work miracles. He had forgotten that his phenomenal success with his own students was based upon his uncanny instinct for picking the right talent imbedded in the right personality.

At about the same time as the Art Students League lecture series, Pyle was in

---

*Reprinted in Pitz, *The Brandywine Tradition*, p. 131.

†Reprinted in Abbott, *Howard Pyle*, pp. 218–19.

‡Ibid., p. 219

Paul Jones.

Heading for "Paul Jones," *Century Magazine*, April 1895.

correspondence with W. M. R. French, the director of the Art Institute of Chicago. In one sentence he stated the kernel of his philosophy of teaching: ". . . It may be well for me to state that in general my opinion is that pictures are creations of the imagination and not of technical facility, and that that which art students most need is the cultivation of their imaginations and its direction into practical and useful channels of creation—."

He was invited to come to Chicago to take charge of a one-week seminar of criticism lectures. He accepted and apparently felt much happier with the results of this venture. The faculty had carefully screened the upper student body—only the most gifted and advanced were allowed to submit pictures and only the most interested were admitted to the auditors' section. At the end of the course a large reception and tea was held so all could meet the distinguished guest. Edith Emerson has told of that crowded gathering. She had been an intent auditor and at the reception was one of the student hostesses selected to pour tea. With Howard Pyle close by her table, the press of students about him caused the large tea urn filled with hot water to totter and tilt toward her. There was a second of terrified horror and then an arm shot out and the heavy urn was tilted back onto its stand. The arm was Pyle's.

The New York and Chicago teaching experiences left their mark. It seems likely that one of his motivations for adding to his already arduous teaching obligations was to have a more widespread influence on the shaping of American art than was possible through the means of his Wilmington and Chadds Ford classes. His letters to men in important positions in the field of art training were critical of many educational practices and tried to explain that his own teaching philosophy was not confined to training illustrators but to training painters and artists in other fields.

In a letter to Dr. James H. Canfield of Columbia University dated April 17, 1905, he expresses critical dissatisfaction with the art schools of New York.

> This winter I have been lecturing in New York, as you know, every two weeks, and have thus come somewhat in contact with the art schools of the Metropolis. I cannot very well make you understand my regret and sorrow at finding them so poor and so inadequate to fill the demands of a progressive art. I doubt if there is a single really excellent art school now available in New York. There is not a New York School comparable either in energy or equipment to the schools of Philadelphia, of Chicago, or even of Brooklyn.*

A few days later in a long letter to W. M. R. French of the Art Institute of Chicago he said:

> My objective in teaching my pupils is that they should be fitted for any kind of art, whether of easel painting or even the minor uses of portrait painting. . . . Among my older pupils, for instance, are Miss Violet Oakley, whose trend is entirely in the direction of mural work and glass; Mr. F. E. Schoonover who, while his work is only just beginning to make an impression, has already received a commission to paint a picture of his own choice of subject, which involves a remuneration to the amount of $1000; and Miss Ida Dougherty, who is devoting herself almost entirely to stained glass.†

*Reprinted in Abbott, *Howard Pyle*, p. 222.
†Ibid., p. 224.

The Trotting Match, illustration for *The Autocrat of the Breakfast Table*, by Oliver Wendell Holmes. Houghton Mifflin Co., 1894. PRIVATE COLLECTION.

There were other expressions of this reaching out toward a broader field of art. In his own pictorial work he was almost entirely the illustrator—there are only a few of his pictures that he might have called "easel paintings," and in truth, where in that crowded life would there have been room for one more major activity? There is little evidence that he had a yearning to paint for painting's sake. He needed a purpose behind the picturemaking urge. There was something of the missionary, the advocate, about him and a puritan instinct that tended to check anything that might be construed as display or self-indulgence. Considering his considerable literary gifts, it followed that they would unite with the picturemaker in him. He was conscious of what seemed to be contradictory impulses within himself; his confrontation with these produced a wealth of great illustrative pictures.

Chapter 11

CHADDS FORD

From the enclave at Franklin Street, little more than a mile up the Kennett Pike came the intersection with the Montchanin road: the favorite way into open country. The old road meandered along the Brandywine. It was a road for artists and nature lovers. It still is.

Pyle students knew every foot of that country road for miles and in every season. They sketched the meadows, the plowed fields, the rounded hills and woodland slopes that stretched off to either side, and the Brandywine itself, sluggish or rampant. Over that road went most of their hayrides in late summer or early autumn and their sleigh rides in winter, and all the way along it were favorite picnic nooks.

The valley had been intimate and loved territory for Pyle from his boyhood days, and its shapes and colors were tightly woven into the expanding experience of his artist's eye. It was home. He drew strength from it and he had turned back to it instinctively after his brief years in New York. Almost all his students came to feel the same affection for it.

Pyle also considered it an indispensable extension of the classroom. The studio was a blessed base for creative work but the steam-heated cube under its northern skylight could also become a trap and prison, particularly for the young and restless. Fortunately, in those earlier days the countryside was only a few steps away.

The two experimental summer sessions with the Drexel students, in 1898 and 1899, had been a brilliant success. The turmoil of building studios and organizing the new school prevented any resumption in the summer of 1900, but everything was ready a year later. Chadds Ford seemed an ideal spot. It was about twelve miles from the Franklin Street studios, walking distance for most of the students. But there were horses and buggies, farm wagons, bicycles, and an occasional automobile; and trains from both Wilmington and Philadelphia stopped at the little Chadds Ford station.

After a summer vacation by the sea at Rehoboth, the large Pyle family found Chadds Ford quite a change but they all loved the ample house with its wide verandas overlooking the Baltimore Pike and the meadows beyond. Behind the house were woodland patches and glens and hillside fields. The first year that the summer school was resumed (1901), Phoebe, the oldest Pyle child, was fifteen and Wilfrid, the youngest, was four. In between were Theodore, twelve, Howard, ten, Eleanor (Nellie), seven, and Godfrey, six. After working hours, the house was a center for the students. Their favorite gathering place in the evenings was on the broad porch or in the big living room, with a log fire in the hearth on cool nights. Family and students mingled together and this was one of the comfortable memories all carried away and recalled in later years.

The same housing arrangements that had been so satisfactory for the two Drexel summer sessions were renewed for the new classes. Two sturdy stone revolutionary farmhouses that had been battle headquarters—one for General Washington and the other for Lafayette—sat on a slope above the Baltimore-Philadelphia Pike, a short walk from Pyle's rented mansion. Both houses were occupied by working farm families who were glad to have young summer boarders. The boys were quartered in Washington's old headquarters. They tossed for choice of rooms and the losers were assigned to the attic. Water for the inevitable washbowl and pitcher was carried upstairs from a hand pump in the kitchen or from the larger one outside. Off to one side was a boarded outhouse. The girls, in the Lafayette house, had similar accommodations. A few students boarded elsewhere. One or two of the boys lived at farmhouses where they could do chores and thus live at reduced rates. Mrs. Imogen Oakley rented rooms for herself and her son Thornton while he was attending the classes.

The long working hours were spent in a gristmill in the long meadow across the road. This was a working gristmill of sturdy random-sized stone, with millstones, wheel, gate, and millrace intact. It was permeated with the smell of grain and flour dust, mixed with the dampness of flowing water below and the sweetness of warm summer breezes blowing through. On the top floor under warped and darkened wooden shingles and hand-adzed rafters was Pyle's studio space, with a desk and filing cabinets at one end where Anna W. Hoopes—"Miss Anna"—attended to her secretarial duties. On hot, humid days the heat was almost unbearable.

The main floor below was where most of the students worked on their own individual compositions or on drawing or painting the posed model. Here, too, the heat sometimes invaded, and some would climb down the stone steps and work beside the cool water and the motionless wheel or set up their easels on the shady side of the mill.

The mill was the center but working territory extended for some miles on all sides. The outdoors was the studio and most working hours were spent under the sky. Pyle encouraged it, for he knew from his own experience how restrictive the winter studio routine could become to creative minds and how painting continuously under a north light led to the use of stereotyped light patterns. Under the sky he could show how light flooded, bounced from, and enfolded every form that it could reach.

A painter's first introduction to the interplaying lights, to the dazzling feast of outdoor light, was almost always confusing. Pyle had to demonstrate how the artist could organize this distracting material. Some of Pyle's students sought to solve the problem by adding pigment after pigment. New colors with strange new names on the tubes were coming from abroad and invited experimentation. This added to the bewilderment. So, to simplify, Pyle ordered his beginners to remove all color from their palettes and limit themselves to black and white alone. This forced them to search for *values,* or the monochromatic equivalents to the colors under study. Gradually the students learned to make accurate distinctions between the degrees of darkness or lightness of each color and they were allowed to restore the full range of pigmentation to their palettes.

It was 1901 and outdoor impressionist painting was at full tide. The work of the pioneer Impressionists had been done; the newer generation were largely followers and consolidators. Pyle had been little touched by the movement. He had inherited a brown palette from his instructor, Van der Weilen. His first true contact with Impressionism was during his New York sojourn when he came to know so many painters who had just returned from the schools and studios of Europe. Later, he became friendly with some of the excellent landscapists who were beginning to settle along and paint the Delaware River Valley near New Hope and Lumberville. But he was never won over. The very highly keyed pastel tints were not his natural color range nor did he care for a canvas covered with small mosaiclike dabs of pigment. As much as he delighted in the alchemy of light, he was unwilling to follow the Impressionists to the point where the passion for light saturation obliterated solid form. To him light was a vehicle, not an end in itself.

As for all illustrators, form was the keystone of his picturemaking, but there was another practical and technical reason behind his predilection for a wider tonal (as opposed to color) range. It permitted richer color and tonal orchestration; it also ensured better results in reproduction. The use of four process plates—red, yellow, blue, and black—was no longer experimental or unreliable, but, in dealing with very intense colors or light, highly keyed hues, the slightest imbalance in the plates could spoil an effect. Results were much more certain in the middle or dark color range, and this accorded with Pyle's instinctive preference for rich, medieval pigmentation.

Pyle's more advanced students were always allowed to select their own sketching locations, but most chose to follow the daily group so as to be within reach of the master's criticisms. A favorite place was Brinton's Mill with its stone granary and miller's house clustered beside the Brandywine about a mile upstream from the Baltimore Pike. Frank Schoonover, in later years, loved to tell of one of his student experiences at Brinton's Mill. Pyle believed in an early start and eight o'clock was the time to be on location in the studio or at the painting site. One morning Schoonover overslept and, disdaining breakfast, gathered his painting traps and jumped on his bicycle. Pedaling madly, he was relieved to note as he approached the mill that H. P.'s bicycle was not among those leaning against the fence. In a minute he had raced down the lane, set up his easel, and squeezed out his pigments. Out of the corner of his eye he could see his teacher pedaling up the road. By the time he heard Pyle's footsteps crunching behind him he had managed to daub in some blue sky and a rough shape of the mill. The footsteps halted behind him. His criticism for the day was "Try and be on time tomorrow."

Of course Pyle was a hard taskmaster, but it was seldom resented. He was giving freely of his own time and energy, and he had his own keen sense of when to relax and relent, when to divert and play. He was not a remote authority. At Chadds Ford particularly, he was with the group, and one of them, most of the time.

Although Pyle, like his pupils, delighted in the relaxed and informal life of the outdoor months, there was no slackening in his creative work. He put in long hours of work at his easel on the top floor of the mill or, when the situation demanded it, before a posed model in the open. Even after supper he would bend over one of his pen illustrations on the front porch or in the living room, conversing all the while with his family and students.

The student class before Brinton's Mill, Chadds Ford, where summer instruction was held from 1898 to 1903.

When he painted his large canvas *The Flying Dutchman*, which was reproduced in *Collier's*, his easel was brought outside the mill. His students set up a tilted platform to simulate a slanting poop deck. John Weller, the family handyman and custodian of the costume chest, mounted it in a suitable pose with a long cloak tied back to a convenient branch to simulate the pull of the wind; and willing students drenched the platform with water from time to time to keep it glistening with reflections. This kind of experience left deep and usable impressions with the students. They could witness the progress of a picture from bare canvas to final brushstroke and then see the reproduced image of it. At that time there was no other school in the country where this would have been possible.

Pyle's ability to create before an audience or to paint and dictate a text at the same time led most to believe that, creatively, he was immune to outside influences. Some believed that his mind worked in separated compartments that did not interfere with each other. Although this was not entirely true, it stimulated the Pyle legend and induced emulation, although none of Pyle's students ever attained the same amazing command over pictorial and literary content.

Who could help but marvel as Thornton Oakley did one summer afternoon as he entered the Pyle house to ask some questions: "On the stairway landing I found my teacher at his easel working on a canvas for his series 'Travels of the Soul,' his young children cavorting about his knees, a model posed nearby in costume to give him some detail of texture, Mrs. Pyle sitting beside him reading aloud proofs from *King Arthur* for his correction, he making comments for her notation."

This is Pyle immersed in two of his most notable creations, the great set of four paintings, *Travels of the Soul*, and the text of *King Arthur*.

The story of another great set of pictures begins with a summer thirst for lemonade and a long bicycle ride. Pyle had a weakness for lemonade—particularly when made with Apollinaris water as dispensed at Anscow's Restaurant and Oyster House opposite the public library in Wilmington. To develop this thirst on a hot August afternoon in Chadds Ford with Anscow's perhaps thirteen miles away was not to give way to home-brewed lemonade made with well water. A party of bicyclists set out for Wilmington, Pyle on his new tandem wheel with young Schoonover on the front saddle. Pyle is to be pictured in his well-worn English knickers and a faded crimson turtleneck sweater, stretched beyond belief, its wide neck hanging down in folds. The party arrived and several pitchers of Anscow's Special were consumed.

A considerably less exuberant group pedaled back—for one thing there was more uphill—and Schoonover, attuned to his teacher's moods, was aware of a quieter than usual Pyle. When he reached the first long hill and rose above his seat to put weight and power on the pedals, he heard Pyle's sharp command, "Frank, sit down and stop swaying from side to side."

Schoonover pedaled the remaining miles in silence, waiting to read the reason for the mood. Pyle jumped off the tandem when they reached the mill, calling up the stairway—"Miss Anna, do you have any academy boards up there?" Miss Anna had a bundle of them in her hand as he reached the head of the stairs. He placed one on his easel and setting his palette began to paint, still in knickers and slouching sweater. Panel succeeded panel until seven were lined up—rough color lay-ins for a new series of paintings. The next morning the stock of seasoned mahogany wood was sorted out and seven panels cut to size. The result was one of the most imaginative and richly colored sets that he ever conceived. They were for the series "The Pilgrimage of Truth." Later, changed to fit the limitations of color reproduction at that time, they appeared in the Christmas issue of *Harper's New Monthly Magazine*.

This seemed to be the pattern of conception and execution for him. Why a major concept should hammer for recognition and clarification in the middle of a long bicycle ride is a mystery to which there is no real answer. The seeds might have been sown days, weeks, or months before, lying dormant in the subconscious, probably shaping itself unsuspected by the conscious mind. Suddenly it rose and demanded attention and all other things were swept aside until it had had its say. By the time seven sketch panels had been brushed in, the mind's vision had reached the first stage of visual expression and at that point Pyle could again become the legendary person who could perform two or three tasks simultaneously.

Yes, the students were closest to him during these summer days. They could watch him at work, see each stage unfold, and compare the progress of their own work with his, enabling them to better understand their own imaginative promptings and how to bring them into fruition. It shortened the inevitable student periods of trial and error.

Work and play dovetailed, and the result was great productivity, steady creative growth, and an accumulated feeling of well-being and boundless futures. The hours of work and study were less rigidly planned and there was room for impromptu enterprises. Pyle liked to organize picnics, and the narrow valley offered scores of accessible nooks. These were sometimes last-minute lunches, sometimes all-day trips to some favorite or important spot like Valley Forge. A whole cavalcade would set out: the family in a large carriage rented for the summer and driven by William, the Negro jack-of-all-trades, and the students on bicycles. Pyle had noticed that some of the girls had to walk their bicycles up the steeper hills, so he bought a new tandem bicycle with the front section minus the usual horizontal bar. A strong boy was elected to furnish most of the motive power from the rear seat while a girl rode in the front.

The weekends were free. That was a time for visitors or visiting. There was more time for games too—baseball, using the makeshift diamond on the flat meadow beside the mill, or some tennis or fishing. There were scarcely enough students to field two full-strength baseball nines, so the old-fashioned game of "movings up" was usually resorted to, but sometimes the village boys were tempted to play. They came with an ingrown belief that "artist fellows" were deficient in muscle, speed, and athletic skill. They had to be taught a few lessons.

Then, the nearby Brandywine always beckoned the swimmers. Some spent a good deal of their spare time in the water, but Pyle's keen nose told him that it would be an excellent idea to organize a regular bath party at the end of sweaty Saturday afternoons. This became a ritual. He would head a procession, carrying a chip basket piled with towels and fresh clothing, and with bars of soap on top as a hint. The dressing rooms were the thickets of pollarded willows that lined the creek in many places. These had been planted by the farmers in the early days of the DuPont powder mills downstream, as a source of supply for charcoal. Emerging from the willow screen in his bathing suit, Pyle would toss the soap bars out into the water and plunge in.

It was a freshened and cleanly clothed group that sauntered back to their farmer's supper. The last touches of dressing up were added—high starched collars, bow ties, and hair parted in the middle for the men; high pompadours brushed over "rats" (pads to hold up the hair) and shirtwaists with high stiffened collars for the women—and an evening of talk, household games, and entertainment was begun at the Pyle house.

The 1903 class at Chadds Ford.

On warm summer evenings they gathered on the wide porch or on the sloping green lawn. Many had good voices and several were musicians. Some were ham actors and mimics. There was enough talent of a kind and a plenitude of good spirits to light up a relaxed summer evening, topped off with cold lemonade or sarsaparilla. And while Mrs. Pyle was usually in her favorite rocking chair on the porch, H. P. often sat inside the screen doors under a lamp, drawing or writing.

A summer highlight was the Fourth of July. There was a great outdoor party from after breakfast until late evening. Pyle always invested heavily in fireworks: packs of red Chinese crackers for the daylight hours and display pieces when dark fell—pinwheels, Roman candles, flares, rockets, and sprays of flaming stars. The eating, shouting, singing, and game-playing came to an end with the final flare. Little was expected of anyone the next day.

These were days of work and play, of awakened sensibilities. Like Thoreau, the students grew like corn in the night. They could repeat Pyle's words to themselves and constantly rediscover their truth: "Look on this, study it, absorb it. Never again will it be the same. If you see it tomorrow the light will be different and you will be different. This moment is unique."

Their eyes were attuned to the never-ending pageant of visual accidentals. Each day exposed its fresh share of pictorial opportunities. Nature was offering them a prodigal wealth of picture material; it was their task to absorb, master, and express it in their pictures. Here was a life's work.

There were five sessions of the Chadds Ford school and they left a deep impression on an important group of young lives. The session of 1903 brought to an end one of the greatest outdoor classes in American art.

Just a year later N. C. Wyeth made one of his many trips out to Chadds Ford and walked slowly through the empty Pyle house. "It seemed so queer to go into that house and not hear the voices and romping of children or not to see Mr. Pyle standing in the doorway beaming all over with joviality."*

Writing almost a quarter of a century later, in the light of long memories, Wyeth said,

> We spent days with him rummaging around old furniture shops, hunting for seasoned mahogany for panels to paint upon, and we spent very much more time with him roaming the gorgeous hills and woods of the Brandywine valley at Chadds Ford.
>
> It was the time spent with him in this remote Pennsylvania village that brings the fondest memories to most of us. I have the keenest and most enjoyable remembrances of him, surrounded by his wife and family of six children, in a large, roomy house that nestled in the trees beneath a great hill, within a stone's throw of General Lafayette's Headquarters. Many jolly evenings did we spend before his crackling log fires, eating nuts, telling stories, or, best of all, listening to his reminiscences, or stories from his full store of knowledge of history and of people. His intimacy with Colonial history and his sympathetic and authentic translations of those times into pictures are known the world over.
>
> Thus to know Howard Pyle—in this country of all countries, where Washington had fought, where from the spacious veranda we looked across the meadows upon Rocky Hill, the very location of the deciding conflict that sent Washington and his men to their memorable winter at Valley Forge—to know Pyle here was a profound privilege.
>
> . . . Here the teacher kept his class intact for five glorious summers. Who of us does not count those as golden days?†

*Quoted in Henry Pitz, *The Brandywine Tradition*, p. 114.
†N. C. Wyeth, "Howard Pyle as I Knew Him," *The Mentor*, June 1927.

Chapter 12

THE CORE OF THE MESSAGE

All the varied facets of the Pyle classes were designed to blend and come to focus in the Monday evening criticism sessions. There, the practice and experience gained in drawing and painting from the model and still life, the exercises in inventing character faces and recording emotions upon them, the outdoor sketching, the lectures on historic backgrounds and costumes, the lessons in proportion and perspective were all intended to provide skills and material for the imagination. Knowledge was important but it was to be commanded by the pictorial imagination.

It was this dual emphasis on deep and wide knowledge, *experienced* knowledge, ignited by the imagination that was at the core of Pyle's message. It meant immersion in one's subject, feeling its mood in one's very bones, acting out its drama and molding it to touch the imagination of others.

Pyle had in him something of the evangelist and prophet, and these latent qualities sprang into life when confronted by a circle of expectant students and a stack of pictures straining for a rich and meaningful utterance. The meetings were called at seven thirty, and long before that the students would gather in several lines of miscellaneous chairs

Illustration for "A Forgotten Tale," by A. Conan Doyle. *Scribner's Magazine*, January 1895.

and stools or on the floor. They faced a pine drawing board fastened to the wall, overhung by a lone electric bulb and with a high stool to one side.

Some finished or partly completed canvases might be in the waiting pile but most offerings would be compositional ideas drawn in charcoal on standard size French charcoal paper. All had been handed in at noontime and at some point during the afternoon Pyle had paused for a half hour of review. Sometimes he would criticize all entries, sometimes he might only choose ten or twelve. He had great patience with clumsy manipulation, inept drawing, or lack of dexterity as long as he could discover a spark of life, a struggle to utter a significant pictorial message. Other things would come, expertise would arrive if the spark could be fanned into flame. He had become an expert at stimulating and nourishing creative possibilities.

Seated on his stool or standing before a hopeful picture on the wall behind him with the overhead light glinting on his bald head with its neat rim of gray hair, Pyle in a strong rich voice would summon up the persuasive possibilities of any picture that had moved him. There was a good deal of the actor in him, a not uncommon trait in an illustrator or painter. An illustrator struggling to evolve a facial emotion upon his canvas often finds his own face contorted in sympathetic response, his own muscles tightening in accord to the ones he is delineating. He would not consider it a foolish action to put brushes or charcoal aside to face a mirror and go through the motions he is trying to imprison in his picture. Pyle was that kind of actor and that was what he meant when he said "Live in your picture—become one with it—feel its mood and action in every part of you."

It was a doctrine that must have seemed more unusual in the early years of the century than today, but it greatly helped to thaw some inhibited natures. And it gained force, coming from such a commanding, controlled, and stalwart personality.

A direct word picture of a typical Monday evening session comes from one of his students, Ida Dougherty Aylward:

> Pyle stood under a strong light usually with one leg on the rung of a stool and he thumbtacked on the wall one composition at a time (big charcoal drawings, covering a sheet) and took it in. Then he asked the maker if what he had gotten—he stated it—was what the maker had intended to show.
>
> If that wasn't it, it was unsuccessful. But that was all to the good, for then he turned toward us in the darkness outside that ring of light, and as we listened, enthralled, he dove into his own profound imagination, and described to us what *he* saw in its depths, as portraying that thing we had tried to show. A wonderful word picture grew before us. We were fired with it. . . . He had gone so much deeper than we could, yet had such a sure grip upon reality, and added mystery and beauty and feeling we hadn't dreamed.*

Quite a number of the students tried to capture the words and phrases that moved them so deeply. Allan Tupper True often tried to set down the actual words immediately after class, before his memory played tricks. Here are some samples of his hasty notes:

> Project your mind into your subject until you actually live in it. Throw your heart into the picture and then jump in after it. Don't take my criticisms as iron-clad rules but more as suggestions, because while you are there [pointing down] and I am here [holding arm horizontal] nature is away up there [pointing up].
>
> Art is not a transcript nor a copy. Art is the expression of those beauties and emotions that stir the human soul. . . .
>
> I criticize these compositions by analysis but an illustration cannot be made that way—it must be made by inspiration.
>
> Make your pictures *live;* there are fifty-thousand artists but how many make their pictures living?†

*Reprinted in R. W. Lykes, "Howard Pyle—Teacher of Illustration" (Paper delivered at the Univeristy of Pennsylvania).

†Wilmington, Delaware. Delaware Art Museum. Pyle papers.

Other notes were taken by Ethel Penniwell Brown and Olive Rush. They tended to concentrate on remarks relating to specific details in certain pictures, which lose a good deal of their pertinence without the pictures before us but some sentences have general importance:

> Make real things, real surroundings, real backgrounds. A tone for a background will not do.
> Paint your picture by means of the lights. Lights define texture and color—shadows define form.
> The student learns rules but all the rules in the world never make a picture.

Young N. C. Wyeth, writing home about his first experience with the Monday evening class, sums up the detail of his description with a sentence: "The composition lecture lasted two hours and it opened my eyes more than any talk I ever heard."

Some of the actual words, such as "Live in your picture" and "Your subjects have had a history—try to reveal it in your picture," we can repeat. The magnetism behind them must be left to the imagination of each reader.

In the realm of picturemaking every outstanding teacher has to possess, as Pyle did, the capacity to rescue a student from despair. Perhaps only those who have struggled through the apprentice years of picturemaking can understand the rock bottom despair of coming to the end of slender resources, of the fright of a seemingly impossible road ahead. Even the greatly talented are not immune from this—indeed, are sometimes the most vulnerable. The early years can sometimes seem a valley of defeats. Pyle's intuitions were acute. He could read the signs, and they brought out his best efforts. He spent little time on routine sympathy but cleared away the fogs of frustration, analyzed the strengths and weaknesses, and planned the next steps. Although he was not prone to demonstrate his own skills, he knew the limitations of words and the time for brush or charcoal to point the way.

He was a builder of futures. Student after student has testified to his power to reinvigorate a despairing spirit and make it believe in itself again. He could read the possibilities in inadequate pictures. And all this was not just an outpouring of groundless optimism. Behind it was a searching, probing, ever sceptical nature, not to be taken in by a passing emotion. Behind it was also a keen, perceptive knowledge of the personality before him. He knew the vulnerable spots, the right chords to touch.

When he said, "Talk about life—but in your own way" or "Paint ideas, paint thought," he spoke to their independence, their uniqueness, qualities he knew they possessed or they would never have been admitted to his class. They were encouraged to tread the paths of self-discovery.

The aura of the school was a quickening thing. One could almost breathe in the feel of effort, devotion, and achievement. There was the authority of the master himself—the authority of one of the greatest illustrators, probably the greatest, of the day. His work was all about them; they saw his latest pictures grow day by day. Each week or month these pictures appeared in the magazines or books. Their own classmates were working for the publishers, the jargon of the publishing world was in their ears, and that world was not a remote and theatrical realm but one almost within their reach.

They knew they were privileged. No school in the country was like it. They had their hours of bragging and strutting but it sprang from pride. They knew they were the survivors of a strict winnowing and their pride was justified.

Chapter 13

THE VINTAGE YEARS

The eighties had flowed into the nineties and the nineties into the new century on a tide of steady, unremitting creativity. Pyle's work habits were set. Most of the daylight hours were for the studio, the evenings for the family, and Sundays for church and friends. There were few exceptions to this routine.

By the beginning of the nineties the name of Howard Pyle was widely known throughout the country. He had a large following of young readers, unique in that it loved both his pictures and prose. With that combination he had no rivals in the field. Some of his early admirers had already grown into their late teens and early adult years and were reading his pirate and other adventure tales. His adult audience was still looking for his latest articles and illustrations, particularly those on early American history. The time would soon come when children brought up on his books would be reading them to their children.

There was little abatement in the books coming from his pen. In 1891 he edited *The Buccaneers and Marooners of America* and the next year his important medieval fiction work for the young, *Men of Iron*, was published.

In the same year as *Men of Iron*, the so-called extravaganza in four acts, *A Modern Aladdin*, appeared and in 1895 a group of three books was published within a few months of each other. They were three quite dissimilar works, typical of Pyle's prolific, versatile mind. The first, a juvenile, *The Story of Jack Ballister's Fortunes*, was an historical adventure tale of the early eighteenth century dealing with a kidnapping from England to the Virginia plantations and with a pirate finale. The story, with its pictures, had been serialized in *St. Nicholas*. The second book was *The Garden Behind the Moon*, and the third was *Twilight Land*, a collection of folktales that had been serialized in *Harper's Young People*. At the end of the eighties came *The Price of Blood*, the title descriptive of its contents.

Many of these books revealed the rapid changes that were sweeping the publication field. Most of the illustrations were halftones. Pyle was working increasingly with painting mediums, gouache or oil, and the illustrations had lost some visual impact as well as appearing almost an afterthought.

In the opening years of the new century, besides the controversial novel *Rejected of Men* came the four books of the Arthurian cycle at intervals of about two years, a collection of four pirate stories under the heading *Stolen Treasure* and *The Ruby of Kishmoor*.

The new century brought a confrontation with new problems and a realization that the channels of his daily life were comfortable and self-planned but confining. He was a victim of success and ingrained work habits. It was exhilarating to feel the demands of a large audience, but they were *demands*. He could scarcely ask for better relations with his publishers but he sometimes felt the prisoner of his obligations. The children were growing and there was need for more space, so in 1896 the family moved to a larger house.

The Pyles' new young neighbor Gertrude Brincklé told me in later years about the move:

> We lived at 1603 Broom Street, from our windows we watched 1601 Broom Street in fascination, to see Mr. Pyle, big and tall; Mrs. Pyle, tall and slim; Phoebe so pretty with yellow hair and blue eyes; Theodore and Howard; Eleanor, a little toddler; Godfrey, the pretty baby; the nurse, the cook, followed by William the colored man and Jacky, the fox terrier. There was no fence between our yards; we children soon made friends. In 1896, I was 11, Phoebe was 9; we went to the Misses Hebb's School together; in the evenings Mrs. Pyle often read aloud to us in the *Wonder Clock* or *Robin Hood*. On the other side of the Pyles, lived the five Moore children, with another little toddler, Constance Moore; we had a lively street corner.

The "little toddler Constance Moore" later became the director of the Delaware Art Center in Wilmington (now the Delaware Art Museum), where she was instrumental in collecting, organizing, and conserving the largest collection of Pyle's works.

The new house was pleasant, in a quiet tree-lined neighborhood within easy walking distance of the studio. The five children fitted into it snugly, the sixth was on the way. Mrs. Pyle managed the large and lively household with great competence and common sense. In the social world of Wilmington she was a great favorite with her beauty, charm, and friendliness. The family had a large circle of friends and their home was a popular gathering place.

Life seemed to have arranged itself most comfortably and satisfactorily for the Wilmington artist with the national reputation. The climate of place and time, of family and friends, of talent and ambition, was all that could be desired. The neighbors who watched the tall, pleasant gentleman walk up the street to and from his studio four times a day saw nothing that jarred with the usual slow Wilmington scene. He was handsome and courteous, with a pleasant word for all; sometimes abstracted, brisk but unhurried. His clothes were of the finest quality, quiet but expertly tailored. Those who knew him well

Pyle with a student group, 1903. *Standing, left to right:* George Harding, Gordon McCouch, Thornton Oakley, N. C. Wyeth, and Allen True.

were aware that he was vain about his dress. It pleased him to be taken for a prosperous man of business. Those who hoped for something more spectacular from an artist and writer were disappointed. Even the stuffiest of Wilmington's inner-core society, hearing of his mounting income, forgave him his odd occupation.

As the new century came nearer, Pyle like every illustrator in the country adjusted to and experimented with the new reproduction methods. The halftone method was now quite reliable, and artists reveled in painting with a full range of the black-and-white palette, knowing the reproduction would be reasonably close to the original and freed from the sometimes unexplained quirks of the engraver's tool. The old feuds between artist and wood engraver were beginning to die out, for wood engraving was a rapidly dying craft and hundreds of men who had spent long apprentice and professional years at an exacting craft were on the streets. For the time being the illustrator made the most of the possibilities. Later he would discover that the halftone process stopped short of perfection and was capable of being bungled in many ways, that the mechanics of the darkroom and the acid-bitten plate could also botch his cherished efforts.

Sir Gawaine finds the beautiful Lady:

Full-page illustration from *The Story of King Arthur and His Knights*. Charles Scribner's Sons, 1903.

Sir Kay interrupts ye meditations of Sir Percival :•

Full-page illustration for *The Story of the Champions of the Round Table*, Charles Scribner's Sons, 1905.

Howard Pyle, circa 1900.

Illustration for "Sinbad on Burrator," by A. T. Quiller-Couch. *Scribner's Magazine*, August 1902.

In the meantime, color reproduction was still very uncertain. For years illustration had been largely an art of black and white. The prospering American magazines had made only a few attempts at color reproduction and then only in a tentative way. The best color reproductions were to be found in the field of children's books and that principally in England. Few American illustrators had been given a chance to experiment in color and Pyle became one of that small number when, in 1881, he produced two sets of pictures for color reproduction for the children's books *Yankee Doodle* and *The Lady of Shalott*. They were not considered to be successful.

Naturally he was hungry to indulge his rich medieval and Byzantine color sense. Although he had seen many disappointments with the new and tentative processes, he was eager to experiment and his opportunity soon came. In his visits with the Harper editors, the growing possibilities of the use of color were constantly under discussion. He knew that it was likely that he would be given one of the first opportunities to experiment. It was impossible for him not to spend hours daydreaming of imaginary color compositions. He was hoping that his first assignment to execute a color picture for magazine publication would furnish him with an inspiring, imaginative text, and so it turned out. Harper asked him to do a set of full-color panels for "The Pilgrimage of Truth," by Erik Bogh. This was planned as a special display feature for the Christmas issue of 1900. The text was scarcely remarkable but it offered many pictorial opportunities and Pyle made the most of them. He painted seven small panels in rich glowing color, measurably different from any of his previous works. He was happy with his effort and so were the Harper editors. The paintings were turned over to the engraving house to be photographed and etched on copper for the new but still uncertain four-color method. It entailed making four plates—one for each color used—red, yellow, blue, and black. Theoretically, by printing the three so-called primary colors—red, yellow, and blue—one over another, a reasonable gamut of the color spectrum could be obtained. The black plate was to give depth and strengthen the very dark colors. To make the negatives for etching the primary color plates, the photographing was done through various filters that would bar out all but the primary color desired. The theory was perfect and was soon to become the dominant method for color reproduction, but at the moment not all the problems had been solved. We have no precise record of what was at fault, but the plates were repeatedly unsatisfactory.

It was a great blow to the editors and to Pyle. If successful, it would have been a conspicuous landmark in the development of an important new method of publishing. But upon reflection both the editors and Pyle decided that the idea of having a color feature should not be abandoned. Disappointed as he was, Pyle was willing to make a second set of pictures, this time abandoning the experimental new process and working with a basic set of black linecut plates over which a number of flat color plates could be printed. Pyle worked determinedly on the black line drawings that were to be filled in with color and they were one of the most stunning sets he had ever drawn. Then, on proofs taken from the drawings, he filled in the white paper areas with experimental washes of flat colors and here again the color effects were glowing. From these color fill-ins it was necessary to trace the exact shape of each separate color and make a separate plate for each color. There is no record to consult as to who did this mechanical chore, Pyle or some engraver or staff artist. But when the series appeared it was a triumph. Today, at the Delaware Art Museum, one can compare the original painted panels with the reproduced, flat color series and form one's own preference, but each set is splendid of its kind.

If, together with this story of an early trying experience with the new method of color printing, we examine Pyle's next two or three encounters with color reproduction, we will have a capsule history of the rapid advance of the four-color method. Pyle, eager to work with color again, was given the chance before another year had passed. He paved the way for it by writing the article "North Folk Legends of the Sea," which was full of imaginative pictorial possibilities. In the short interval of about a year the publishers had learned to expect a higher degree of reliability in the new method. The decorative series, painted in color, included pictorial panels, margin decoration, headpieces, decorative titles, and initial letters. Pyle used a restricted color range suited to the mood of his subject—mostly greens and cool grays with some bright red accents. Only three color plates were used—red, yellow, and blue; the black plate was eliminated to preserve the cool green rhythms of the sea. All in all, it was a quite successful effort. True enough, a comparison of scattered copies of this January 1902 issue of *Harper's Monthly* reveals variations of color, impression, and registration, but with the exception of a few extreme cases, the world of deep sea rhythms and misty, elusive color is well maintained and the mood and spell of the artist's conception is well expressed.

Both Pyle and the publishers were heartened by this marked improvement. Pyle immediately began brooding on new color possibilities and looking for a theme that would justify a set of paintings. It was *Century Magazine* that offered him his third opportunity. The publishers were looking for a spectacular color display as a focal point of their Christmas issue of 1902. Pyle was prepared with a theme that offered wide pictorial opportunities for imaginative color and design. His theme was *The Travels of the Soul*, a title that held all kinds of metaphysical promise, and he furnished his own text. That text was short, but elaborated not only by four full-color panels but by black-and-white page decorations, title page, headpieces, and initial letters. Of course the crown of the whole project was a group of color panels glowing like rich Byzantine enamels. Their titles give a hint of their imaginative content, *The Wicket of Paradise*, *In the Meadows of Youth*, *In the Valley of the Shadows*, *At the Gates of Life*. They created a sensation in the publishing world. They were something new in American illustration. American magazine color illustration was now mature and more than ever the envy of Europe. The technical reproduction was not quite perfect but it was a remarkable achievement and ahead were the golden years of American color illustration.

All the problems of color reproduction were by no means completely solved but from this point on the method was largely dependable. Practicing illustrators were adapting their procedures to the new requirements and both engravers and printers were becoming versed in the new skills. Wood engraving had almost vanished from book and magazine pages and American illustration had a new look. The American magazine, brash, aggressive, inventive, and conscious of its mounting popularity and power, was the astonishment of the Western world.

Pyle, rather late in his creative life, was now able to indulge his craving for color expression. That rich color sense, held in leash for so many years until technological opportunities opened the way for its expression, came as a surprise to many. Like his occasional forays into rampant bloody tales of pirate adventure, it contradicted the notion of many who, perhaps from outward appearance, conceived of him as an apostle of simplicity and decorum. His seeming contradictions, the complexities of a widely gifted character, were a worry to some but a delight to most. Perhaps some expected his palette to be a range of Quaker grays. The grays were there, to be used when appropriate, but his delight was in a sumptuous palette.

In the following year, making four paintings for another medieval subject, "Peire Vidal, Troubadour," for *Harper's Monthly*, he was still indulging a rich palette but with modifications for the more tender and subtle passages. In one picture, at the gate of the castle, the chill of approaching winter is beautifully conveyed by lucid passages of modified color. One can feel that he is not only immersed in expressing the light and feel of a time of year but also testing the capabilities of the new intoxicating medium. The reproduction is almost all that one could ask for, and this, together with the three previous color groups, shows how in the space of about three years American color reproduction had moved into maturity.

Now there was ample opportunity to use his tubes of pigment. He had a contract with Harper for a minimum of three illustrations a month for use in their magazines. These were largely to be color paintings. The subjects were mostly historical, often a type of light and affected costume fiction. His name became linked with those of a number of popular writers of that genre, particularly James Branch Cabell. In spite of the fact that

Illustration for "Peire Vidal le Troubadour," by Olivia H. Dunbar. *Harper's Monthly*, December 1903.

Illustration for "Swanhild," by Brian Hooker. *Harper's Monthly*, January 1910.

Burning of the Gaspé illustration for "Colonies and Nation," by Woodrow Wilson. *Harper's Monthly,* January 1901. BROWN COUNTY LIBRARY, GREEN BAY, WISCONSIN.

several of Pyle's adventure novels fell into this category, he had no great admiration for the school. Perhaps his taste was changing.

But these were prime years. He still had a great reservoir of energy, a head full of plans and projects (too many for one man to carry into completion), and an admiring audience across the country. Surrounding and supporting him were a fond and capable wife and family, a great circle of friends, and helpers on all levels, from Katie the cook and William the black handyman to Anna Hoopes, his secretary, and John Weller, the answer to every problem and emergency. Gardener, carpenter, butler, child-watcher—let the list

Illustration for "The Coming Tide." *Harper's Monthly,*

grow—John could fill any role. He was the emergency model, ready for any pose, any character. He had worn every male costume in the large costume chest and countless others, contrived from odds and ends. He was the custodian of the chest, aware of the dates and purpose of every costume, and he doled them out to students with words of advice. John kept an eye on the whole mechanism of home and studio and usually had problems solved before others were aware of their existence.

Pyle was upset when Anna Hoopes, his experienced secretary, decided to retire, but he discovered the perfect answer, virtually in his own household. The daughter of his friends and neighbors, Gertrude Brincklé had been the constant playmate of the Pyle children for years. Gertrude at nineteen was looking for interesting work, and Pyle could see her as the ideal secretary.

He wrote to Major Brincklé, her father:

> I believe Gertrude has written you about her helping me as a sort of secretary— I do not think that I should be an exacting taskmaster, but if she should undertake such duties it should have to be as a matter of business. It would require that she should give me every morning except the usual times. She will find, I think, that her position with me would add to her social pleasures rather than detract, and the earning of spending money in such a way is a thing very much to be desired by any girl. I should be glad to send her to a good school to learn the rudiments of shorthand and typewriting.*

So it came about that Gertrude attended classes at Goldeys Business College and thereafter spent her mornings in the studio on Franklin Street. She discovered that writing shorthand notes and typing were only part of her duties. There was also reading. Pyle had a passion for being read to while he worked. When other chores were out of the way, that was often Gertrude's occupation. Pyle's repertoire of authors was not voluminous but those who struck a chord within him, he read repeatedly and in depth, searching for inner meanings. Gertrude found herself receiving an extension of her education, ranging from Swedenborg to Darwin, from Thackeray to Joseph Conrad, from William Dean Howells to Theodore Roosevelt's *Winning of the West.*

She was also expected to be a model for female roles. Age, size, or character did not mean too much; Pyle needed only a general suggestion, the fold of a skirt or a turn of a hand—his imagination and experience could improvise the rest.

Occasionally he felt his imagination needed more accurate support from reality. When *Harper's Monthly* gave him the story "Lola," the characterization of the central figure, a Spanish dancer, seemed to demand a more authentic model. Pyle heard that Miss Taylor, an actress, was in Wilmington and she looked the part. Gertrude was sent to persuade her to pose. Miss Taylor was located in an old-fashioned house downtown. Gertrude was shown into a small overstuffed parlor where she waited endlessly, wedged between the wall and a grand piano. When Miss Taylor finally appeared she was in a vile mood. She disliked having to stay in Wilmington—"It smells of fish," she said—but she softened at the proposal to pose—she was flattered. Gertrude discovered that her new job was not all routine. Her good nature and diplomacy solved many problems.

Toward the end of the 1903 Chadds Ford class, Pyle began plans for another family move. What had once seemed ample family quarters in the Broom Street house were now overcrowded. He found a much larger house with grounds at 907 Delaware Avenue, not far from his studio. He felt the property needed additions and other improvements and since this would take some months, it became convenient to remain in the large rented house in Chadds Ford throughout the winter.

When the family installed itself in the new house they could count heads—it was a

*In the possession of the Brincklé family.

sizable establishment. Besides the parents and six children, there were Anne's mother, an invalid, and her nurse, a nurse for the younger children, a cook, upstairs maid, and downstairs maid and, later, a butler. A gardener came by the day as did a "mother's helper." Pyle's income was mounting but so were the weekly payroll and household expenses.

The family was living in an ample way that delighted Pyle. He was a gourmet and enjoyed good company; the dinner parties at 907 Delaware Avenue soon became talked about in Wilmington. They were usually formal. The women assembled in the parlor, the men in the drawing room where they picked up the cards giving the names of their dinner partners. Then, two by two, the hosts and their guests, walked into the candlelit dining room, while, from the floor above, the younger children peered down through the banister rail at the procession.

It was a comfortable and comforting home life that fortified the long intense hours at the easel or with the students, and Pyle was aware of his blessings. There were daily problems, both at the easel and in the classroom, but they were the stuff of life, to be taken in stride. Wilmington seemed a sheltered place, a protected enclave of family and friends where one read the newspapers to discover there was an outside world.

As insular as Wilmington was, however, Pyle could not help but be aware of the changing scene in American publishing as he worked. Although his contract with *Harper's* for three pictures a month was now his principal creative concern, it did not consume all his time and, moreover, he needed more income. He accepted additional assignments from time to time, from editors who were eager to have his name in their publications. *Collier's Weekly* was one he liked to work for. The Colliers, father and son, had made the *Weekly* into one of the country's most spectacular magazines. They had adopted a large page format (9 × 12 rather than the usual 7 × 10) using oversize illustrations, often with full-page paintings by the country's best illustrators. Pyle was proud to be in a group that included Frederic Remington, Walter Appleton Clark, Edward Penfield, William Smedley, his old friend A. B. Frost, and his former student Maxfield Parrish.

At the moment, in the churning world of American magazine publishing, with new vehicles constantly entering the field, each with fresh, extravagant, or experimental ideas, *Collier's* was a showpiece, a monument of native enterprise, skill, and the ability to sense and lead the taste of millions. The illustrative talent was of a very high quality and being constantly renewed, but even that opportunistic company was startled by the emergence of a new talent that America suddenly took to its heart. The new idol was Charles Dana Gibson.

The older illustrators, strong as their hold was upon large American audiences, were eclipsed in popularity by the younger man. In a few years the young Gibson, even to his own astonishment, had captured the interest and adulation of the American public. He had done this through the medium of a galloping and spectacular pen line, which brought to life, among other characterizations, two invented young types—the so-called Gibson Girl and Gibson Man. This pair was elegant and assured, noble featured and nobly proportioned, aloof and superior. They wore their clothes with nonchalant distinction, moved with easy assurance, and rarely betrayed any emotion beyond the ghost of a smile or a slight crease of the brow. Most of young America and much of its middle-aged lovingly attempted to model themselves upon these prototypes. Tens of thousands of American girls fought nature to coerce their bodies into the Gibson formula: a narrow waist and long shapely legs, a full but trim bosom, clearcut, aloof features, and that princess gaze.

This was no longer showing admiration for the artist by cutting out his reproductions and pinning them up on one's wall. This was changing one's appearance and even way

Illustration for "The Nation Makers." *Collier's Weekly,* June 2, 1906.

of life at the behest of a pictorial formula. And the Gibson formula did not confine itself to the magazine pages. The favorite pictures were assembled in large horizontal volumes for the parlor table; special editions of prints were issued. Gibson heads were found on saucers, ashtrays, decorative plates, china mugs, and glasses. There was a Gibson Girl wallpaper aimed at the bachelor trade. She was on pillow covers, scarves, hangings, and leather novelties. She made certain popular songs and the musical comedy stage. In short, Gibson, quite unwittingly the benefactor and victim of having given life to one of America's smoldering dreams, was leaving his imprint upon an age as no previous American artist had done.

When he moved to the pages of *Collier's Weekly* after having developed his technique and content on the pages of *Life,* he set in motion a revolution in publication economics. The Collier family, eager to lure Gibson away from *Life,* gradually bid up the price per drawing. When they passed the five-hundred-dollar figure they were already well above the three hundred that Pyle was receiving for a drawing and that was already much higher than average. But the bidding went on to eight hundred and then to nine. By this time the competition was public news, and the Colliers became aware of the value of all this free publicity. They conceived the bombshell effect of offering a full thousand dollars and better still, a contract of a hundred thousand dollars for a hundred pictures. Gibson agreed to this providing he could still contribute pictures to *Life.* The Colliers accepted this and bought newpaper space to broadcast their triumph.

Now the illustration and editorial world was shaken. Every illustrator began to reestimate his worth. Every editor and publisher faced an increased budget. Good illustrators were in short supply and prices did go up, but it was many years before a thousand dollars was anything but very exceptional in the art departments of New York City.

The publicity generated by the Gibson affair penetrated all levels and for a few weeks was a common topic of conversation. Friends asked cautious or pointed questions of Pyle. He admitted very readily that he cared little for the work of Gibson and the financial figures seemed a bit extreme. But he couldn't escape the inevitable comparison with his own remuneration. *Harper's* made no offer of an increased contract but *Collier's* and *McClure's* were paying more. Then, out of this sharply competitive turmoil came a tempting offer that could only be accepted by making a major change in the pattern of his life.

A typical Gibson drawing employing two of his typical characters that delighted large American audiences in the early years of the present century. Gibson was the envy of his fellow illustrators for the extraordinary prices paid by his publishers, but eventually they raised the scale for all.

Pen drawing by Charles Dana Gibson.

Chapter 14

THE McCLURE'S INTERLUDE

In the winter of 1906 the buzz of rumor, gossip, and conjecture that constantly circulated through the student body on Franklin Street began to center about the frequent and excited visits of the master to New York. Of course, visits to New York were part of the pattern—the publishers were there—but in recent years Pyle had reduced his trips to only those of great necessity. His completed illustrations were now usually delivered by one of his senior students, often Frank Schoonover or Stanley Arthurs. This not only saved Pyle precious hours for his studio work but brought the more professional students in contact with the editors. The carriers were always sent off with detailed instructions, including where to eat and what was best to eat, for Pyle believed in fine food and special dishes. He was always generous in money for food but all other expenses were expected to be minimal.

Whether the news leaked through the carrier's contacts with New York or from Pyle himself is unimportant; the facts seemed to be that he had been offered the unheard of salary of $36,000 a year to act as full-time art director of *McClure's* magazine. This remarkable offer was part and parcel of the booming times in the publication field and the resulting sharp and bitter competition among the contending magazines, old standbys and newcomers alike. *McClure's* was essentially a magazine dominated by its agressive founder and owner, S. S. McClure. He was after big names and in his mind may have been the hope of cornering the market in Pyle School graduates.

The offer was enormously tempting and Pyle was in an agony of indecision. His anxiety and touchiness were noticeable to those about him, although they did not at first know the reasons for it. Financially it offered rescue for he was deeply concerned about mounting expenses and the lack of any financial reserve. The Howard Pyle look was now apparent on the pages of many magazines and books, but he may have craved more exposure or could he have been somewhat dazzled by the power that an editor was supposed to exert? But the other side of the picture was frightening. He would have to live in New York except, perhaps, for weekends. The family roots were all in Wilmington. He might as well close his studio door. The classes would have to be disbanded. All this was unthinkable, and he refused the offer.

But S. S. McClure was stubborn and willful. He made another offer of half salary—$18,000—for half a week's work, and Pyle capitulated. The salary would take care of all expenses and much more, and he persuaded himself that in three days he could take care of his studio and teaching commitments and have Sundays with his family. There seems to be no record of a contract or a dated agreement but the new arrangement appears to have gone into effect in the early spring of 1906.

Whatever mixed imperatives were behind Pyle's plunge into the *McClure's* assignment, we have a statement of some of them in a late March 1906 letter to his old friend Arthur B. Frost.

> Dear Frost:—
>
> I do not know whether you have heard that I have taken up a sort of art directorship at *McClure's*—which at present is perhaps the most inartistic of all the magazines published.
>
> I think I am going to have good backing, and I am very much interested in the work. To so old a chum as you I would like to explain that I am doing some very large mural work, and as long as I undertook to do illustration as well I found that I could not bend my mind to larger projects. So I cut loose from illustration, earning a living at *McClure's* by giving them one half of my time, and coming back the other half of my time to Wilmington with renewed vigor and energy. I hope I am wise in operating it that way. At least I find, after having made the departure, that a good deal of rather large and interesting work is drifting my way.
>
> There is a little group of stories that has come up in *McClure's* that would exactly fit you. They are very charming and very humorous, and are going to make a hit. The central figure is a little darky boy. The scene is Hampton, Va., with the Northern people who have drifted there, and the Southern people who are there, and the little boy is the creator and teller of a series of grotesque negro stories which only you could possibly touch.
>
> For it is not necessary for me to tell you, my dear fellow, that you are the one and only real artistic humorist in the country, and that your humor is of a sort that is as broad and as deep as the great American heart. It has always been my opinion that long after the great raft of American painters and illustrators have passed away into oblivion, your work will remain as typifying the great American sense of humor which stands rooted in our humane American heart, and blossoms in a wit that is to be found nowhere else.
>
> So now that I am drifting into this new work, I want you to help me if you can possibly do so.
>
> At any rate, I want you to come and see me, and have a talk with me, for somehow my thoughts turn much toward you of late, and I feel myself (now that the years are advancing on me) to reach out for the old friends of earlier days.
>
> Please remember me most kindly and sincerely to Mrs. Frost, and believe me to be, dear fellow,
>
> *Fraternally yours,*
> *Howard Pyle.**

*In the possession of the Pyle family.

Scrawled under the signature in difficult penmanship is this message: "I write so badly[?] nowadays that I have to take to the typewriter with even such a dear friend as you."

Frost's reply came promptly and it helps to indicate some of the difficulties Pyle was to face in his new position. It also casts light upon the thinking of some of Pyle's own generation about illustration and painting. It forecasts Frost's future as a painter, but not his comparative failure at it.

April 1st 1906.

Dear Howard,

I am mighty glad to get your letter and thank you sincerely for the kind things you say in it. I will answer the business end of it first. I am very sorry I can't make your pictures. I have an exclusive arrangement with *Collier's Weekly* that has nearly a year to run, after that I am not going to make any more illustrations. I am going to paint, so you see I am not to be an illustrator much longer. I am very much interested in your new move and am very glad you are going to paint or are painting, it confirms me in my belief that it is the thing to do. We all drift that way, all the men who have anything in them drop illustration as soon as they can, Reinhart tried and failed, Abbey next and succeeded, Alexander, Robert Blum, Irving Wiles, Smedley is painting and illustrating, Gibson will paint, to a certainty; it is the natural yearning for something better, I am not as young as the other fellows, but I am not old, by a good deal.

I am very *glad* you have the work to do. It is such a great thing to have the work in hand. I am sure you are doing the right thing in taking this position with McClure's. Your mind will be free to work out your big work. You can't work and illustrate, I have tried it and can't make it go.*

Frost, with his family, moved to Paris and out of Pyle's life, discarding his remarkable power to delineate with sly humor American backwoods life and wasting his last years on run-of-the-mill impressionist landscapes. His refusal to join *McClure's* was one of a series of similar shocks for which Pyle was not prepared.

A few excerpts from several of young Wyeth's letters to his mother help to round out the picture. On March 5, 1906, Wyeth was telling of the beginning of the new art editor's campaign: "Tuesday I received an 'art director's' letter from *McClure's*, signed Howard Pyle, and I can tell you it looked strange. His letter was worded in the same sing-songy way that characterizes all editors' letters. He evidently has got into the art editor atmosphere."

Two weeks later he was saying, "Mr. Pyle is anxious for me to contract half my time with *McClure's*, but I shall *most decidedly* stick out against it. It will tie me down too much, that is it will limit my chances of picture-making as it will bind me to illustrations. Of course he claims that I would have the rest of my time to paint, but I want to be seen in the different magazines and, besides, it would sacrifice all my chances for trips for *Outing*."

Then in early April, he notes a confrontation. "Today I faced Mr. Pyle with my final decision in regards to the *McClure* contract. It was as I said it t'would be—a refusal. I made a very logical and reasonable stand and for once he saw my position and agreed with me that I was in the right. Mr. Pyle told me how much they wanted me and that I must talk with him about some sort of an agreement in June. So things will rest until June."

In a May first letter there are two brief sentences relating to the McClure problem: "Mr. Pyle is clean off his trolley these days. All worked up over the *McClure's* business."†

There are repeated references in many letters during May and June, including an announcement that he is about to sign an agreement to devote thirty weeks during a year

*In the possession of the Pyle family.
†N. C. Wyeth, *The Wyeths*, ed. by Betsy James Wyeth (Boston: Gambit, 1971), pp. 152, 153, 155–156.

The young N. C. Wyeth, circa 1908.

beginning July 15 for a remuneration of $4000. On August 10, there comes an explosion of anger:

> Mr. Pyle has sent in his resignation to *McClure's*—which was prophesied by all magazine men before he actually took office there. His reasons for leaving are very many and intricate; the magazine's reason is just one big fact—H. P. is not the man for the place. He is too impractical, too radical in his views, and too perceptible, and over all he has *no* business sense.
>
> Of course this all results in my overthrow as far as the *contract* goes. . . .
>
> It's what I prepared for and expected and to tell you the truth I'm tickled to death. The stringent obligation I was under was like a millstone around my neck. Not the obligations to *McClure's* so much, but to Howard Pyle. . . . Mr. Pyle has been using me for his personal betterment and yesterday I told him so.*

*N. C. Wyeth, *The Wyeths*, pp. 173–174.

There were difficulties with Frank Schoonover and Allen True also, and strained relations existed for a while; but shortly we have instances of Pyle's renewed concern and kindnesses to his now professional students and the breach seemed to be healed.

The *McClure's* interval was a mistake, even a disaster. It came at what might be considered the peak of Pyle's career. He was fifty-three with an extraordinary life of accomplishments behind him, with widespread fame on every side and undiminished ambition. But he was also beset with inner dissatisfactions. His lack of a financial reserve gnawed at him. The illustrative world was changing, new faces were replacing old ones, the stories that the editors turned over to the picturemakers often required new types, new costumes, new backgrounds. The whole field was more competitive. There was the lure of mural decoration and that too was highly competitive. He was working on *The Story of Sir Launcelot and His Companions*, the third in the King Arthur series, but there was diminishing vigor in some of the pictures and the text seemed repetitive. He must have been aware that the imaginative fire that had warmed both text and picture in the first two volumes was burning lower.

In the few months that Pyle officiated as art director, it is impossible to trace his every move. Except in a few instances there is no record of what artists he chose for what texts. Examining the bound volumes of the magazine for the few months that he officiated, and for a year or two before and after, arouses some speculations—but they are only speculations.

In the light of Pyle's assertion to his friend A. B. Frost that "*McClure's* . . . at present is perhaps the most inartistic of all the magazines published," the files of the four most competitive magazines can be consulted—*Harper's Monthly*, *Century*, *Scribner's*, and *Collier's Weekly*. The paper of those older magazines is yellowing, the pages smudged and dog-eared—pristine copies are hard to come by. But side by side, the paper of *McClure's* seems somewhat inferior, the presswork less crisp, the page layout humdrum, and certainly the color pages are considerably below standard.

Is this what Pyle meant or was he thinking more of illustration values? Certainly type selection, magazine page layout, and the supervision of presswork were not his intimate experiences but pictorial evaluation was. All four of the competitive magazines contain the work of some very excellent artists and so does *McClure's*, judging from the issues of 1905 and early 1906, before Pyle assumed office. In this period Pyle and several of his students are represented—N. C. Wyeth, Percy Ivory, Charlotte Harding, and William Aylward. The work of other outstanding American illustrators is also shown such as Frank Walter Taylor, Ernest Blumenschein, and André Castaigne. A goodly number of excellent British artists had been appearing in *McClure's* for several years.

Since there are no accurate dates for Pyle's assumption of office or resignation, we can only guess that his authority lasted but five or six months at most. In that interval the quality and kind of *McClure's* illustration remained about the same. There was no increased invasion of Pyle students. There was perhaps a slightly higher percentage of British illustrators such as Edmund Sullivan, Frank Craig, William Hatherill, and L. Raven-Hill, but *McClure's* had always been partial to the British. Other regular choices were William Glackens, Thomas Fogarty, and John Sloan. In short, it is difficult if not impossible to detect the Pyle touch upon *McClure's* pictorial pages. True enough the general page layout showed improvement, the printing and paper quality were better. Perhaps this was Pyle's contribution.

It seems likely that until Pyle actually sat in the art editor's chair he had no notion of the flood of niggling details that were so much a part of that office and only bitter experience drove home the lesson that an art editor was not a sovereign but a subordinate.

Chapter 15

THE LATE YEARS

The *McClure's* interlude was brief but it left a mark. It was the only conspicuous failure in a long line of successes and not easily brushed out of the mind. Outwardly the intent was to carry on as before—inwardly there was a growing awareness that things were not the same.

Pyle, now in a mood of recapitulation, realized that in the heat of problems and anxieties, in the haste and desperation of trying to salvage a mounting failure, he had bruised some old friendships. He handsomely admitted his mistakes and gradually the breach with his former students, N. C. Wyeth, Frank Schoonover, and Allen True, was healed.

Being back in the accustomed rhythms of Wilmington life was a comfort but one that could not completely conceal some growing dissatisfaction. The financial problems, which were to have been handsomely solved by the magnificent *McClure's* fees, were still there. He was fifty-three. Creative ideas were still abundant and energy had not slackened greatly, but the resilience of youth was gone. The content of his teaching had not changed, but its audience had. That dictated certain changes in approach. The company of bright young spirits with high promise and malleable talents ready for the shaping were still crowded in the three student studios, and there were seldom any openings for new recruits. But dotted around Wilmington was now a considerable body of newcomers, schooled professionals already earning their way in the publication world but dissatisfied with the quality of their work. They sought out Pyle for inspiration, for guidance in making the most of their talents. Those talents had already taken professional form—the master was not expected to remake them, just add a final polish. This was an utterly different problem from the earlier one of shaping into maturity, and a less inviting and challenging one.

These professionals mixed to some extent with the younger students, but essentially they were a group apart. They added a new element to the art life of Wilmington. There were many private houses where rooms and meals were available, but studio space was more difficult. There were all kinds of makeshifts. Sheds, stables, sign painter's lofts, and empty stores were used. Edward Wilson and his friend William H. Foster found theirs in the old slave quarters of the Rodney estate. These professionals felt no need for sessions of model study, head construction, or theoretical problems; besides, there was no room for them in the crowded studios. They had their own assignments from various publishers and although they sometimes attended the evening composition classes, they preferred to arrange for individual conferences and criticisms from Pyle. This was an outgrowth that Pyle had not planned or foreseen and it encroached more and more upon his own creative time.

With a few exceptions, they were a richly endowed company and they benefited from association with each other. Some experienced new growth in their association with Pyle, some expected the impossible. Edward Wilson, with a buoyant romantic temperament somewhat akin to Pyle's, expanded in the Wilmington atmosphere and left, fortified for a

Pen illustration by John Wolcott Adams for *Harper's Monthly*.

The Charge, illustration for *Harper's Monthly*, November 1904. PRIVATE COLLECTION.

Attack on a Galleon, illustration from "The Fate of a Treasure Town." *Harper's Monthly,* December 1905. DELAWARE ART MUSEUM.

The Coming of Lancaster, illustration for *Harper's Monthly*, May 1908. DELAWARE ART MUSEUM.

Illustration from "The Grain Ship." *Harper's Monthly*, March 1909. DELAWARE ART MUSEUM.

The Shell, illustration for *Harper's Monthly*, December 1908. PRIVATE COLLECTION.

Illustration from "The Salem Wolf." *Harper's Monthly*, December 1909. DELAWARE ART MUSEUM.

They Scrambled Up the Parapet and Went Over the Crest, illustration from "Colonies and Nation," by Woodrow Wilson. *Harper's Monthly,* January–December 1901. DELAWARE ART MUSEUM.

The Battle of Bunker Hill, illustration from the "Story of the Revolution." *Scribner's Magazine,* January–December 1898. DELAWARE ART MUSEUM.

Illustration from "Fate of a Treasure Town." *Harper's Monthly*, December 1905. DELAWARE ART MUSEUM.

His Army Broke Up and Followed Him, illustration for *Harper's Monthly*, February 1911. COLLECTION OF
MRS. PHILIP D. LAIRD.

The Mermaid, a decorative panel, 1910. DELAWARE ART MUSEUM.

Canadian Trapper and Wolf, oil painting by Frank E. Schoonover. COLLECTION OF MR. AND MRS. ANDREW WYETH.

General Harrison and Tecumseh at Vincennes, oil painting by Stanley Arthurs. DELAWARE ART MUSEUM.

Buffalo Bones Are Plowed Under, oil painting by Harvey Dunn. SOUTH DAKOTA MEMORIAL ART CENTRE.

La Fee and Bertrand, painting by Elizabeth Shippen Green. DELAWARE ART MUSEUM.

Ore Wagon, illustration for *McClure's Magazine* by N. C. Wyeth, 1907. COLLECTION OF THE SOUTHERN ARIZONA BANK & TRUST CO., TUCSON, ARIZONA.

Street in Siena. Pen drawing by Ernest Peixotto for *Harper's Monthly*.

long lifetime of distinguished illustration that included many classics for the Limited Editions Club. His exuberant *Iron Men and Wooden Ships* became almost as famous as Pyle's *Book of Pirates*. John Wolcott Adams was another congenial talent who was fired by Pyle's great knowledge of the early history of the country and who based his own delightful pen technique upon that of his master. Olive Rush, attracted by the great success of so many of Pyle's women students, found her work rejuvenated within about a year's time and moved into her most accomplished period.

Ernest C. Peixotto came with a high reputation and a record of being a regular contributor to the important magazines. He had a brilliant pen-and-ink technique that sprang from the Vierge–Martin Rico tradition and which he used to depict scintillating architectural subjects. For years he had been sought after to illustrate travel articles, but reputations in the publishing world could be chancy. Pen and ink had been a popular illustrative medium for a long time but the rise of the halftone had brought with it an appetite for tonal drawings, and pen drawings faced a declining market. In addition there was less demand for travel illustrations and Peixotto, although a splendid architectural draftsman, had limited command of the human figure. He needed to reorient his illustrative abilities and so he came to Wilmington. Pyle labored with him, but Peixotto never attained the same kinship with the brush that he had come by naturally with the pen. And his command of the figure never reached the level of ease, mobility, characterization, and authority that defines first-rate illustration.

An artist with a different background, Anton Otto Fischer, came with his intimate experience of the sea and ships. He was a capable if somewhat matter-of-fact picturemaker with a leaden gray palette. Pyle helped him release more of the inherent drama of his subject matter, and, although more intense pigments were added to his palette, they were usually mixed with each other to the point of neutralization. Still another artist, Henry J. Soulen, who had a natural zest for brilliant color combinations, was encouraged to exploit it in his pigment-loaded canvases, and for years his sumptuous color plates were a welcome contrast to the more orthodox pictures in the *Saturday Evening Post*.

These professionals came and went as they pleased, but the colony grew and presently Wilmington could claim that, after New York, Philadelphia, and Boston, it was the fourth most important center of illustration in the country. Many other well-known names came like Remington Schuyler, Douglas Duer, Herman Pfeifer, Will Colby, and Harold M. Brett; and some like Gale Hoskins, Herbert Moore, Charles DeFeo, Howard E. Smith, and Charles A. MacLellan made Wilmington their home for long periods of time, even for life.

Unwittingly, Pyle found himself committed to two schools; the first was the old, intimate, almost familylike group of eager young talents; the other, a kind of finishing or postgraduate assembly. In the late years, the first was dwindling and the second growing. It was the greatest compliment to have so many important names gather about one from a distant publishing center, but a price was paid—the spontaneity of young life was on its way out; the newcomers were bent on business.

In his studio hours Pyle faced a steady stream of assignments coming from *Harper's*, to which were added intermittent commissions from other publishers. It was the work coming in from other publishers that he began looking forward to with more expectancy, simply because it was less predictable and offered greater variety. *Harper's* was sending him the kind of assignments that reflected his reputation and which they thought he would be most happy to execute. As a matter of fact, they were beginning to bore him.

It was a period in which the historical adventure story was still in ascendancy, but showing signs of delicately perfumed decay. The genre was moving farther and farther from credible history, its characterizations had more and more a mannequin air, the conversations were stilted, contrived, and artificial. It had become a tawdry type of storytelling.

Although Pyle knew that it was not impossible for a masterpiece of illustration to spring from a tawdry manuscript, he knew the handicap of feeling resentful of an assignment. Although he had written a goodly amount of historical adventure fiction himself, it was of a hearty and more straightforward kind. A certain inner probity kept him from the precious language and posturing stagestruck characters of the times. He found his gorge rising when he read some of the manuscripts sent him.

Although he had painted some excellent pictures for this series of stories and had received letters of praise from both editors and authors, he was far from satisfied and fearful of repetition. He seemed happiest with the series of Joan of Arc pictures he had painted for Mark Twain's "Saint Joan of Arc," in the Christmas 1904 issue of *Harper's Monthly*. The other medieval and eighteenth-century stories were by a number of authors but most were from the pen of James Branch Cabell and it was upon this writer that his dissatisfaction centered.

In a 1907 letter to Wells, the *Harper's* editor, he wrote,

> I am in great danger of grinding out conventional magazine illustrations for conventional magazine stories. I feel myself now to be at the height of my powers, and in the

So the treasure was divided, illustration for "The Fate of a Treasure Town." *Harper's Monthly*, December 1905.

next ten or twelve years I should look to do the best work of my life. I do not think it is right for me to spend so great a part of my life manufacturing drawings for magazine stories which I cannot regard as having any really solid or permanent literary value. Mr. Cabell's stories, for instance, are very clever, and far above the average magazine literature, but they are neither exactly true to history or exactly fanciful, and, whilst I have made the very best illustrations for them which I am capable of making, I feel that they are not true to medieval life, and that they lack a permanent value such as I should now endeavor to present to the world.*

With that letter his pictures for Cabell's stories and similar ones came to an end. Some of Cabell's stories, together with Pyle's color pictures had already appeared in book form under the title *The Line of Love*. Later three more of these books appeared: *Gallantry, An Eighteenth Century Dizain*, 1907; *Chivalry*, 1909; and *The Soul of Melicent*, 1913.

Pyle was not planning an escape from all medieval themes—only those of a certain caliber. In all his spare time he was working on the texts and pictures of his four King Arthur volumes. In addition came an interesting commission from the Bibliophile Society to make a set of illustrations for Thomas Frognall Dibden's *The Bibliomania or Book-Madness*. These four paintings rank with his best and attracted so much admiration that it was decided to issue them in portfolio form. Large etching plates were made by W. H. Bicknell and printed in a limited edition. It is interesting to note that the Albrecht Dürer

*Reprinted in Abbott, *Howard Pyle*, pp. 125–26.

influence, so apparent in the drawings for *Otto of the Silver Hand*, crept back into this later Bibliophile series.

The letter to editor Wells is one indication of the self-searching and reevaluation Pyle was experiencing in his mid-fifties. He could now cast his mind back over a long journey on a clearly defined road, crowded with incessant activities, achievements, and honors. Ahead the road would be shorter and some uncertainties lurked there. For the moment he could bask in the knowledge that he had probably surpassed even the more expansive dreams of his youth. In all modesty, he could not help but know that he was a hero in America's countless family reading circles. His reading public included children and adults, from the youngest to the oldest. From this audience came a steady flow of appreciative letters.

The demand for his pictures was unceasing, and his books were reviewed as important events. There were articles about him and his work in *The Literary Digest, Harper's Weekly* and *Monthly, The Independent, New York Times, The Bookmart, The Book Buyer, The Dial,* and other magazines. His pictures were welcomed in exhibitions—there were two large one-man shows of his work in Macbeth's Gallery and the gallery of Pratt Institute. In 1907 he was elected Academician of the National Academy of Design. He was the friend of many important persons: artists such as Winslow Homer, Daniel Chester French, George De Forest Brush, Augustus Saint-Gaudens, and Frederic Remington; writers such as William Dean Howells, Mark Twain, Oliver Wendell Holmes, Edwin Markham, and S. Weir Mitchell; figures in public and political life such as Henry Cabot Lodge, Presidents Theodore Roosevelt and William Howard Taft, as well as President-to-be Woodrow Wilson.

These were some of the rewards and satisfactions he could savor when in a relaxed and mellow mood. But he was acutely conscious that these things had been possible because he had been fortunate enough to have caught the tide of the times. America had been preparing its audience for him—he had been born at the proper hour with the proper attributes. Simply by following his own star, heeding the nudgings of his instincts, he had shaped his words and pictures to touch the thought and feelings of a whole generation.

It had not been a simple and obvious passage. He could chart the patient exploration of his own diverse talents, the recognition of the apparently opposing traits of his nature, and the remarkable coordination of his plural selves. The irresistible imaginative and romantic side was foreordained to verbal and pictorial utterance and drawn to elegant clothes, a splendid house, and fine food. But the pull of those past generations of restrained Quakers demanded its own satisfaction and found it in the usefulness of word and picture and the whole conduct of his life. An embarrassment of creative and emotional talents that might have been self-frustrating was handsomely disciplined and coordinated.

When the inward look shifted to scan the outside world of publishing, it found that world still straining to satisfy a mounting hunger for the printed word and picture. The roster of American illustrators now contained many illustrious names; not only was Pyle's among the highest but there were many new promising ones displaying their Pyle schooling. Pyle's influence in the field of illustration was becoming the most important one in the country.

Whether Pyle was fully conscious of it or not, in his middle fifties his illustrative work was at high tide. He was, however, increasingly restless with the repetitive and confining aspects of it and his mind was exploring other pictorial possibilities. The turn of the century promised new possibilities to artists of all media. The great World's Columbian Exposition in 1893 in Chicago, the famous White City, had broadcast visions of beauty and a more fruitful life to millions. The great white buildings of the exposition, all designed

The King glared down at her, illustration for "The Noble Family of Beaupertuys," by Stephen F. Whitman. *Harper's Monthly*, July 1907. DELAWARE ART MUSEUM.

Illustration for "When All the World Was Young." *Harper's Monthly*, August 1909. DELAWARE
ART MUSEUM.

Illustration for "The Salem Wolf." *Harper's Monthly*, December 1909. PRIVATE COLLECTION.

Marooned. Hitherto unreproduced easel oil painting, 1909. DELAWARE ART MUSEUM.

by American architects and mirrored in the waters of a chain of lagoons and fountains, the numerous white statues, the murals, easel pictures, and artifacts inside the great buildings carried a message of what the American city could become if its artists could be mustered for the task. Even those who did not make the journey to Chicago could pore over the endless pictures.

Pyle, too, was caught up in the general wave of optimism. That wave did not die down immediately—it generated a new high regard for monumental sculpture and mural decoration. America suddenly discovered that it possessed a large company of architects, sculptors, and decorators of high talent. An enthusiasm for the possibilities of mural decoration had been dormant in Pyle's mind for some years, pushed back into a dark corner by the presence of other work and other problems, but now it began to reassert itself.

He was spurred on, too, by the knowledge that so many friends and associates from his youthful New York days were now immersed in painting and mural projects, men like Walter Shirlaw, Charles Reinhart, Frank Vincent Du Mond, Francis D. Millet, and J. Alden Weir. So were some later friends such as Gari Melchers, Kenyon Cox, Edwin Blashfield, George Maynard, and Walter McEwen.

His old friend Edwin Abbey had been commissioned to paint a frieze of the Holy Grail for the Boston Public Library. Similar panels in the library were allotted to John Singer Sargent for a frieze of the Prophets and to the Frenchman Puvis de Chavannes for his then startling primitive figures frozen in their chalky landscape. Blashfield now had a busy studio turning out drapery-wrapped female figures bearing certain symbols that might help to differentiate the Spirit of Democracy from the Art of Drama, or Roman Law from Civic Virtue. Artists were learning to cultivate the architects of public projects in hopes that the budgets contained funds for art. The grapevine that linked studio to studio was now concerning itself with mural decoration.

Some friends of Pyle, learning of a mural project for the Massachusetts Capitol building in Boston, advocated his retention to the powers that be. Apparently the project never reached the point of submitting a sketch or plan. In a letter to Winthrop Scudder, a friend and advocate, Pyle stated his position in the matter:

> As Governor Walcott writes, the space upon the walls of the House of Representatives is proposed to be filled by a decorative or allegorical subject and not by historical subjects. I think I could paint a Battle of Bunker Hill; I think I could paint a picture of the smoke, the thunder, the roar of the battle, the bareheaded, wounded and shattered columns of British advancing, the trampled grass, the smoke of the burning houses and over beyond all the quaint town reposing silently and peacefully in the afternoon sunlight. The image is very clear in my own mind and if I could materialize it upon canvas I think I might be able to show the sunlight, the heat and the desperate human earnestness of the grim red-coated heroes marching up that hill to their death.
>
> I doubt whether I could paint, "Massachusetts Crowned with Plenty," or "Massachusetts Standing a Bulwark for Freedom against Tyranny." I do not know whether I could paint a decorative subject in tones of blue and silver or blue and gray, but I am very sure I should not venture to make the attempt.*

This was a very clear statement of his feeling about allegorical subject matter at the moment, although he could scarcely have forgotten the number of illustrative problems that he had solved, and brilliantly, with allegorical material. He realized only too well that mural painting involved more than the mere enlarging of a pictorial subject. The size and placement of a mural brought into play all kinds of complicated factors—the varying distances from the spectator, the involvement with architectural forms, the possibility of curious shapes, of slanted or curved surfaces, the lighting factor, and many others.

*Abbott, *Howard Pyle*, pp. 229–30.

For practice he planned some experimental panels in his own home as a background for his daughter's coming-out party. After the letter to Winthrop Scudder, it is interesting to scan the titles of the new panels: *The Birth of Literature, The Gems of Art, Music,* and *Drama*—all indicating allegorical subjects.

They were lively and charming and fitted the place and purpose completely but they were too small and intimate to relate to the spatial problems of large public projects. The largest panel of the set, *"The Gems of Art"* (12'6" × 5'5"), was exhibited in 1905 in the galleries of the Society of Architects. It attracted a good deal of favorable attention, particularly among architects, and Pyle was persuaded that some concrete commitments would come from it.

They did, and he suddenly found himself plunged into the problems of his first authentic mural commitment. Cass Gilbert, a great admirer of his work, had the giant task of designing and supervising the construction of the Minnesota State Capitol at St. Paul. In the plans was a provision for a horizontal mural panel in the governor's reception room. The subject was to be The Battle of Nashville. The same sense of immersion in the actual happening, which permeated Pyle's description of the Battle of Bunker Hill in his letter to Winthrop Scudder, saturated the Nashville painting. It was in no sense a decoration but a splendid battle piece, perhaps the best painted by an American artist. Pyle had extended himself, and it was rightfully admired.

This was in 1906 and almost immediately Cass Gilbert asked him to plan another horizontal panel for the new Essex County Courthouse in Newark, New Jersey. This panel was larger, twenty by six feet, and the subject was The Landing of Carteret. Again he researched his picture as carefully as any historian. Two letters written to friends at this time describe the problems of these two large canvases in detail. It is obvious that the elements of deepest concern to him were to give a gripping portrayal of two stirring historical events and to amass all relevant material in order to fortify a sense of conviction. There is no mention of any concern with the architectural elements of the settings. The panels were stirring pictures placed on a wall.

When a third, and more extensive, mural commission arrived, it seemed as though mural painting was to be an important part of Pyle's artistic life. His old friend Frank Millet had selected him to paint five panels—three large horizontals and two small verticals—for the Hudson County Courthouse in Jersey City, New Jersey. The largest panel was thirty-five by seven feet and the subjects were again historical. The major panel was *Life in an Old Dutch Town;* the two smaller rectangles were *Hendryk Hudson and the Half-Moon,* and *Peter Stuyvesant and the English Fleet.* Each of the small upright panels contained a single soldier's figure, one English and one Dutch. This was Pyle's most extensive mural undertaking and the studio was filled with the five sizable canvases. He engaged Stanley Arthurs and Frank Schoonover as assistants. They transferred his full-size cartoon drawings onto the canvas surfaces and painted in many of the background areas and even some of the finished portions. This was the most exacting of the three mural assignments. This time with five separate elements to harmonize, he had to be more aware of decorative demands, and the end result did not entirely satisfy him. This experience gave him a deeper insight into mural problems, and he realized that the richer and longer European tradition might provide answers not yet assimilated by the American newcomers.

This was only one of the questions nagging at his mind. Although he had been teaching and practicing an indigenous American art for years, he could not deny that at least two areas of European tradition had played important parts in shaping his own style. English art, particularly of the Pre-Raphaelite period, and German medieval art, from the prints of the Little Masters to the work of Albrecht Dürer and Holbein, had left their marks upon many of Pyle's compositions. He had been scornful of the Italian masters at one time but suppressed doubts were coming back. His life was moving into

The Landing of Carteret. Oil study for mural in Essex County Court House, Newark, New Jersey, 1907. DELAWARE ART MUSEUM.

The Battle of Nashville. Mural panel in Governor's Reception Room, Minnesota State Capitol, Minneapolis, Minnesota, 1906. THE MINNESOTA HISTORICAL SOCIETY.

Pyle at work upon the historical mural for Hudson County Courthouse, Jersey City, New Jersey, 1910.

its later years, and the questions had to be met face to face. Europe seemed a possible answer to his problems.

Since he was now living in an atmosphere of plans and hopes for mural projects, promises and half promises from architects and public authorities, rumors of coming projects, and constant accounts of mural awards, it seemed likely that this was where his future lay. He followed Abbey's work in the Pennsylvania State Capitol and knew that he had that artist's recommendation for additional projects. Although there is no record of his making any official application, he was surprised, complimented, and somewhat chagrined to learn that the contract had been awarded to his former student Violet Oakley.

But if mural painting was to become an important part of his future, his Franklin Street studio might not be suitable for the very large projects. He listened to some of his artist friends returning from Europe and heard of vast studio spaces to be rented for a pittance and the low cost of living there. Added to this was constant financial worry. In spite of an outward appearance of prosperity, and in spite of a rather handsome income, expenses seemed to consume it all, leaving him without any reserve. Italy seemed to promise an answer to many problems and included the wonderful possibility that living among the acclaimed masterworks of the Renaissance and reading their lessons might rejuvenate his own creative powers.

Talking over all these factors with Anne, he found her in accord with the experiment. Italy was to be their home for at least a year.

Chapter 16

MYSTIC AND REALIST – SWEDENBORG AND WILLIAM DEAN HOWELLS

All through Pyle's life ran the strains of the mystic and the realist. The two seemingly disparate strains appear in his work, sometimes one, then the other, but frequently blended by the alchemy of a diversified personality. There are pictures and writings of his that are permeated by an atmosphere of the unseen, of a world beyond and behind our touchable world; there are other creations of his that are saturated with the concreteness of the everyday world and there are many more that partake of both.

He said, more than once, that he was obsessed, even as a child with the mystery of death. His early Quaker training was more a natural blood inheritance than a result of formal teaching; it was an ancestral transfer. The Swedenborgianism of slightly later years was an acquired attitude and faith, congenial to his nature but to the very end an exploration and something of a puzzle.

Quakerism satisfied much of the mystic in him but not all. He was a born maker of pictures, both in paint and words, but the Quaker primness toward imagery and the seeming self-indulgence of the artist struck at the very roots of his talents. Fortunately the artist triumphed, but with a condition: the Quaker urge toward a useful life was satisfied by channeling his dual talent to serve the multitude, by way of the printed book and magazine. By that adjustment he entered into a life of most fruitful accomplishment and inner satisfaction.

Swedenborg half satisfied him and half tormented him, half exalted and half mystified him. He had worked through the Swedenborg volumes, *Divine Love and Wisdom, Heaven and Hell, The True Christian Religion, Divine Providence,* and *Arcana Coelestia,* first with his family and then by himself. He could say of *Heaven and Hell* at one point: "I think it is an awful book. . . . To my mind there is little choice in the eternity of discomfort between the Heaven and the Hell that Swedenborg pictures."*

But he could say about the *Arcana Coelestia* that although he had not finished the third volume, "next to the Bible upon which it stands it is the greatest book I have ever read." In later years he would often have Swedenborg read to him while he painted and he frequently read passages to his students. Baffling as he sometimes found the Scandinavian mystic he responded to the clearly stated portions of his vision, those that painted verbal pictures:

> The things I have habitually seen are not visions but things seen with the highest wakefulness of the body . . . the outward face of the spiritual world resembles the natural world . . . a man's spiritual body appears precisely similar to his natural body. . . . Be it known that the spiritual world in outward appearance is entirely similar to the natural world. There are countries, mountains, hills, valleys, plains, fields, lakes, rivers, and streams of water as in the natural world; thus all things of the natural kingdom. There are parks, gardens, groves, woods, and in them all kinds of trees and shrubs bearing fruits and seeds, plants, flowers, herbs and grasses; thus all things of the vegetable kingdom. Man is there an angel or spirit. This preliminary statement is made to show that the universe of the spiritual world is entirely similar to the universe of the natural world, with this difference only, that things there are not fixed and settled like those in the natural world, because everything there is spiritual and not natural.†

This kind of statement appealed to Pyle's picturemaking sense. But even with one of Swedenborg's books always close at hand and with quite regular attendance with his parents at the new Swedenborgian church on Fourteenth Street, when it came time for his marriage with Anne Poole, it was in the Friends' manner in the Poole home. Later, when writing to his wife at Rehoboth he used the Quaker *thee,* and a little later, writing to his friend A. B. Frost, he referred to "my Quaker family." It was not a question of abandoning one for the other—he would encompass both although he was no longer a recognized member of the Society of Friends.

It was in the latter part of 1890, at this point of self-questioning, that a friendship developed that helped him greatly. He had discovered the writings of William Dean Howells and read them intently. He admired Howells's depiction of ordinary American personalities facing the unexaggerated problems of their lives against a believable American background. It was a reaction against the sentimental, the unduly contrived, and the overly romantic literature of the time. All this was in accord with his own feeling for exact observation and accurate description.

Harper and Brothers was the publisher for both men, and it seemed inevitable that their ways might cross there and so they did. They met and seemed to like each other, but that first meeting was only a passing contact. Sometime later, a story of Howells's, "The Shadow of a Dream," appeared in *Harper's Monthly.* Pyle was struck by the speculative bent of the story and in April of 1890 wrote a letter of approval and

---

*Quoted in Abbott, *Howard Pyle,* p. 184.
†Emanuel Swedenborg, *Divine Providence.*

questioning to the author. This was the beginning of a long and amicable correspondence. Pyle was delighted to discover that Howells was also a deep student of Swedenborgian lore. Here, in many ways was his counterpart in another creative personality. It gave him great comfort and apparently Howells shared that feeling. Another bond was the discovery that both suffered from interludes of melancholia, resulting from the death of a beloved child.

Howells, for his part, was greatly interested in discussing the often obscure preachings of Swedenborg and the entire field of human groping that might be covered by the word mysticism. He was also struggling to probe the workings of the artist's mind, since he was impelled to write about art but conscious of the limitations of being a layman. He hoped for enlightenment from Pyle. So their exchange of letters ranged over the vast territories of Life, Death, and the Afterlife, of the functions of the writer and artist, of the release of strange and wonderful energies in the human psyche, even analyses of certain characters in some of Howells's stories. They undoubtedly fed upon each other's minds with benefit. They both were in agreement that their messages should reach a broad public, not just an elite.

Howells's influence on Pyle, at the time of Pyle's return from New York and before their meeting, had been in the direction of imitating Howells's realistic short stories. This influence faded, but, as their friendship developed, Pyle felt the encouragement of Howells as he struggled to put his speculative thoughts about life and death into some communicable order. One such untitled subject was discussed and apparently abandoned. They were both wrapped up in the old struggle of the mystic to describe the presence without name. The vocabulary of realism seemed inadequate. But two short stories grew under Howells's encouragement, "In Tenebras" and "To the Soil of the Earth." The first was published in *Harper's New Monthly Magazine,* February 1894, and the second was selected for *Cosmopolitan* by Howells and published in June 1892.

The most ambitious effort that passed under Howells's critical eyes was Pyle's religious novel *Rejected of Men.* Pyle expended great effort on this—writing and rewriting it over a period of about nine years. The idea had been pressing him for a long time. He was advancing into a strange domain, distrustful of every step. This was the same man who stood before his easel with such confidence, eager for the attack.

The story was of the last days of Jesus and the Crucifixion, but the setting was the New York of Pyle's time, the last decade of the nineteenth century. The execution was not upon the cross but in an electric chair. It was told from the viewpoint of Pharisees who were ordinary business and religious types. The Pharisees were not portrayed as wicked or vindictive men, but men who, given what they were, inevitably arrayed themselves against the revolutionary, the threatening destroyer of their society. The book was not as much of a bombshell as might have been expected upon publication in 1903, but it attracted some attention. There were some good reviews with reservations, as well as some sharply negative ones, but, in any case, the book was quickly forgotten. The modern setting chosen by Pyle lacked bite and conviction, the Pharisee types lacked believability, and the accumulating tension leading up to the execution failed to grip.

Henry Mills Alden, after reading an earlier version of the manuscript, had written: ". . . it jars upon some sacred inviolable sense of the Christ and in some passages—especially the electrocution—it is a profound shock." This general opinion was reiterated by other critics. Naturally, at the time of its publication, Pyle went through a difficult period, but he seems to have been prepared for it and he could say, looking backward, "I do not know that it would ever have been completed had it not been for the encouragement given me from time to time by my friend W. D. Howells. I don't suppose Mr. Howells has any idea how much he has heartened me as to the progress of my work from time to time, and by telling me how much he liked the method in which I was trying to embody my thoughts."

This compulsion for probing into life beyond its everyday dimensions and the scrutiny of religious answers seems to have been part of the texture of Pyle's mind always. But its greatest visible activity seems to have manifested itself roughly from the time of his friendship with Howells to the publication of *Rejected of Men*. It also had found prominent expression in the book *The Garden Behind the Moon* published in 1895. The story is usually called a fairy tale and certainly it is full of poetic imagination, but it is also an allegory that searches for the meaning of life and death. Sadness permeates it and there are intimations of social consciousness—in all, an amalgam that reveals the depths of Pyle's nature.

Attempting to pick apart some of the important threads of Howard Pyle's creativity has its rewards and is certainly one approach to understanding, but it must be remembered that they did not exist in isolation—they interwove to form a design, a picture, an utterance of a very complex man.

Chapter 17

ITALY

The entire family was enlisted to help prepare for the move to Italy, a major one in their lives. The two girls, Phoebe and Eleanor, with Wilfrid, and their youngest brother, accompanied their parents as did faithful and indispensable Gertrude Brincklé. The three older boys, two of them at Yale, were to remain in America until the close of college in early summer and then join the others. Everyone of the family was to share the European experience.

For the children it was an expectant adventure, for their father a questionable one. There was no question in his mind but that the unprecedented move was a necessary one, but this was his season of doubt. Only his brother Walter, to whom he was entrusting his affairs while gone, knew that Howard had placed a mortgage upon the studio buildings to raise money for the trip, so short was the cash reserve. The main studio was to be rented and lived in by Olive Rush and Ethel Penniwell Brown, and the student studios were also rented.

There were no mural contracts to take abroad, although there seemed to be a number of hopeful possibilities. The *Harper's* editors promised to send some illustrative assign-

Anne and Howard Pyle in 1910, just before leaving for Italy.

Pyle with family group, 1910. *From left to right:* Phoebe, Theodore, Howard, Jr., Godfrey, Mrs. Pyle, Wilfrid, and Bijou with Pyle.

ments when he was ready for them, and his idea of writing and illustrating some articles on the old Italian cities was encouraged.

When the family boarded the small steamer *Sant' Anna* and it moved down the waters of New York harbor, Pyle, for the first time in perhaps thirty-five years, had no immediate work on his hands. All the speculation and unanswered questions that had been held at bay for years by incessant creative work were now demanding attention. Outwardly, he impressed one as a man of single mindedness and purpose; this was true but an oversimplification. It tended to conceal a mind subject to contradictory pulls.

His love for his native and historic valley and his pride in the long line of Quaker ancestors, stretching back to the earliest days, was part of his very fiber, but so was the pictorial memory of his young days when he pored over the reproductions of Pre-Raphaelite and early German pictures, until he could shut his eyes and recall every one in all detail. Both had blended in his own work, which could be called nothing but American. Why should he fear that Renaissance art should be alien? He had scant interest in later schools—baroque, rococo, neoclassic, or romantic. He had some kinship with Impressionism, particularly as it was practiced in its late stages by the American landscape painters, but the only European Impressionist he spoke of with great admiration was Segantini, the painter of Alpine meadows. He admired Adolf Menzel, the draftsman and pen artist but he knew little of his paintings.

Perhaps he had delayed the confrontation too long. Would some lifelong convictions be overthrown or was his mind too set to embrace new experiences? Had the grooves of habit become his enemies? But he was now convinced that his future lay in mural painting and he must know at first hand the acknowledged masters of it.

His introspection often took a gloomy turn because of bouts of ill health. The *Sant' Anna* was small, slow, and economical; ship life was pleasant enough and an exciting adventure for the children. The steamer stopped in Boston to take on many returning Italian immigrants who filled the steerage deck, and Pyle found himself watching their volatile life with great interest. As they left the Gulf Stream the weather turned cold and damp, and the seas became rough causing bouts of seasickness. But they moved into balmy winds as they approached the Azores, and going ashore at Terceira restored all spirits. It was the first foreign port for the children and Gertrude, and even Pyle felt better basking in the warm sunlight.

Gertrude Brincklé kept a terse daily diary of the entire trip so the catalog of events is quite complete. For example:

> Nov. 29—Seasick. No church, too many passengers sick, hymn singing not a success either. Rough, regular storm at night, pitching today; I the worst sailor, Mrs. Pyle next; elaborate meals, olive oil; Azores tomorrow. Mr. Pyle sent me champagne on deck.
>
> Dec. 1, 1910—Land, Flores, Azores. 300 steerage bound for Azores. Our cockney steward said a "decent, civil lot." Mr. Pyle sick. Very enthusiastic over seeing steerage, said one of the finest things he ever heard was the way these poor things felt about coming home. Binoculars, to Terceira, Azores; little flags of new Portuguese Republic to wave; red, blue and green; ships almost never stop here. Little Azores dogs for sale looked like white, wooly dachshunds with pink noses like rubber; Wilfrid went up to two officers and said, "Hurrah for Manuel!" and they laughed.
>
> Dec 4th—Gibraltar. Poor Mr. Pyle looked so ill, soon went below; his eyes have a blue glassy look; ill two hours in the night. French doctor; Phoebe had enough French to translate symptoms and remedies.
>
> Dec. 7—Doctor prescribed opium. Mr. Pyle's illness no better than on *Sant' Anna*. French doctor good. Even a mustard plaster. They even thought of stopping in Naples, but he got up early, with the light of determination in his eyes; rough passing Sardinia. Floods of rain, circle of lights, Naples harbor. I was busy paying bills and tipping. Luggage off. 14 bags and as many trunks.*

*In possession of Gertrude Brincklé.

Pyle managed the journey to Rome with the others but it was with pain and a clouded mind. In Rome he scarcely left his room. When somewhat recovered, he went on to Florence and the family settled in a pension while a search was made for more permanent living and studio quarters. His mood was still dark, but there were now gleams of appreciation and delight.

A letter to Stanley Arthurs dated December 16, 1910, paints a picture of his mood:

> I have been knocked up with a bilious attack or a stomach attack or something of the kind, and have had a two weeks siege of it which has prevented my doing any work—or my doing anything. . . . It [Florence] seems to be a wonderful place, and very interesting, but it is dirty and ramshackle compared to our American ideals. In fact, Italy, especially the southern part, impresses me as a great charnel house, full of the dead and chiefly of the dead bones of the past, and while northern Italy, and especially Florence, is much more prosperous, still the charnel house idea remains with me, and I think I shall use it in an article.
>
> As for Rome, I hate it. I was in my room all the time but twice, and when I went out I saw the Roman ruins and not Saint Peters and the great pictures and statues. The "Moses" was the only thing I saw. As for the Roman ruins, they are without shape, weatherworn, and channeled by the rivulets of centuries of rain. They are black in some places and white in others, and are, I think, ugly and disagreeable. I saw nothing beautiful in them, but only the weatherworn remnants of a past and forgotten age.
>
> In contrast to this I like Florence very much, and am sure that I shall like it better as time goes on. I want to get to the Garden of the Medici's and the place where Lorenzo di Medici breathed his last, and I am going to make my first article on it.*

His letter showed that at the first sign of better health he was planning his creative work. But he missed the amenities of his own home and he speaks of this in another letter to Arthurs a week later.

> I like Florence very much, but have not yet seen it under the best auspices. We are just now in a pension or boarding-house, and I am not very fond of boarding-house life—in fact, my long domestic life has unfitted me for it. I get along pretty well excepting at mealtimes and in the evening. At meals we form a part of a long *table d'hote* of uninteresting people, and though they are now more interesting than they were at first, they are not thrillingly so. In the evenings we have a very uncomfortable sitting room where the family gathers and where Mrs. Pyle reads to us. But we have found now a furnished apartment which I think will be very nice. . . .
>
> I wished a great many times that I had you boys here to enjoy this with me. I also wish that my strength would come back to me, for I am as yet quite weak—too weak to work—for I had a very sharp and intense illness while it lasted, and it seems to have cut away nearly all of my virility and strength. I am much better, however, and expect each week to find a studio and do at least some work. . . .
>
> I think, however, that both you and Frank ought to come over here to Italy. It will be a great lesson to you in the way of color, composition, etc., for the old masters were glorious painters and I take back all I ever said against them.†

His capitulation to the old masters was reiterated in a letter to Ethel Penniwell Brown:

> You know I did not think much of the Old Masters, seeing them in black and white, but in color they are so remarkable that I do not see how any human being painted as they did. You stand among them and you feel you are surrounded by a glow of soft ardent colors in which the yellows and browns are the predominant tone and the wonderful blues and crimsons are the relieving note. Two pictures of Botticelli I saw yesterday are the most remarkable pieces of color work that I have ever seen in my life. One of them in particular, a rich, dark gray with a crimson tone is so remarkable a piece

*Reprinted in Abbott, *Howard Pyle*, pp. 240–41.
†Ibid., pp. 241–42.

of color that I do not think of anything to parallel it. All the time I was there, I kept thinking of my pupils and wishing that they could see these pictures.*

A happy accidental meeting paved the way to obtaining a suitable apartment and established a valuable friendship. From the cab that was taking Gertrude Brincklé and the children from the railway station in Florence to their pension, Gertrude had caught sight of and hailed an old friend, an American girl from Bryn Mawr. Not only were they overjoyed to find an American friend in the strange city, but their new friend's uncle was an answer to a prayer. He was Dr. Charles R. Parke, a practicing physician. He was invaluable in dealing with Pyle's worrisome illness, and he and his family became fast friends of the new arrivals. Moreover, they occupied a delightful small palazzo on the Via Garibaldi, which had an ample vacant apartment on the third floor, a perfect answer to the Pyle family's needs.

A studio was also found and Gertrude Brincklé tells about it in a later account.

> In 1910 in December, when we first reached Florence, he began at once to hunt for the perfect studio, high-ceilinged and large enough for the big mural he expected to paint; he wanted so much to have Frank Schoonover and Stanley Arthurs come to Italy to help him work on this commission from Cass Gilbert.
>
> In January he found what he wanted in the Piazza Donatello. Imagine him installed there, enjoying the large rooms, directing us in unpacking the studio gear, overseeing the hanging of costumes in the huge wardrobe. The former owner had left some of his belongings, some furniture, his mistress as landlady, and Carlo the janitor. The studio boasted a lovely garden with laurels and bamboos; I cut him a mahlstick the first morning. He liked the lizards sunning on the stonewall, and a whistling blackbird in a wicker cage, like one of his own drawings.
>
> We would arrive early, he would dictate letters, I would typewrite, read aloud, and sometimes pose; Phoebe and Wilfrid would sometimes stop in, and every morning at eleven Eleanor would come to read with us, while Mr. Pyle painted from Italian models. One was a black-eyed girl with too much perfume and chilblains, and a young man who refused to cut off his mustache and complained that his costume was too loose. Mr. Pyle gave me 4 lire to go out and buy suspenders—that was hard, what are suspenders in instant Italian?
>
> Imagine Mr. Pyle standing on his studio steps, making me with Carlo's help stop a passing carter to ask if he would bring his horse to pose in the garden the next day.
>
> For Mr. Pyle was beginning work on a picture familiar to you all, the last commission he ever filled; the DuPont Powder Wagon, War of 1812, which painting now hangs in the Hotel. It was made for the Company's 1912 calendar. You can see that very horse, six horses in the painting—that very horse, with his red Italian tassels.†

His spirits rose with the coming of spring and he was writing:

> Already the spring is beginning to approach—one feels it in the air. It is not like the spring in America, when the south wind comes up from the Caribbean Islands and makes you think of foreign parts; but it is just a balmy glow that seems to cover and embrace everything. [And a little later] We do not know in America how beautiful fifty generations of culture will make a country. You have to see the surroundings of Florence in springtime for that. The quaint sight of the peasantry doing their work—the men ploughing with a single-handed plough; and once we saw a man and a woman dragging a plough, while another man directed it. Of course the soil is very light and generous, or they could not do it. It is all exceedingly beautiful, and all I want now is plenty of work to keep me busy.‡

*Reprinted in Abbott, *Howard Pyle*, pp. 242–43.
†Diary of Gertrude Brincklé.
‡Reprinted in Abbott, *Howard Pyle*, p. 245.

Italian villa outside Florence where the Pyles lived.

The Pyle family in Italy at their villa in 1911. *From left to right:* Theodore and Howard, Jr. (*at back*), Wilfrid, Phoebe, Gertrude Brincklé, Howard Pyle, Godfrey, Mrs. Pyle.

The Old World had conquered in the end but he was disappointed in his desire for work. He began a travel article but was not encouraged to do more. He heard little from the American editors. A mural commission that seemed to be promised by Cass Gilbert never materialized. His funds were dwindling, but the commission from the DuPont Company came in time.

They gave him for subject matter a train of Conestoga wagons laden with powder from the Brandywine mills at the time of the War of 1812. It was a large horizontal panel, 18'3" × 14', and a good example of his historical work. The picture is bathed in a golden light, the direct effect of his admiration for the Botticelli and other Renaissance pictures of the Uffizi. The panel was painted in his large, high-ceilinged studio and in the adjoining garden where he had persuaded an Italian carter to drive his team in and pose.

The panel was finished and shipped to the States, and with no other commissions at hand he asked Gertrude to pose for a painting he planned to give to Dr. Parke. The doctor was now a close friend and Pyle's physician, and Mrs. Parke was equally friendly and generous with all kinds of helpful suggestions to ease the difficulties of living in a strange country and dealing with a strange tongue. There was a Parke automobile and chauffeur that were frequently placed at the Pyles' disposal. For a while the master's health seemed improved and had not his destiny been shaped by a lifetime of constant creativity, he might have relaxed and indulged himself in the intoxication of new experiences. But he fretted at the lack of new assignments.

With the coming of summer the parents looked forward to seeing their son Howard, now released from school. His ship was to dock in Genoa, and they took the train to meet him. The heat was stifling, the journey long and exhausting. In Genoa, Pyle suffered a severe attack of renal colic. Partly recovered, the return journey brought on another. The heat was heavy in the bowl of Florence and they fled to the hills at San Domineo and later to Siena. Here the distress abated enough for him to enjoy the beauty of that hill town.

But the journey back to Florence brought on another attack. The illness was diagnosed as Bright's disease, an ominous kidney infection. He slipped into a coma that was punctuated intermittently by slurred words, and he died a few days later on November 9, 1911. His ashes are in the American cemetery outside Florence on the road to Chertosa.

Chapter 18

THE PYLE LEGACY

Only a few of Pyle's friends, students, or admirers knew of his last illness. The news of his death abroad came as a surprising shock to almost all. The family and those close to it rallied to the task of bringing the widow and children home, selling property, settling the estate, and helping them through the difficult period of readjustment. There was a group of students clustered in or near Wilmington hopeful for the friendship and occasional criticisms of Pyle upon his return. Some left for their homes or for New York, but a nucleus remained, having formed an attachment for the city and the valley behind it that were filled with the landmarks of their common experience and purpose.

Almost immediately plans were undertaken to celebrate and perpetuate Howard Pyle's memory and achievements. A group of the concerned and energetic met and formed The Delaware Art and Library Association. Their first project was a large retrospective exhibition of Pyle's work. It opened on March 13, 1912, in the ballroom of the Hotel DuPont and included the largest collection of work shown up to that time. It attracted endless throngs daily. The Wilmington papers carried headlines such as:

GREAT CROWD VIEWS PICTURES
About 10,000 Saw the Howard Pyle Art
Collection during Yesterday
MANY COULDN'T GET IN

A fund was started for the purchase of a permanent collection, and by fall of that year forty-seven paintings and thirty pen drawings had been acquired. This nucleus, together with many others loaned for the occasion, was shown in another large exhibition at the Hotel DuPont in November of 1912. It was now realized that the city needed a new museum with suitable exhibition facilities and proper housing of a permanent collection. The association changed its name to The Wilmington Society of the Fine Arts, and for some years, without a permanent home, its principal activity was an annual exhibition of the work of Pyle and his former students. A few years later this was extended to include the work of other Delaware artists and still later the museum came to include out-of-state members and began to invite guest artists.

In 1923 it found a temporary home in three rooms on the second floor of the large, just completed Wilmington Institute Free Library facing Rodney Square. Here it could house its growing permanent collection and begin a season of changing exhibitions. Eight years later, the estate of Samuel Bancroft, Jr., gave the society a large plot of land on Kentmere Parkway for the erection of a museum building. With it went the Bancroft Collection of Pre-Raphaelite paintings, books, and memorabilia, as well as an endowment for a wing to house and maintain the collection. On June 5, 1938, the new Art Center was opened.

The new building, besides housing the Bancroft Collection and the constantly growing Howard Pyle collection, had a large central gallery for rotating exhibitions. The center expanded its activities and enlarged its collections under the directorship of Miss Constance Moore, a friend since childhood of the Pyle family. Art classes were begun and when they outgrew their first basement studios, a new wing was built to house them. Educational activities for public and private school children also grew apace. Additions were made to the Pyle collection from time to time, making it by far the largest assemblage of its kind in the country, a mecca for admirers and students of illustration. His library is also housed there together with a collection of memorabilia, records, and many works by his students.

Miss Moore retired in November of 1957, having seen the Pyle collection grow from its very inception and having built the Art Center into a thriving organization. She was succeeded by Mr. Bruce St. John, under whose directorship an important John Sloan collection was added, the building enlarged, and its name changed to The Delaware Art Museum. Just at the time of his retirement, in the spring of 1973, the largest and most comprehensive exhibition of Pyle's works was staged by Mr. Rowland Elzea, the curator of collections and acting director. This was the most important collection ever assembled and its catalogue is a valuable contribution to Pyleana.

A few miles upstream from the Delaware Art Museum is the newly established Brandywine River Museum at Chadds Ford. This concerns itself with environmental and conservation matters relating to the valley area and also to its cultural resources. There, a continuing series of exhibitions have dramatized the work of the Brandywine artists; Howard Pyle, his students and followers and, particularly, the talents of three generations of the Wyeth family have been featured.

Documentation upon the work of Pyle and the Brandywine artists has grown during the years. In a little over a decade after Pyle's death four important publications laid a foundation for future research and appraisal. The Wilmington Society of the Fine Arts early realized the great importance of compiling a complete bibliography of Pyle's pictures and writings. Gertrude Brincklé, for many years Pyle's secretary and a friend of the family, and Willard S. Morse, a close friend of Pyle and an avid collector of his work, were chosen for the task and in 1921 their *Howard Pyle, A Record of His Illustrations and Writings* was published. It is an invaluable record of an amazingly fruitful career and an indispensable source book for students. A few years later a full-length biography, *Howard Pyle—A Chronicle,* was published by Harper. It was written by young Charles D. Abbott with the approval of Mrs. Pyle, who placed a large collection of family and publisher's letters at the author's disposal. Two other Harper books, published about the same time, gathered together important aspects of Pyle's illustrations and of his writing. *Howard Pyle's Book of Pirates,* 1921, was a collection by Merle Johnson of the best of the pirate tales, with an abundance of grim and roistering pictures. *Howard Pyle's Book of the American Spirit,* compiled by the same author, gathered together a fine selection of the historical pictures, accompanied by some explanatory text by Francis Doud. In recent years new material has appeared. There has been a volume upon the whole regional group of Brandywine artists, *The Brandywine Tradition,* by Henry C. Pitz, and books dealing with the life and works of N. C. Wyeth, Harvey Dunn, Violet Oakley, and Frank Schoonover. The renewed interest in the whole extensive subject of American illustration has resulted in an increasing number of articles and references to the Pyle circle as in Walt Read's *The Illustrator in America,* published by Reinhold Publishing Corp. in 1966.

It was, of course, natural that all this interest—the large collections and the memories—should be centered in Wilmington and the Brandywine country. Descendants of the Pyle clan were still there, as was an enclave of former students and their descendants, not to mention the very background that had found its way into so many pen and brushstrokes. The valley had its own history, its anecdotes, yarns, and folktales, and Pyle was now becoming the dominant figure in its legend.

Out in the broad area of the country, American illustrators were spreading more and more of their illustrations in weekly and monthly publications. The country was still picture-hungry and there was an abundance of talent and the technological knowledge and equipment to supply it. And the Pyle students were the single most important factor on the creative side. In the years following their master's death they came into their artistic maturity, and for over two decades they were to leave an unmistakable imprint. But much of Pyle's work had a continuing life after his death. His children's books with their unforgettable pictures found their audiences generation after generation, but it is possibly his pictures of America's early history that have carried the most potent messages and opened aroused minds to receive the words that accompanied them.

His exhortations to his students—"The characters in your pictures have had a past and will have a future. Think of that! You have caught a moment in some lives, but there have been moments before and some will come after,—feel as if you could tell their past history and their future"—quite perfectly describes the working of his own creative mind. He automatically brooded upon the ancestry of a pictorial moment and its aftermath. Almost always his pictures take their place in time, his moment of depiction carrying with it a feeling of past and future. His best pictures are not pictorial anecdotes but histories.

And his historical pictures were just as much history as the lines of text that surrounded them. He was in his way a scholar, for he knew more about the story of his country than some who taught it, and in certain ways he knew it better than some who wrote it. When painting the illustrations for Woodrow Wilson's *George Washington,* he pointed out certain discrepancies and questioned some of the author's facts, which Wilson responded to by rewriting portions of the text. In addition Wilson thanked him, saying, "I can say with all sincerity that the more you test my details the more I shall like it. I am not in the least sensitive on that point," and ". . . you understand the objects I have in view quite as sympathetically as I do myself." That sentence seems to indicate that Wilson and Pyle shared the same attitude toward the historical writer and picturemaker. Some eight years later Wilson was putting it in the plainest words, "The historian needs something more than sympathy, for sympathy may be . . . pitying, contemptuous . . . it must be the sympathy of the man who stands in the midst and sees like one within, not like one without, like a native, not like an alien."

Pyle's letter was a helpful criticism based upon a memory of facts, but Pyle's historical faculty sprang from a broader base than that, fortified by more than study and memory—*the power of identification*. This is the knowledge learned by the bone and sinew, by the penetrating eye, by the test of all the senses—not of the studious mind alone, the homely knowledge that the same pair of legs moves differently in moccasins than in jackboots, that a body takes a seat differently in a farthingale than in an Empire shift, that lace ruffles at a velvet cuff dictate the gestures of a hand and arm within. This is the instinctive knowledge that good actors have, and good illustrators are good actors, but it is scarcer in the academic world. This was the kind of intimate, day-by-day living and participatory awareness, that opened insights into the past and enabled Pyle to portray verisimilitudes of another age. To him, the way people looked and moved was a revelation of ancestral urges and immediate pressures and hopes.

Pyle had his moments of irritation at some historians and writers of historical fiction, for their sense of unreality, for the smell of the library, for pontification by circumscribed minds, for contriving a charade of manipulated puppets. The pageant of the past was not remote for him; he was a part of it as he painted.

Out of that combination of splendid aptitudes came hundreds of historical paintings and drawings, a great volume of pictorial re-creation and stirring projection. And that stream of pictorial history immediately reached tens of thousands of readers. One glance of the eye and an impression was recorded. Even the nonreader received a message. Over the years many of these pictures were reproduced again and again, and still they appear. The picture of the tense groups on the rooftops of Boston watching the attack on Bunker Hill, of Washington and Steuben at Valley Forge, of Arnold telling his wife that he must flee, of the fight on Lexington Common, have helped to shape the vision of our earlier days in the minds of several generations. And to this was added the contributions of the many Pyle students who had absorbed their master's teaching and purpose.

This is not to forget the many contributions of scores of other illustrators to picture America. Over the years the illustrator of American history has amassed a monumental record of the country's triumphs and disasters, its hopes, failures, accomplishments, yearnings, and follies. From this body of work has emerged the prototypes that stick in our minds—the frontiersman, the rugged patriot, the plantation owner, the slave, the emigrant, the frontier wife and mother, the whole kaleidoscope of our history's pageantry. This is the power of the picture, that it can inform at a glance and the image can persist.

This is one phase of Pyle's pictorial reach and of his followers'. His kind of history reached not only the students, the seekers, but the casual and even the unaware. The power of the historical picture, with its possibility of endless reproduction and distribution as practiced in affluent America, seems never to have been studied by the social historians, whose faith seems limited to the printed word but blind to the printed picture. The pedantic historian talks grandly of the facts of his material, seemingly oblivious that the central *fact* of his whole enterprise is *reconstruction* and *interpretation*. Picturemaking is an excellent method of conveying these characteristics.

Pyle and his followers left an imprint of the life of their ancestors in the minds of many thousands of Americans, and the end is not yet in sight. But the Pyle influence extended well beyond the field of history and was readily visible in the broad area of American illustration. Publishers were eager to commission work from his students, and several scores of them were actively giving a kind of "Pyle look" to a large segment of periodical and book illustration.

Even as they worked, the times were changing, and illustration was sensitive to change. Some had made their ultimate pictorial commitments and found them inelastic and uncongenial to change, others had the strength to impose their vision and play their parts in directing the newer influences. The sudden irruption of World War I had an enormous effect. George Harding and Harvey Dunn were given captain's commissions and sent to France as official war artists, together with other commissioned artists, and these two came back with probably the most convincing and compelling of the official war pictures. Others such as Schoonover, Wyeth, Aylward, and Edward Wilson were illustrating war texts, and several were making their first efforts in poster design as that field proliferated with the need to arouse people to support the war effort.

To a great extent the war acted as an historic watershed—things were not the same after, not even illustration. N. C. Wyeth began to take his place at the head of the romantic school. His creative powers had blossomed almost overnight under the warmth and persuasions of Pyle. After only a brief student apprenticeship he moved into the ranks of sought-after illustrators.

Drawing by Captain George Harding as official war artist in World War I.

Cover design in two colors for *American Artist* by Edward A. Wilson.

There was a group that exhibited strong decorative abilities. Violet Oakley developed rapidly into a distinguished draftsman with an innate design sense that craved space. Mural decoration was her destiny and after a series of smaller ventures, she received her lifetime opportunity when given important commissions to decorate the governor's reception room, the Senate chamber, and the Supreme Court chambers in the newly erected Pennsylvania State Capitol in Harrisburg. These were her most important works, where she was given themes that responded to her predilection for the religious, the philosophical, and the universal. George Harding, after years as an active magazine illustrator, gradually turned toward mural decoration. He executed a long list of decorations for schools, banks, and offices: the Montgomery County Court House in Norristown, Pennsylvania; the Audubon Shrine in Audubon, Pennsylvania; and the Hotel Traymore in Atlantic City. Stanley Arthurs painted a large decoration for the State Capitol at Dover, Delaware. Both Ida Dougherty and Frank Schoonover created designs in stained glass, and Maxfield Parrish, always the decorator whether in the small compass of an illustration or the expanse of a wall, also experimented with Tiffany glass mosaic in a large lobby mural in the Curtis Building in Philadelphia. The list of mural decorations by the Pyle school is a long one ranging from the extensive series by Violet Oakley in the Pennsylvania State Capitol to the dining room frieze in the Philadelphia Art Alliance by Richard Blossom Farley.

Many of the male students had had their boyhood interludes of cowboy and Indian infatuation but only a few carried that over into their professional artist lives. Wyeth was one of them, and in his student days he traveled to the West for the first time and experienced the life. He came back with his enthusiasm fired and a mind crammed with impressions. In no time he had established himself as a painter of western themes. After some years of continuing success with western subject matter he turned away from it toward the historical and legendary. The cowpuncher and frontiersman West was safely left in the hands of a large company of capable artists but no one replaced Wyeth's poetic vision of the early Indian, alone with nature. These paintings were among his finest. By the time he put down his roots in the Brandywine Valley, his interest had waned and his horizon had widened. He began his long, fertile series of picture-book classics that have been growing-up food for several generations of young readers. To these were added hundreds of magazine pictures—mostly in color—numerous advertising paintings, and the mural decorations of his later years. Always he sought relief from commissioned subject matter in easel painting. He seemed to be moving toward new levels of expression at the time of his sudden death, but he bequeathed a painter's outlook to his talented children, to daughters Henriette and Carolyn, and his young son Andrew.

In contrast, the West was William Henry Koerner's first love and his last—almost all his creative life was spent delineating it. Philip Goodwin and a number of others treated some western subjects in passing, but it was Harvey Dunn who was filled to the brim with its wonder, its poetry, and terror and his canvases are eloquent of these things.

His early life in a sod house on the Dakota plains had left its mark upon his nature. He knew the limitless out-of-doors, its peace and its rages, even the pitiless imprisoning winters and scorching summers. After hundreds of lusty action paintings for the large circulation magazines, he loved to come back to his broadly painted canvases of the prairie lands of his youth. The largest public collection of his work is in the South Dakota Art Center in Brookings, South Dakota.

The sea and its life were the background for another group. Clifford Ashley, raised on the deep-sea lore of New Bedford, Fair Haven, and Mattapoisett, naturally turned his increasing pictorial skills in that direction. Most of his pictures recreated those old sailing days, the New England coast, and its old ports. He wrote two notable books about seafaring life: *Yankee Whaler* and *The Ashley Book of Knots*. His friend William Aylward was

The Slave Ship Ransomed. Mural panel on the theme of Quaker protest against slavery, by Violet Oakley, in the Supreme Court of the Pennsylvania State Capitol, Harrisburg.

One panel of a series upon the life of William Penn executed by Violet Oakley in the Governor's Reception Room in the Pennsylvania State Capitol, Harrisburg.

L'Allegro. Color illustration for *Harper's Monthly* by Maxfield Parrish.

When American Ships Were Found in Every Part of the World. Watercolor by W. J. Aylward for *Scribner's Magazine.*

likewise a student and recorder of America's sailing past and its great inland waterways. He was a brilliant watercolorist whose limpid, dashing technique concealed the accurate student behind the brush. Anton Otto Fischer served time before the mast even as he was struggling to teach himself to draw. He came to Pyle to find his way into greater freedom and spontaneity and a more adventurous color range.

Edward Wilson also had his reputation as a painter of the sea. His most famous book, *Iron Men and Wooden Ships,* illustrated with boldly colored woodcuts, has become a collector's item. Wilson was a versatile technician and far-ranging in his pictorial interests. His first reputation was made largely in the advertising field but later he turned to book illustration. He did a long series of classics for the Limited Editions Club that earned him an important place among our romantic book illustrators.

A contrasting talent was that of Thornton Oakley. He had almost none of Wilson's versatility and innate dexterity but he found congenial subject matter in contemporary industrialism. He rendered the smoke, clutter, and menace of our invading industry with a kind of blunt power and conviction.

A Monster Skeleton of Steel Where Steam Caravans Come and Go.
Two-color illustration by Thornton Oakley for *Harper's Monthly.*

Frank Schoonover, who had the longest productive life of any of the Pyle students, began by following closely the picturemaking of his master, but after trips to the Canadian wilderness and the bayou country of the South he moved into the full-bodied, painterlike expression of his maturity. He painted a wide gamut of subject matter over the years, although most of it could be characterized as masculine, out-of-doors, action, and romance picturemaking. He meticulously numbered his pictures as they came from his easel, banishing headaches for future catalogers. He worked steadily through the years at his magazine and book commissions and when they began to taper off he gave more time to landscape painting, to teaching, and to designing stained glass. From his earliest student days, Pyle had relied upon him for certain kinds of help; he was closely associated with the master until he died, and later he was in the center of all activities to keep green Pyle's memory.

Schoonover did his share of American historical painting but several of his colleagues made an almost total commitment to it. His close friend Stanley Arthurs, in his nearby studio, painted his carefully researched canvases of America's past and many of them were collected and reproduced with text in a handsome volume, *The American Historical Scene*. John Wolcott Adams, with his descent from a famous New England family, had history in his blood. He came late to Pyle's class, was fascinated by his looser, fine-line pen technique, and evolved one of his own based upon the master's. He became adept at the vignette form, with groups of animated figures moving naturally and spontaneously, free of pomposity or theatricality. His small, unpretentious drawings are little gems. Clyde DeLand was another student who devoted most of his creative life to picturing the American historic scene. Elizabeth Shippen Green, Sarah Stillwell Weber, and the Betts girls could not be called historical picturemakers in the strict sense of the word but they all depicted the charm and domestic side of mid- and late-Victorian life.

Pyle's two giant talents, with words and pictures, were scarcely duplicated in his students. They were all essentially picturemakers, although a few such as Harding, Arthurs, and Schoonover wrote journalistic texts to accompany some of their pictures, and several had a book or two to their credit. In spite of the brilliant reach of Pyle's illustration for children, he had few followers there. Wyeth and Schoonover painted many pictures for the teen-age audience, but the most famous and consistent talent devoted to children was that of Jessie Wilcox Smith. She illustrated a goodly number of children's classics, such as Stevenson's *A Child's Garden of Verses* and Louisa May Alcott's *Little Women*. Her pictures were very popular and in her later years reached an adult audience through her long series of colored covers for *Good Housekeeping*. The atmosphere of her pictures was essentially Victorian, a neat, charming world of decorum.

This was almost the last lingering of Victorian illustration, although officially that period had ended. Pyle's own sturdy texts and pictures for children had played their part in revealing a new horizon for children's literature, and the war had accelerated a change of character in adult books and periodical illustration. There was increasing emphasis upon the contemporary scene. The old favorite magazines were fading—*Century*, *Scribner's*, and *McClure's*. The larger-format magazines like *Collier's*, *The Saturday Evening Post*, and a host of so-called women's magazines such as *The Ladies' Home Journal*, *Woman's Home Companion*, *Good Housekeeping*, *Delineator*, and *Pictorial Review* were crowding them out. This was a symptom of the country's rapidly expanding readership. More pictures were needed, more illustrators were busy.

These magazines were now vehicles for the work of many of Pyle's pupils, among them Arthur Becher, Chester Ivory, Walter Everett, Herman Pfeifer, Herbert Moore, Emlen McConnell, Harry Townsend, Henry Peck, Douglas Duer, H. D. Koerner, Frances Rodgers, Henry Soulen, and Leslie Thrasher. This was the period, in the decade after the war, when the Pyle influence upon American illustration was unmistakable. Pyle himself, in his late years, as he watched one after another of his pupils win attention by editors and public, could read something of the future of illustration. But he died a few years before he could have realized that he had also generated a group of teachers of illustration and that a certain teacher-student chain was itself evolving that would last for several generations.

Quite a number of the former students felt an obligation to pass on the benefits of their own training. Most taught only in a peripheral way, to a few students in their own studios. A few more taught for short periods in organized classes in school or studio. For instance, William Aylward taught a class in composition for a number of years in the Newark School of Art; Violet Oakley had students in decoration at the Pennsylvania Academy of the Fine Arts, Frank Schoonover held classes in his Wilmington studio for years, and N. C. Wyeth accepted a few students from time to time, mostly from his own talented family—his two painter daughters, Henriette and Carolyn, his to-be-famous son Andrew, and his future sons-in-law, John McCoy and Peter Hurd. But it so happened that four of Pyle's group devoted a goodly portion of their time to large classes that were

Nelly Custis in the Mount Vernon Garden. Color drawing by Anna Whelan Betts for *Harper's Monthly*.

Aren't They Just Splendiferous? Charcoal illustration by Charlotte Harding for *Harper's Monthly*.

available in organized art schools. And, as a result, a very sizable new generation of picturemakers was shaped to enter into America's illustration, painting, and teaching in its turn.

The established art schools had been very sluggish in their recognition of the need and importance of illustrator training. Pyle's classes at Drexel Institute had been the first of their kind in the country, and, when word-of-mouth reports of his Wilmington school spread, it is little wonder that it became the mecca of all young, ambitious would-be illustrators. Gradually some of the art schools began to set up classes in illustration, but in fumbling, unknowing ways. They were often headed by some third-rate, conventional painter who fell back upon the cozy routine of copying the model—sometimes hoping to give an impression of illustrative instruction by clothing the model in modern dress.

The first break in this sterile vacuum came when the Pennsylvania Museum School of Industrial Art selected Walter Everett, one of Pyle's older Drexel students, to form a new illustration department. In a few years a large proportion of Everett's graduates were

The Prodigal Son. Illustration (in oil) by Herbert Moore for *Ladies' Home Journal,* 1912.

moving into the professional field—illustrators like Maurice Bower, Robert McCaig, Frederick Anderson, Ralph B. Coleman, and Charles Chickering were beginning their careers. There was no question about the effectiveness of the new teacher; the news spread and better than average talent came crowding in. Everett was no counterpart of Pyle. He was different in almost every way—temperamental, whimsical, and enormously vain, but able to impart purpose, ambition, and drive. He was a daydreamer who put off the hour of facing his own empty canvases. When he approached the deadline for the delivery of a set of illustrations, he often fled the studio with his fishing gear to escape the importunate telephone. But when cornered at last, he had the fierce drive to stand before his canvas and paint swiftly, forcefully, and unremittingly, all through the night if necessary. Some of his favorite students liked to stay with him in these frantic but amazing sessions, then carefully pack his wet canvases as he changed his clothes, carry them to the station, buy his ticket, and see him off on the New York train, breathless.

His quirky character attracted his students or sometimes repelled, but he had a great deal to impart and no one who studied under him forgot him. He was widely talked about in art circles and his classes grew in size. He might have gone on for many years building a reputation as a famous teacher, but the size of the increasing classes annoyed him and he withdrew from the faculty to dream of never-to-be-painted masterpieces. A few years later he took over classes at the Spring Garden Institute that had been taught by a former pupil, Maurice Bower, who had to leave them for war duty. Here he repeated his earlier successes.

When Everett resigned from the faculty of the Pennsylvania Museum School of Industrial Art in 1914, its illustration department was the largest in the school. For a suitable replacement they went again to a Pyle graduate, Thornton Oakley, who was making a reputation with his pictures of industrial America. None of the Pyle protégés could have been more idolatrous of the master, and Oakley did his utmost to revitalize the Pyle message. But good intentions were not enough; he was not another Howard Pyle. He was part pedant and part evangelist. The Pyle message, always spontaneously springing from the spirit of the moment, was now prepared and doctrinaire. The intangibles, the instinctive awareness of the audience, the faculty for touching the imaginative chords of the mind—these were scarcely present. The fervor was there, but hampered by the urge to present it in the form of a neat, ritualistic doctrine. The inspiration hardened into a formula of ten commandments tacked high on the classroom wall. But Oakley was a personality and although a controversial figure left an imprint upon most of his pupils.

It was during these years that the expanding of the illustration field prompted art school after art school to set up classes to satisfy the demand for competent picturemaking instruction. Scarcely a mile away from the Pennsylvania Museum School was the famous Pennsylvania Academy of the Fine Arts and that, too, had succumbed to the demand. Again a Pyle graduate was in charge of the class. George Harding—forceful, direct and a driver—was fast building his own reputation as an instructor in illustration. The two nearby schools had been rivals for years although their basic philosophies differed, but now the two illustration courses had to be judged on the same grounds. The academy was one of the country's fine art centers: Did that mean that illustration was now accepted as a fine art, no longer to be sneered at as entirely utilitarian? Answers were evasive, for a positive answer in either direction posed a dilemma for the fine arts schools. Naturally there were other reasons for rivalry but quite a number of the students achieved the best of two worlds by taking advantage of loose supervision in both schools and slipping unobtrusively into a rival session, thus having a taste of the rhetoric of two instructors.

Harding and Oakley, of course, had been side-by-side colleagues in Pyle's classes and ostensibly they were friends, but temperamentally they had little in common. Harding was brisk, direct, and hardheaded—lean, active, and with a certain cynical air that concealed sensitivity. He looked for practical answers to pictorial problems. He was a man's artist (his female types were unremarkable), at ease with muscle and movement, but recoiling from emotionalism and sentimentality. He enjoyed the artist-reporter assignments that took him from the Grand Banks of Newfoundland to Borneo, and the war-artist experience in World War I. In his sixties he accepted a major's commission to picture World War II in the South Pacific. He had an innate decorative sense that led him into mural painting in his middle years and he was busy at this and easel painting until his last illness.

The fourth important teacher of the Pyle tradition was Harvey Dunn and once again we encounter another and very different personality. He resembled none of the other three but he had an abundance of Pyle's magnetism. He was in all things his own man, unforgettable in appearance and manner. A former student of his and a well-known

Biblical illustration by Walter Everett.

illustrator in his own right, Grant Reynard, gave me an accurate and penetrating description of Dunn:

> He was a whale of a man, a veritable pioneer hulk of a man with a head reminding you of a cross between an Indian chief and a Viking. He looked as though he could easily bite a spike in two with one crunch of his broad jaws. You couldn't dress him up in city clothes. But in loose country clothes or a smock he was a king of men. . . . It was years before I came to know that he was as gentle as a lamb under that steel frame and as sensitive in emotion as the artist he was. To discover this was like finding lilacs in a boiler factory.

He had Pyle's faculty of being able to swing from the most minute and particular, the most practical and timely to the heights of the imagination, from the intimate to the visionary. A favorite phrase of his was "the mysterious people," which he used to call attention to the unexplored depths of even the most ordinary folk, the mystery behind the facade of the uncelebrated, the ignored—everybody. He felt the awe of simple things.

He loved all aspects of nature, but nature was only the dictionary. Once the artist had some command of that dictionary, miracles were possible.

Teaching first in his own school near Tenafly, New Jersey, he was soon overwhelmed by numbers, and he accepted the offer of the Grand Central School of Art to join its faculty and so escape the harassments of administration and the lack of proper space and facilities. His students were numbered in the hundreds and he became the greatest teacher of illustration in his era. Among his students were Dean Cornwell, Mario Cooper, Harold Von Schmidt, Clark Fay, John Steuart Curry, Grant Reynard, Arthur D. Fuller, Saul Tepper, and Albin Henning. These and others made a mark upon American illustration particularly during the nineteen thirties and forties.

So the two or three decades after Pyle's death saw our illustration strongly conditioned by his philosophy through the medium of these teachers, their own work, and the work of their students. And even a second generation of such teaching developed as these men retired and were succeeded by former students: Dunn by Dean Cornwell, Oakley by Henry Pitz, and Harding by Edward Shenton. But this transfer through the generations must not be thought of as the passing on of a tight doctrine or a codified set of principles. As these artists worked, natural changes were appearing under their creative fingers. Growth and new horizons were revealing themselves; maturity and the persuasions of the times were working into their pictures. A hundred other influences were in the air, mingling and blending, changing the face of American illustration. Pyle's whole philosophy had been predicated upon the awakening of the imagination, the exploration for and development of individual utterance, the immersion in any chosen subject, and the revelation of that immersion to the limits of one's capacity. And always there was the concern for human values. There could be no pat formula for reaching these goals. It had to be a transfer of spirit and that opened the achievement to the whole spectrum of human diversity. The Pyle message, now constantly cross-fertilized, became a potent motif in a much larger pattern.

The Pyle impulse tended largely toward the illustrative, but even from the first there were those with painterlike talents who followed their own stars—Violet Oakley, George Harding, and Frank Schoonover, William Hekking, and Richard Blossom Farley. And then, N. C. Wyeth with his partly suppressed desire to paint, his finding of a gifted painterly family growing about him, began a dynasty of three generations of famous painters that has spread the Brandywine influence all over the country.

All those threads have found their way through many aspects of American life but one of the most important has been that impressive mass of pictorial documentation of the country's history that came from the studios of Pyle and his followers and passed under the eyes of untold thousands. Among other things this was an important segment of social history, although as yet scarcely discovered by the social historians themselves.

When a deep, widespread, and abiding hunger in society for pictorial enlightenment, information, and delight is satisfied so well, we have an important chapter in the history of a time. It helped the American people know their country and themselves. It was an informal education offered to all, young and old—even the unlettered. Its effect has not ceased accumulating. History does not lie in words alone.

The later gradual shift of emphasis from illustration to painting was a combination of two influences: the gradual fading in importance of illustration, the growth of photography, and the remarkable upspringing of nationwide appreciation for the paintings of Andrew Wyeth, his sisters, and brothers-in-law. An interest was rekindled in the work of earlier generations of Brandywine artists and like innumerable instances in the story of other cultural and historical interludes, the Pyle achievement is recovering its freshness after a period of neglect.

Although Andrew Wyeth has never taught, hundreds of hopeful artists have and are learning from him by the most ancient of all methods—imitation. Some have passed through the stage of imitation, have used it as a firm foundation and as an entry into their own individual versions. His paintings have been examined inch by inch by thousands of hungry eyes that are unaware for the most part that the secret lies elsewhere. But let us not give the impression of subscribing to the modern notion of imitation as a reprehensible thing. Imitation is imbedded in all learning, from learning to walk and talk to training for the Olympics. Imitation is a law of life, deeply implanted in the genes; without it there is no survival. Do not have hasty scorn for the imitator—he is yourself.

Howard Pyle the person and his work evade a neat summary. His career was a demonstration of the miraculous unexpectedness of high talent. Looking backward, a picture is given in a few lines by one who knew him closely and became very famous himself. N. C. Wyeth, late in life, writing from Chadds Ford to his wife in Maine about the poetry that was being written by their daughter Carolyn, says: "Somehow, I feel that Caroline [sic] has inherited an important gift from Howard Pyle, and I have a strangely significant feeling that if I have succeeded in starting this talent toward something *good*, that it will give me a certain mystical gratification and the sense that in some degree I have perpetuated something of the spirit of my old teacher and master, who, as the years roll by is assuming greater and greater proportions as an artist, as a man, and as my benefactor."

APPENDIX

1853   Born March 5, in Wilmington, Delaware, son of William Pyle and Margaret Churchman Pyle.

1869   Starts to art classes under Van der Weilen in Philadelphia. Attends for almost three years.

1871–72   Worked in father's leather business. Drew and wrote small projects.

1876   Journey to Chincoteague Island, Virginia, to draw the annual wild pony roundup. Wrote story with pictures which was accepted for *Scribner's Magazine.* Wrote and illustrated a little poem, also published by *Scribner's Magazine.* October—moved to New York City to write, illustrate, and study.

1877   Professional career launched: Illustrations and little tales published in *Harper's Weekly* and *St. Nicholas,* children's magazine.

1878   First full-page illustration, untouched by other artists, published in *Harper's Weekly.* June—large full page of Philadelphia Carnival 1778, published in *Harper's New Monthly Magazine.* Studied in evening classes at Art Students League.

1879   Firmly established as professional, moved back to Wilmington, continuing his work with New York publishers.

1881   Married Anne Poole, April 12. Moved to 607 Washington Street. First color illustrations for books, *Yankee Doodle* and *The Lady of Shalott.*

1882   Son Sellers born, June 4. A busy year with illustration.

1883   Studio built at 1305 Franklin Street. The first book written and illustrated by Pyle, *The Merry Adventures of Robin Hood*, published by Charles Scribner's Sons. Well over one hundred illustrations published.

1885   *Within the Capes*, the first adventure novel published.

1886   Daughter Phoebe born, December 28. Collection of tales, written and illustrated by Pyle, were published by Harper and Brothers.

1888   *The Wonder Clock* and *Otto of the Silver Hand*, both written and illustrated by Pyle, were published as were over two hundred illustrations.

1889   Young son Sellers died, February 22, while the Pyles were in Jamaica. Son Theodore born August 19.

1891   Son Howard born, August 1.

1892   Illustrated Oliver Wendell Holmes's "The One-Hoss Shay." A prolific year of over one hundred and fifty illustrations.

1894   Daughter Eleanor born, February 10. Began teaching career at Drexel Institute, Philadelphia. A prolific year in illustration.

1895   Son Godfrey born, October 15. Published *The Twilight Land* and *Garden Behind the Moon*, both written and illustrated by Pyle. Another prolific year in illustration.

1897   Gave commencement address at Delaware College, exhibitions at St. Botolph Club, Boston, and Drexel Institute. Son Wilfrid born, October 29.

1898   First summer class at Chadds Ford for ten scholarship students from Drexel classes.

1899   Second summer class at Chadds Ford.

1900   A prolific illustration year. Resigned from Drexel Institute faculty. Planned his own school for illustrators in Wilmington with student studios next to his own on Franklin Street.

1901   Teaching his own summer class at Chadds Ford.

1902   Gave annual address at the art school of Yale University. His story and illustrations for *The Story of King Arthur and His Knights* appeared serially in *St. Nicholas*, the next year in book form.

1903   The last summer class at Chadds Ford. Novel, *Rejected of Men*, published.

1904   Became friend of Theodore Roosevelt. Began weekly lectures to students of Art Students League, New York.

1905   Became art editor of *McClure's Magazine* in spring; resigned August 1906. Executed group of decorations for home, 901 Delaware Avenue. Painted mural panel, *The Battle of Nashville*, for the Minnesota State Capitol. Published the second of the King Arthur series, *The Story of the Champions of the Round Table*. Elected Associate of National Academy of Design. Gave composition lectures at Chicago Art Institute.

1907   Mural of *The Landing of Carteret* for the Essex County Court House, New Jersey. Published *The Story of Sir Launcelot and His Companions*. Elected Academician of National Academy of Design.

1908   Exhibited at Macbeth Gallery, New York. Diminishing number of illustrations.

1910   Completed mural for Hudson County Court House, Jersey City, New Jersey. Published *The Story of the Grail and the Passing of Arthur*. Sailed for Italy, November 2, to resolve his ambivalent feelings about the art of Europe.

1911   Died November 9, in Florence, Italy. Buried in Protestant cemetery outside the city.

APPENDIX

HOWARD PYLE STUDENTS

Abbott, Eleanor Plaisted
Adams, J. Wolcott
Ahrens, Ellen W.
Arthurs, Stanley M.
Ashley, Clifford
Aylward, William
Barber Stephens, Alice
Barrett, Watson
Beard, Alice
Becher, Arthur E.
Betts, Anna Whelan
Betts, John H.
Betts Bains, Ethel F.
Bonsall, Elizabeth
Brett, Harold
Brincklé, Gertrude
Brown, Ethel Penniwell
Cahill, W. B.
Chase, Sidney
Clements, Ruth
Colby, Will
Collins, J. Edes
Cross, Ernest J.
Crownfield, Eleanor F.
Day, Bertha Corson
deFeo, Charles
DeLand, Clyde
Demarest, Alfredo
Dougherty, Ida
Dougherty, Louis R.
Duer, Douglas
Dunn, Harvey E.
Edwards, Edward
Everett, Walter
Farley, Richard B.
Fisher, Anton Otto
Fithian, Frank

Gage, George W.
Goodwin, Philip R.
Graff, James Bell
Green, Elizabeth Shippen
Gurney, Elizabeth
Harding Brown, Charlotte
Harding, George
Hekking, William M.
Hinchman, Margaretta
Hoskins, Gayle
Hoyt, Philip
Ivory, P. V. E.
Johnson, Mary Craven
Kay, Gertrude A.
Kemp, Oliver
Kerr, Balfour
Koerner, W. H. D.
Lackman, Harry B.
Leasey, Elizabeth
Leonard, Helen
Lukens, Winifred S.
McBurney, W. E. (James)
McConnell, Emlen
McCouch, Gordon M.
McKernan, Frank
MacLellan, Charles A.
Masure, Robert
Masters, Frank B.
Mhoon, Anne A.
Moore, Anne
Moore, Herbert
Newton, Francis
Oakley, Thornton
Oakley, Violet
Palmer, Samuel
Parrish, Maxfield
Peck, Henry

Peixotto, Ernest
Perritt, Louise
Pfeifer, Herman
Pierson, Katherine G.
Pyle, Katharine
Richards, Harriett
Robinson, Robert P.
Rogers, Frances
Rosin, Theodore
Rush, Olive
Russell, Walter
Schoonover, Frank E.
Schrader, E. Roscoe
Schuyler, Remington
Seldon, Henry Bill
Skidmore, Thornton
Smith, Howard E.
Smith, Jessie Wilcox
Smith, Sarah K.
Smith, Wuanita
Soulen, Henry
Squires, C. Clyde
Stadelman, Henryette
Stillwell Weber, Sarah S.
Stitt, Herbert
Thompson, Ellen Bernard
Thrasher, Leslie
Townsend, Henry E.
True, Allen Tupper
Tyng, Griswold
Wall, Herman C.
Warren, Dorothy
Whitehead, Walter
Wilson, Edward A.
Wireman, Katherine Richardson
Wyeth, Newell Convers

APPENDIX

BOOKS

ABBOTT, CHARLES D. *Howard Pyle—A Chronicle.* New York and London: Harper and Brothers, 1925.

APGAR, JOHN F., JR. *Frank E. Schoonover: Painter-illustrator. A Bibliography.* Privately printed. 1969.

ARTHURS, STANLEY. *The American Historical Scene.* Philadelphia: University of Pennsylvania Press, 1935.

BLAND, DAVID. *A History of Book Illustration.* Cleveland and New York: The World Publishing Company, 1958.

CANBY, HENRY SEIDEL. *The Age of Confidence.* New York: Farrar and Rinehart, 1934.

————. *The Brandywine.* New York: Farrar and Rinehart, 1941.

CRANE, WALTER. *The Decorative Illustration of Books.* London: George Bell and Sons, 1896.

ELLIS, RICHARD WILLIAMSON. *Book Illustration—A Survey of Its History & Development shown by the work of Various Artists together with Critical Comments.* Kingsport, Tennessee: Kingsport Press, 1952.

FURTHEY, J. SMITH, AND COPE, GILBERT. *History of Chester County, Pennsylvania.* Philadelphia: Privately printed. 1881.

HOLME, CHARLES. Editor. *Modern Pen Drawings, European and American.* London: The Studio, 1901.

KENT, NORMAN. Editor. *The Book of Edward A. Wilson.* New York: The Heritage Press, 1948.

KIRK, CLARA MARBURG. *W. D. Howells and Art in His Time.* New Brunswick, New Jersey: Rutgers University Press, 1965.

KLEMIN, DIANA. *The Art of Art for Children's Books.* New York: Clarkson N. Potter, Inc., 1966.

————. *The Illustrated Book.* New York: Clarkson N. Potter, Inc., 1970.

LARKIN, OLIVER W. *Art and Life in America.* New York: Rinehart and Company, 1949.

LEHMANN-HAUPT, WROTH and SILVER. *The Book in America.* New York: R. R. Bowker Co., 1951.

MacELREE, WILMER W. *Down the Eastern and up The Black Brandywine.* West Chester, Pennsylvania: Privately printed. n.d.

MAHONY, BERTHA E.; LATIMER, LOUISE PAYSON; FOLMSBEE, BEULAH. *Illustrators of Children's Books.* Boston: Horn Book, Inc., 1947.

MORSE, WILLARD S. and BRINCKLÉ, GERTRUDE. *Howard Pyle—A Record of His Illustrations and Writings.* Wilmington: Wilmington Society of the Fine Arts, 1921.

MUIR, PERCY H. *Victorian Illustrated Books.* London: B. T. Batsford, Ltd., 1971.

NESBITT, ELIZABETH. *Howard Pyle.* New York: Henry Z. Walck, Inc., 1966.

PENNELL, JOSEPH. *Modern Illustration.* London: George Bell and Sons, 1895.

————. *Pen Drawing and Pen Draughtsmen.* London: Macmillan and Company, 1889. Revised edition. New York: The Macmillan Company, 1920.

PITZ, HENRY C. *The Brandywine Tradition.* Boston: Houghton Mifflin Company, 1969.

————. *Illustrating Children's Books.* New York: Watson-Guptill Publications, 1963.

————. *A Treasury of American Book Illustration.* New York: Watson-Guptill Publications and American Studio Books, 1947.

READ, WALT. *The Illustrator in America.* New York: The Reinhold Publishing Corporation, 1965.

RICHARDSON, E. P. *Painting in America.* New York: Thomas Y. Crowell Co., 1965.

SIMON, HOWARD. *500 Years of Art and Illustration.* Cleveland and New York: World Publishing Company, 1942.

THOMPSON, W. FLETCHER, JR. *The Image of War.* New York and London: Thomas Yoseloff, 1959.

WYETH, BETSY JAMES. Editor. *The Wyeths.* Boston: Gambit, 1971.

ARTICLES, CATALOGS, AND PAMPHLETS

"Celebrating the 100 Anniversary of the Birth of Howard Pyle." Wilmington Society of the Fine Arts, Wilmington, Del., March 5, 1953.

"Charles Parsons and His Domain." Exhibition catalog, Montclair Art Museum, Montclair, N. J., April 1958.

"Children's Books and Their Illustrators." (Mention of many of Pyle's books.) *International Studio,* Winter Number 1897–1898.

Coffin, William A. "American Illustration of Today." *Scribner's Magazine,* March 1892.

Drexel Institute of Art, Science and Industry, Records (1894–1900).

The Garden Behind the Moon. (Review.) *The Book Buyer,* December 1895.

Garrett, Charles Hall. "Howard Pyle." *The Reader,* May 1903.

"The Golden Age of American Illustration." Catalog, Delaware Art Museum, Wilmington, Delaware, 1972.

Hawthorne, Hildegarde. "Howard Pyle—Maker of Pictures and Stories." *St. Nicholas,* May 1915.

Hawthorne, Julian. "Howard Pyle—Illustrator." *Pearson's Magazine*, September 1907.

"Howard Pyle Collection." A catalog. Delaware Art Museum, Wilmington, Del., 1971.

"Howard Pyle—Diversity in Depth." Delaware Art Museum, Wilmington, Del., March 1973.

Howell, Edgar M.. "The Look of the Last Frontier" [Pictures of Harvey Dunn]. *American Heritage*, June 1961, p. 41.

Koerner, W. H. D.. "Howard Pyle." *New Amstel Magazine*, November 1911, p. 477.

Lunt, Dudley. "The Howard Pyle School of Art," *Delaware History*, Historic Society of Delaware, March 1953, p. 151.

Lykes, Richard Wayne. "Howard Pyle—Teacher of Illustration." Paper, University of Pennsylvania, 1947.

Men of Iron. (Review.) *Harper's Monthly*, December 1891.

Moore, Constance. "The Wilmington Society of the Fine Arts 1912–1962." Published by the Society. 1962.

Oakley, Thornton. "Howard Pyle–His Art and Personality, An Address." Free Library of Philadelphia, November 8, 1951.

The Merry Adventures of Robin Hood. (Review.) *The Critic*, November 1883.

———. (Review.) *Harper's Weekly*, November 28, 1885.

———. (Review.) *Literary World*, December 15, 1883.

Otto of the Silver Hand. (Review.) *The Book Buyer*, December 1888.

———. (Review.) *The Bookmart*, December 1888.

Pitz, Henry C. "American Illustration: Then and Now." *American Artist*, June 1962, p. 51.

———. "The Brandywine Tradition." *American Artist*, December 1966, p. 29.

———. "Frank E. Schoonover: An Exemplar of the Pyle Tradition." *American Artist*, November 1964, p. 64.

———. "George Harding." *American Artist*, December 1957, p. 29.

———. "Howard Pyle: American Illustrator." *American Artist*, December 1951, p. 44.

———. "Millions of Pictures" (two parts). *American Artist*, November 1961, p. 35; December 1961, p. 52.

———. "N. C. Wyeth." *American Heritage*, October 1965, p. 34.

———. "N. C. Wyeth and the Brandywine Tradition," Harrisburg, Pennsylvania, William Penn Memorial Museum, 1965.

The Price of Blood. (Review.) *The Dial*, December 1899.

Pyle, Howard. "When I Was a Little Boy." *Woman's Home Companion*, April 1912.

"Report of the Private View of the Exhibition of Works by Howard Pyle." Philadelphia Art Alliance, 1923.

Rhoads, Eugenia Eckford. "A Master Returns to His Studio," *Delaware Today*, December 1964, p. 16.

The Ruby of Kishmoor. (Review.) *Harper's Monthly*, February 1909.

Schoonover, Frank E. "Howard Pyle," *Art and Progress*, October 1915, p. 431.

Stolen Treasures. (Review.) *The Literary Digest*, July 6, 1907.

———. (Review.) *The New York Times*, July 6, 1907.

Trimble, Jessie. "The Founder of an American School of Art." *The Outlook*, February 23, 1907, p. 453.

Twilight Land. (Review.) *Harper's Monthly*, November 1894.

Wyeth, N. C. "Howard Pyle as I Knew Him." *The Mentor*, June 1927.

Young, Mahonri Sharp. "Catalogue of Pictures by Howard Pyle." Wilmington Society of the Fine Arts, Wilmington, Del., 1926.

BIBLIOGRAPHY

BOOKS WRITTEN AND ILLUSTRATED (UNLESS NOTED) BY HOWARD PYLE

The Merry Adventures of Robin Hood. New York: Charles Scribner's Sons, 1883.

Within the Capes. No illustrations. New York: Charles Scribner's Sons, 1885.

Pepper & Salt. New York: Harper & Brothers, 1886.

The Wonder Clock. Embellished with verses by Katharine Pyle New York: Harper & Brothers, 1888.

The Rose of Paradise. New York: Harper & Brothers, 1888.

Otto of the Silver Hand. New York: Charles Scribner's Sons, 1888.

Men of Iron. New York: Harper & Brothers, 1892.

A Modern Aladdin. New York: Harper & Brothers, 1892.

The Story of Jack Ballister's Fortunes. New York: The Century Co., 1895.

The Garden Behind the Moon. New York: Charles Scribner's Sons, 1895.

Twilight Land. New York: Harper & Brothers, 1895.

The Ghost of Captain Brand. Wilmington: John M. Rogers Press, 1896.

A Catalogue of Drawings Illustrating the Life of Gen. Washington. Wilmington: printed for the St. Botolph Club by John M. Rogers Press, 1897.

The Divinity of Labor: an address delivered by H. Pyle at commencement exercises of Delaware College. No illustrations. Wilmington: John M. Rogers Press, 1898.

The Price of Blood. Boston: Richard G. Badger & Co., 1899.

Some Merry Adventures of Robin Hood. New York, Chicago, and Boston: Charles Scribner's Sons, 1902.

Rejected of Men. No illustrations. New York and London: Harper & Brothers, 1903.

The Story of King Arthur and His Knights. New York: Charles Scribner's Sons, 1903.

The Story of the Champions of the Round Table. New York: Charles Scribner's Sons, 1905.

Stolen Treasure. New York and London: Harper & Brothers, 1907.

The Story of Sir Launcelot and His Companions. New York: Charles Scribner's Sons, 1907.

The Ruby of Kishmoor. New York and London: Harper & Brothers, 1908.

The Story of the Grail and the Passing of Arthur. New York: Charles Scribner's Sons, 1910.

The Merry Adventures of Robin Hood. No illustrations. Embossed in Braille type for use of the blind. Boston: Perkins Institution and Massachusetts School for the Blind, 1910.

BOOKS CONTAINING WRITINGS BY HOWARD PYLE AND OTHER AUTHORS

The Elocutionist's Annual: Number 10, edited by Mrs. J. W. Shoemaker. Contains "Tilghman's Ride," by Howard Pyle, without illustrations. Philadelphia: National School of Elocution and Oratory, 1882.

Sport with Gun and Rod in American Woods and Waters, edited by Alfred M. Mayer. Contains "Among the Thousand Islands," written and illustrated by Howard Pyle. New York: The Century Co., 1883.

The Buccaneers and Marooners of America, edited by Howard Pyle. Introduction and frontispiece by Howard Pyle. London: T. Fisher Unwin; New York: Macmillan & Co., 1891.

School and Playground, by Howard Pyle and Others. Contains "Lambkin: Was He a Hero or a Prig?" by Howard Pyle, without illustrations. Boston: D. Lothrop Co., 1891.

First Year Book, The Bibliophile Society. Contains "Concerning the Art of Illustration" and frontispiece by Howard Pyle. Boston: 1902.

Strange Stories of the Revolution, by Howard Pyle and Others. Contains "Nancy Hansen's Project," by Howard Pyle, without illustrations. New York and London: Harper & Brothers, 1907.

Shapes that Haunt the Dusk, edited by William Dean Howells and Henry Mills Alden. Contains "In Tenebras," by Howard Pyle, without illustrations. New York and London: Harper & Brothers, 1907.

Adventures of Pirates and Sea-Rovers, by Howard Pyle and Others. Contains "The Buccaneers—Wolves of the Spanish Main" and "The Fate of a Treasure Town," written and illustrated by Howard Pyle. New York and London: Harper & Brothers, 1908.

The Book of Laughter, edited by Katherine N. Birdsall and George Haven Putnam. Contains "Hans Gottenlieb, the Fiddler," "Robin Goodfellow and His Friend Bluetree," and "Drummer Fritz and His Exploits," by Howard Pyle, without illustrations. New York and London: G. P. Putnam's Sons, 1911.

BOOKS, BY OTHER AUTHORS, CONTAINING ILLUSTRATIONS BY HOWARD PYLE

Note: Several books in this list also contain illustrations by other artists.

McGuffey's Fifth Eclectic Reader. Cincinnati and New York: Van Antwerp, Bragg & Co., 1879.

McGuffey's Sixth Eclectic Reader. Cincinnati and New York: Van Antwerp, Bragg & Co., 1879.

Art in America, by S. G. W. Benjamin. New York: Harper & Brothers, 1880.

Old Times in the Colonies, by Charles Carleton Coffin. New York: Harper & Brothers, 1881.

Yankee Doodle: An Old Friend in a New Dress. New York: Dodd, Mead and Co., 1881.

Phaeton Rogers, by Rossiter Johnson. New York: Charles Scribner's Sons, 1881.

The Lady of Shalott, by A. Tennyson. New York: Dodd, Mead and Co., 1881.

Harper's Popular Cyclopaedia of United States History, by Benson J. Lossing. New York: Harper & Brothers, 1881.

Farm Ballads, by Will Carleton. New York: Harper & Brothers, 1882.

The Story of Siegfried, by James Baldwin. New York: Charles Scribner's Sons, 1882.

The Chronicle of the Drum, by William Makepeace Thackeray. New York: Charles Scribner's Sons, 1882.

Under Green Apple Boughs, by Helen Campbell. New York: Fords, Howard, & Hulbert, 1882.

New England Bygones, by E. H. Arr (Ellen H. Rollins). Philadelphia: J. B. Lippincott & Co., 1883.

Swinton's Fifth Reader and Speaker. New York and Chicago: Ivison, Blakeman, Taylor and Co., 1883.

Building the Nation, by Charles Carleton Coffin. New York: Harper & Brothers, 1883.

BIBLIOGRAPHY

A History of the United States of America, by Horace E. Scudder. New York and Chicago: Sheldon & Co., 1884.

Art Year Book. Boston: New England Institute, 1884.

Illustrated Poems of Oliver Wendell Holmes. Boston: Houghton, Mifflin and Co., 1885.

Indian History for Young Folks, by Francis S. Drake. New York: Harper & Brothers, 1885.

A Larger History of the United States of America, by Thomas Wentworth Higginson. New York: Harper & Brothers, 1886.

City Ballads, by Will Carleton. New York: Harper & Brothers, 1886.

Swinton's Advanced Third Reader. New York and Chicago: Ivison, Blakeman, Taylor and Co., 1886.

The Inca Princess. Philadelphia and London: J. B. Lippincott Co., 1886.

A History of New York from the Beginning of the World to the End of the Dutch Dynasty, by Diedrich Knickerbocker [Washington Irving]. New York: Printed for the Grolier Club, 1886.

The Closing Scene, by Thomas Buchanan Read. Philadelphia: J. B. Lippincott Co., 1887.

A Story of the Golden Age, by James Baldwin. New York: Charles Scribner's Sons, 1887.

Storied Holidays, by Elbridge S. Brooks. Boston: D. Lothrop Company, 1887.

The Star Bearer, by Edmund Clarence Stedman. Boston: D. Lothrop Company, 1888.

Old Homestead Poems, by Wallace Bruce. New York: Harper & Brothers, 1888.

Harper's Fourth Reader. New York: Harper & Brothers, 1888.

Library of Universal Adventure by Sea and Land. Edited by William Dean Howells and Thomas Sargeant Perry. New York: Harper & Brothers, 1888.

Pen Drawing and Pen Draughtsmen, by Joseph Pennell. London and New York: Macmillan & Co., 1889.

Recollections of a Minister to France, by E. B. Washburne. New York: Charles Scribner's Sons, 1889.

Youma: The Story of a West Indian Slave, by Lafcadio Hearn. New York: Harper & Brothers, 1890.

In the Valley, by Harold Frederic. New York: Charles Scribner's Sons, 1890.

The Captain's Well, by John Greenleaf Whittier. New York: New York Ledger, 1890.

Flute and Violin, by James Lane Allen. New York: Harper & Brothers, 1891.

The True Story of the United States of America, by Elbridge S. Brooks. Boston: D. Lothrop Co., 1891.

Works of John Greenleaf Whittier: The Poetical Works, vol. 1. Boston and New York: Houghton, Mifflin and Co., 1892.

Works of John Greenleaf Whittier: The Poetical Works, vol. 2. Boston and New York: Houghton, Mifflin and Co., 1892.

The One Hoss Shay, by Oliver Wendell Holmes. Boston and New York: Houghton, Mifflin and Co., 1892.

American Illustrators, by F. Hopkinson Smith. New York: Charles Scribner's Sons, 1892.

Works of Oliver Wendell Holmes: The Poetical Works, vol. 12. Boston and New York: Houghton, Mifflin and Co., 1892.

Works of Oliver Wendell Holmes: The Poetical Works, vol. 13. Boston and New York: Houghton, Mifflin and Co., 1892.

A Tour Around New York, by John Flavel Mines. New York: Harper & Brothers, 1893.

Abraham Lincoln, by Charles Carleton Coffin. New York: Harper & Brothers, 1893.

Dorothy Q with *A Ballad of the Boston Tea Party* and *Grandmother's Story of Bunker Hill Battle,* by Oliver Wendell Holmes. Cambridge: Riverside Press, 1893.

A School History of the United States, by William Swinton. New York, Cincinnati, and Chicago: American Book Company, 1893.

Giles Corey, Yeoman, by Mary E. Wilkins. New York: Harper & Brothers, 1893.

In Old New York, by Thomas A. Janvier. New York: Harper & Brothers, 1894.

Transactions of the Grolier Club of the City of New York, Part 2. New York: The Grolier Club, 1894.

The Art of the American Wood Engraver, by Philip Gilbert Hamerton. New York: Charles Scribner's Sons, 1894.

First Lessons in Our Country's History, by William Swinton. New York, Cincinnati, and Chicago: American Book Company, 1894.

The Autocrat of the Breakfast-Table, by Oliver Wendell Holmes. Cambridge: Riverside Press, 1894.

Great Men's Sons, by Elbridge S. Brooks. New York: G. P. Putnam's Sons, 1895.

The True Story of George Washington, by Elbridge S. Brooks. Boston: Lothrop Publishing Co., 1895.

Stops of Various Quills, by W. D. Howells. New York: Harper & Brothers, 1895.

The Parasite, by A. Conan Doyle. New York: Harper & Brothers, 1895.

History of the United States, by E. Benjamin Andrews. New York: Charles Scribner's Sons, 1895.

Modern Illustration, by Joseph Pennell. London: George Bell & Sons, 1895.

Kidnapped, by Robert Louis Stevenson. New York: Charles Scribner's Sons, 1895.

The Merry Men and Other Tales and Fables and *The Strange Case of Dr. Jekyll and Mr. Hyde,* by Robert Louis Stevenson. New York: Charles Scribner's Sons, 1895.

David Balfour, by Robert Louis Stevenson. New York: Charles Scribner's Sons, 1895.

In Ole Virginia, by Thomas Nelson Page. New York: Charles Scribner's Sons, 1896.

The History of the Last Quarter-Century, by E. Benjamin Andrews. New York: Charles Scribner's Sons, 1896.

Writings of Harriet Beecher Stowe: Oldtown Folks and *Sam Lawson's Oldtown Fireside Stories*, vol. 9. Cambridge: Riverside Press, 1896.

Writings of Harriet Beecher Stowe: Oldtown Folks and *Sam Lawson's Oldtown Fireside Stories*, vol. 10. Cambridge: Riverside Press, 1896.

Hugh Wynne, Free Quaker, by S. Weir Mitchell, M. D. New York: The Century Co., 1897.

Works of Francis Parkman: LaSalle and the Discovery of the Great West, vol. 5. Boston: Little, Brown and Co., 1897.

Works of Francis Parkman: LaSalle and the Discovery of the Great West, vol. 6. Boston: Little, Brown and Co., 1897.

Works of Francis Parkman: A Half-Century of Conflict, vol. 11. Boston: Little, Brown and Co., 1897.

George Washington, by Woodrow Wilson. New York: Harper & Brothers, 1897.

The First Christmas Tree, by Henry Van Dyke. New York: Charles Scribner's Sons, 1897.

Quo Vadis, by Henryk Sienkiewicz. Translated by Jeremiah Curtin. Boston: Little, Brown and Co., 1897.

Works of Francis Parkman: Montcalm and Wolfe, vol. 15. Boston: Little, Brown and Co., 1898.

The Book of the Ocean, by Ernest Ingersoll. New York: The Century Co., 1898.

The Story of the Revolution, by Henry Cabot Lodge. New York: Charles Scribner's Sons, 1898.

Odysseus, the Hero of Ithaca, by Mary E. Burt. New York: Charles Scribner's Sons, 1898.

Silence and Other Stories, by Mary E. Wilkins. New York: Harper & Brothers, 1898.

Old Chester Tales, by Margaret DeLand. New York: Harper & Brothers, 1899.

Good for the Soul, by Margaret DeLand. New York: Harper & Brothers, 1899.

Janice Meredith, by Paul Leicester Ford. New York: Dodd, Mead & Co., 1899

To Have and to Hold, by Mary Johnston. Boston and New York: Houghton, Mifflin and Co., 1900.

The Man with the Hoe and Other Poems, by Edwin Markham. New York: Doubleday McClure Co., 1900.

Works of John Lothrop Motley: The Rise of the Dutch Republic, vol. 5. New York and London: Harper & Brothers, 1900.

Complete Writings of Nathaniel Hawthorne: A Wonder Book for Girls and Boys and *Tanglewood Tales*, vol. 13. Boston and New York: Houghton, Mifflin and Co., 1900.

Sir Christopher, by Maud Wilder Goodwin. Boston: Little, Brown, and Co., 1901.

The Odes & Epodes of Horace. Edited by Clement Lawrence Smith. Boston: Bibliophile Society, 1901.

Captain Ravenshaw, by Robert Neilson Stephens. Boston: L. C. Page & Co., 1901.

A History of American Art, by Sadakichi Hartmann. Boston: L. C. Page & Co., 1901.

Modern Pen Drawings, European and American. Edited by Charles Holme. London: The Studio, 1901.

Character Sketches of Romance, Fiction and the Drama. Edited by Marion Harland, vol. 2. New York: Selmar Hess, Publisher, 1901.

A History of the American People, by Woodrow Wilson. New York and London: Harper & Brothers, 1902.

The Struggle for a Continent. Edited by Pelham Edgar from the writings of Francis Parkman. Boston: Little, Brown & Co., 1902.

Harper's Encyclopaedia of United States History, based upon plan of Benson John Lossing. New York: Harper & Brothers, 1902.

The Blue Flower, by Henry Van Dyke. New York: Charles Scribner's Sons, 1902.

A Report of the truth concerning the last sea-fight of the Revenge, by Sir Walter Raleigh. Cambridge: Riverside Press, 1902.

The Bibliomania or Book Madness, by Thomas Frognall Dibdin. Boston: The Bibliophile Society, 1903.

Etchings, by W. H. W. Bicknell (after original paintings by Howard Pyle). Boston: The Bibliophile Society, 1903.

The Eclogues of Vergil. Translated by Baron Bowen. Boston: privately printed by Nathan Haskell Dole, 1904.

Poetical Works of James Russell Lowell, vol. 10. Cambridge: Riverside Press, 1904.

Poetical Works of James Russell Lowell, vol. 11. Cambridge: Riverside Press, 1904.

How to Draw, by Leon Barritt. New York: Harper & Brothers, 1904.

A History of the United States, by Wilbur F. Gordy. New York: Charles Scribner's Sons, 1904.

The Island of Enchantment, by Justus Miles Forman. New York: Harper & Brothers, 1905.

The Line of Love, by James Branch Cabell. New York: Harper & Brothers, 1905.

The One-Hoss Shay, by Oliver Wendell Holmes. Illustrated in color. Boston and New York: Houghton, Mifflin and Co., 1905.

BIBLIOGRAPHY

History of the United States, by Thomas Wentworth Higginson. New York: Harper & Brothers, 1905.
Snow Bound, by John Greenleaf Whittier. Boston: Houghton, Mifflin & Co., 1906.
The First Book of The Dofobs. Chicago: printed for the Society of the Dofobs, 1907.
Gallantry, an Eighteenth Century Dizain, by James Branch Cabell. New York: Harper & Brothers, 1907.
Dulcibel, by Henry Peterson. Philadelphia: John G. Winston Co., 1907.
Chivalry, by James Branch Cabell. New York: Harper & Brothers, 1909.
Lincoln and the Sleeping Sentinel, by L. E. Chittenden. New York: Harper & Brothers, 1909.
Harper's Book of Little Plays, by Margaret Sutton Briscoe, John Kendrick Bangs, Caroline A. Creevey,
    Margaret E. Sangster and others. New York: Harper & Brothers, 1910.
The Works of William Makepeace Thackeray, by Lady Ritchie. New York: Harper & Brothers, 1910.
On Hazardous Service, by William Gilmore Beymer. New York: Harper & Brothers, 1912.
The Buccaneers, by Don C. Seitz. New York: Harper & Brothers, 1912.
Catalog of Pictures by Howard Pyle, The Wilmington Society of the Fine Arts. Wilmington: 1912.
Founders of Our Country, by Fanny E. Coe. New York: American Book Company, 1912.
The Soul of Melicent, by James Branch Cabell. New York: Frederick A. Stokes, 1913.
Etchings, by W. H. W. Bicknell. Boston: The Bibliophile Society, 1913.
Theatrical Bookplates, by A. Winthrop Pope. Kansas City: H. Alfred Fowler, 1914.
Some American College Bookplates, by Harry Parker Ward. Columbus, Ohio: 1915.
Around Old Chester, by Margaret DeLand. New York: Harper & Brothers, 1915.
Stories of Later American History, by Wilbur F. Gordy. New York: Charles Scribner's Sons, 1915.
American Art by American Authors. New York: P. F. Collier & Son, 1915.
A History of the American People, by Woodrow Wilson. New York: Harper & Brothers, 1918.
Saint Joan of Arc, by Mark Twain. New York: Harper & Brothers, 1919.

MAGAZINE ARTICLES WRITTEN AND ILLUSTRATED (UNLESS NOTED) BY HOWARD PYLE

Note: Periodicals are listed alphabetically.

THE AUTOGRAPH
"Ye Pirate Bold." Jan.-Feb. 1912.

THE BOOK BUYER
"American Wood Engraving of the Present." No illustrations by Pyle. Dec. 1887.
"Holiday Books for Young People." No illustrations by Pyle. Dec. 1894.
"An Old Friend with a New Face." Illustrated by Albert Herter. Dec. 1897.

BOOK NEWS
"Fairy Tales." No illustrations. Dec. 1904.

THE CENTURY MAGAZINE
"A Set of Sketches." Dec. 1893.
"Hope and Memory." Nov. 1901.
"The Travels of the Soul." Dec. 1902.

COLLIER'S WEEKLY
"The Price of Blood." Dec. 17, 1898.

THE COSMOPOLITAN
"To the Soil of the Earth." June 1892.
"A Modern Magian." Aug. 1894.

FRANK LESLIE'S POPULAR MONTHLY
"The Romance." Illustration by Henry J. Peck. Aug. 1903.

HARPER'S BAZAR
"The Flight of the Swallow." Nov. 27, 1886.
A Modern Aladdin. May 23, 1891–July 11, 1891.

HARPER'S NEW MONTHLY MAGAZINE
"A Peninsular Canaan." May 1879–July 1879.
"The Last Revel in Printz Hall." Sept. 1879.

"Bartram and His Garden." Feb. 1880.
"Old-Time Life in a Quaker Town." Jan. 1881.
"Tilghman's Ride from Yorktown to Philadelphia." Nov. 1881.
"Autumn Sketches in the Pennsylvania Highlands." Dec. 1881.
"The Early Quakers in England and Pennsylvania." Nov. 1882.
"A May-Day Idyl of the Olden Time." May 1884.
"Stephen Wycherlie." June 1887.
"Buccaneers and Marooners of the Spanish Main." Aug. 1887 and Sept. 1887.
"On the Outposts—1780." Feb. 1888.
"A Peculiar People." Oct. 1889.
"Jamaica, New and Old." Jan. 1890 and Feb. 1890.
"Chapbook Heroes." June 1890.
"A Famous Chapbook Villain." July 1890.
"Among the Sand Hills." Sept. 1892.
"Retribution." April 1893.
"The Cocklane Ghost." Aug. 1893.
"A Soldier of Fortune." Dec. 1893.
"In Tenebras." No illustrations. Feb. 1894.
"By Land and Sea." Dec. 1895.
"Through Inland Waters." May 1896 and June 1896.
"The Romance of an Ambrotype." Dec. 1896.
"Love and Death." March 1897.
"A Puppet of Fate." Dec. 1899.
"The Angel and the Child." Illustrations by Sarah S. Stilwell. May 1900.

HARPER'S MONTHLY MAGAZINE
"North Folk Legends of the Sea." Jan. 1902.
"The Fate of a Treasure Town." Dec. 1905.
The Ruby of Kishmoor. Aug. 1907.
"The Mysterious Chest." Dec. 1908.
"The Salem Wolf." Dec. 1909.
"The Dead Finger." Sept. 1911.
"The Painted Pitcher." Nov. 1911.
"The Evil Eye." Feb. 1912.
"The Die of Fate." May 1912.
"Huntford's Fair Nihilist." June 1913.

HARPER'S ROUND TABLE
"Tom Chist and the Treasure Box." March 24, 1896.
"The Buccaneers." June 29, 1897.

HARPER'S WEEKLY
"St. Valentine." Feb. 24, 1877.
"The Robin's Vesper." June 7, 1879.
"The Milkmaid's Song." July 19, 1879.
"The Song of the Whippoorwill." June 12, 1880.
"Washington's Birthday." March 4, 1882.
"The Sea-Gull's Song." Nov. 25, 1882.
"Christmas Time Two Hundred Years Ago." Dec. 9, 1882.
"Ye True Story of Granny Greene of Salem Town." Dec. 1, 1883.
"The Strange Adventures of Carl Spich." Jan. 3, 1885.
"Squire Tripp's Old Arm Chair." Dec. 12, 1885.
The Rose of Paradise. June 11, 1887–July 30, 1887.
"The Great Snow Storm in Lewes Harbor." March 31, 1888.
"A Transferred Romance." April 9, 1892.
"A Thread Without a Knot." Sept. 3, 1892.
"Stamford's Soprano." June 24, 1893.
"Sailors and Landsmen—A Story of 1812." Dec. 15, 1894.
The Ghost of Captain Brand. Dec. 19, 1896.
"A Small School of Art." Illustrated with pictures by students of H. Pyle. July 17, 1897.
"A True History of the Devil at New Hope." Dec. 18, 1897.
"St. Valentine's Day." Illustrated by picture by Miss Mhoon. Feb. 19, 1898.

BIBLIOGRAPHY

HARPER'S YOUNG PEOPLE

"Nancy Hansen's Project." April 13, 1880.
"A Christmas Carol." Dec. 21, 1880.
"The Magic Wand." March 29, 1881.
"Jeremy Black's Fourth of July." July 5, 1881.
"Merry Adventures of Robin Hood." Jan. 9, 1883, and Jan. 16, 1883.
"Ye Romantic Adventures of Three Tailors." Aug. 28, 1883.
"Two Opinions." Oct. 9, 1883.
"A Victim to Science." Nov. 20, 1883.
"A Disappointment." Dec. 25, 1883.
"The Accident of Birth." Jan. 29, 1884.
"A Verse with a Moral but No Name." March 11, 1884.
"A Tale of a Tub." April 8, 1884.
"Pride in Distress." May 6, 1884.
"Moral Blindness." June 3, 1884.
"Serious Advice." June 24, 1884.
"Three Fortunes." July 15, 1884.
"Ye Song of Ye Gossips." Aug. 5, 1884.
"Venturesome Boldness." Aug. 26, 1884.
"Ye Song of Ye Foolish Old Woman." Sept. 16, 1884.
"Ye Song of Ye Rajah and Ye Fly." Oct. 21, 1884.
"Ye Two Wishes." Nov. 4, 1884.
"Superficial Culture." Nov. 18, 1884.
"Play and Earnest." Dec. 2, 1884.
"The Force of Need." Dec. 30, 1884.
"Ye Story of a Blue China Plate." Jan. 20, 1885.
"Ye Sad Story Concerning One Innocent Little Lamb and Four Wicked Wolves." Jan. 27, 1885.
"Overconfidence." Feb. 10, 1885.
"Hans Hecklemann's Luck." Feb. 24, 1885.
"Profession and Practice." March 10, 1885.
"How Dame Margery Twist Saw More Than Was Good for Her." March 17, 1885.
"A Newspaper Puff." March 24, 1885.
"Clever Peter and the Two Bottles." April 7, 1885.
"Fancy and Fact." April 21, 1885.
"Farmer Griggs's Boggart." April 28, 1885.
"The Skillful Huntsman." May 19, 1885.
"Claus and His Wonderful Staff." July 14, 1885.
"The Apple of Contentment." Aug. 18, 1885.
"The Bird in the Linden Tree." Sept. 15, 1885.
"The Swan Maiden." Oct. 13, 1885.
"How One Turned His Trouble to Some Account." Nov. 10, 1885.
"How Boots Befooled the King." Dec. 1, 1885.
"How Three Went Out into Ye Wide World." Dec. 29, 1885.
"The Princess Golden Hair and the Great Black Raven." Jan. 26, 1886.
"The Clever Student and the Master of Black Arts." Feb. 23, 1886.
"Peterkin and the Little Gray Hare." March 23, 1886.
"How the Good Gifts Were Used by Two." April 27, 1886.
"Mother Hildegarde." May 25, 1886.
"Master Jacob." June 29, 1886.
"How Three Little Pigs Had the Best of the Great Wicked Ogre." July 27, 1886.
"The Staff and the Fiddle." Aug. 31, 1886.
"The Simpleton and His Little Black Hen." Nov. 2, 1886.
"King Stork." Nov. 30, 1886.
"How the Princess's Pride Was Broken." Dec. 28, 1886.
"Dame Bridget's Prophecy." Jan. 4, 1887.
"How Two Went into Partnership." Jan. 25, 1887.
"Bearskin." March 1, 1887.
"Cousin Greylegs, Ye Great Red Fox and Grandfather Mole." March 22, 1887.
"Which Is Best?" April 19, 1887.
"The Best That Life Has to Give." May 17, 1887.

"The Water of Life." June 24, 1887.
"The Stepmother." Aug. 2, 1887.
"The White Bird." Sept. 6, 1887.
"One Good Turn Deserves Another." Oct. 11, 1887.
"The Three Fortunes." June 26, 1888.
"The Princess on the Glass Hill." July 24, 1888.
"That Which Is Done Never Dies." Aug. 27, 1889.
"Ill-Luck and the Fiddler." Oct. 15, 1889.
"Wisdom's Wages and Folly's Pay." Nov. 5, 1889.
"The Salt of Life." Jan. 7, 1890, and Jan. 14, 1890.
"Empty Bottles." Feb. 18, 1890.
"Where to Lay the Blame." March 25, 1890.
"Not a Pin to Choose." June 10, 1890, and June 17, 1890.
"Woman's Wit." July 29, 1890.
"Good Gifts and a Fool's Folly." Sept. 9, 1890.
"All Things Are as Fate Wills." Oct. 14, 1890.
"Much Shall Have More and Little Shall Have Less." Nov. 4, 1890.
"The Stool of Fortune." Dec. 23, 1890.
"The Fruit of Happiness." Jan. 13, 1891.
Men of Iron. Jan. 20, 1891–June 9, 1891.
"The Enchanted Island." Dec. 15, 1891, and Dec. 22, 1891.
"The Talisman of Solomon." March 29, 1892, and April 5, 1892.
"So It Is with Them All." Nov. 1, 1892.
"A Piece of Good Luck." April 10, 1894, and April 17, 1894.
"The Good of a Few Words." July 17, 1894, and July 24, 1894.

THE NORTHWESTERN MILLER

"Blueskin the Pirate." Dec. 1890.
"Captain Scarfield." Dec. 1900.

ST. NICHOLAS

"The Crafty Fox." Feb. 1877.
"The Fox and the Tablet." April 1877.
"Hans Gottenlieb, the Fiddler." April 1877.
"Pictorial Puzzle." July 1877.
"Drummer Fritz and His Exploits." Sept. 1877.
"The Stork and the Crane." Jan. 1878.
"Wise Catherine and the Kaboutermanneken." April 1878.
"The Fox, the Monkey, and the Pig." Sept. 1878.
"The Gourd and the Oak." May 1879.
"Robin Goodfellow and His Friend Bluetree." June 1879.
"Fables." Dec. 1879.
"A Fable from Deacon Green." Feb. 1881.
"The Soldiering of Beniah Stidham." Dec. 1892.
Jack Ballister's Fortunes. April 1894–Sept. 1895.
The Story of King Arthur and His Knights. Nov. 1902–Oct. 1903.

SCRIBNER'S MAGAZINE

"A Pastoral Without Words." Dec. 1890.
"Beneath the Mask." Aug. 1893.
"A Life for a Life." Jan. 1900.

SCRIBNER'S MONTHLY

"The Magic Pill." July 1876.
"Chincoteague, the Island of Ponies." April 1877.
"Among the Thousand Islands." April 1878.

WIDE AWAKE

"Lambkin: Was He a Hero or a Prig?" Dec. 1889

WOMAN'S HOME COMPANION

"When I Was a Little Boy." April 1912.

BIBLIOGRAPHY

MAGAZINE ILLUSTRATIONS, NOT ACCOMPANIED BY TEXT, BY HOWARD PYLE

Note: Periodicals are listed alphabetically.

THE CENTURY MAGAZINE
"Three Pictures of Don Quixote." Nov. 1901, p. 41.

CHICAGO TRIBUNE
"Christmas Morn." Dec. 20, 1903. Issued as supplement.

COLLIER'S WEEKLY
"The Flying Dutchman." Dec. 8, 1900.
"How Are We Going to Vote This Year?" Nov. 5, 1904.
"The Burning Ship." Dec. 10, 1904.
"The Minute Man." Feb. 17, 1906.
"The Nation Makers." June 2, 1906.

HARPER'S BAZAR
"The Rejection." Dec. 9, 1882, p. 777.
"A Quaker Wedding." Dec. 12, 1885, p. 802.

HARPER'S NEW MONTHLY MAGAZINE
"A Glimpse of an Old Dutch Town." March 1881, p. 524.
"Spring Blossoms." May 1885, p. 825.
Cover design. Dec. 1896.

HARPER'S MONTHLY MAGAZINE
"Pictures from Thackeray: Beatrix and Esmond." Aug. 1906, p. 327.
"Pictures from Thackeray: Becky Sharp and Lord Steyne." Dec. 1906, p. 3.
"Pictures from Thackeray: Pendennis." March 1907, p. 497.
"Pictures from Thackeray: The Newcomes." June 1908, p. 3.
"When All the World Was Young." Aug. 1909, p. 327.
"Pictures from Thackeray: The Virginians." July 1911, p. 165.

HARPER'S WEEKLY
"Queen of the May: Unpropitious Skies." May 12, 1877, p. 365.
" 'One of Those City Fellows.' " Sept. 8, 1877, p. 701.
"Entangled." Drawn by E. A. Abbey from sketch by H. Pyle. Jan. 19, 1878, p. 52.
" 'Wreck in the Offing!' " March 9, 1878, p. 202.
"Lost in the Snow." March 16, 1878, p. 212.
"A Matrimonial Difficulty: Legal Intervention." April 6, 1878, p. 272.
"A Love Affair of the Olden Time: Consulting the Wise Woman." July 12, 1879, p. 509.
"The Dance of the Veterans." Drawn from a sketch by Louis Joutel. July 26, 1879, p. 592.
"Breaking the News." Aug. 16, 1879, p. 649.
"The Outcast's Return." Jan. 10, 1880, p. 24.
"The Circus: An Interrupted Performance." July 31, 1880, p. 488.
"Women at the Polls in New Jersey in the Good Old Times." Nov. 13, 1880, p. 724.
"Christmas Morning in Old New York." Dec. 25, 1880, p. 828.
"New Year's Day Seventy Years Ago: The Last Evening Caller." Jan. 8, 1881, p. 24.
"St. Valentine's Day in the Morning." Feb. 26, 1881, p. 136.
"A Presidential Progress: Politics in the Olden Times." March 12, 1881, p. 164.
"Shad-Fishing on the Lower Delaware at Night: The Last Haul before Dawn." April 30, 1881, p. 284.
"The Surrender of Cornwallis." Oct. 22, 1881, p. 705.
"A Love Feast Among the Dunkers." March 17, 1883, p. 169.
"The Mysterious Guest." March 24, 1883, p. 185.
"The First Visit of William Penn to America." March 31, 1883, p. 199.
" 'Autumn Leaves.' " Nov. 24, 1883, p. 740.
"Washington Taking Leave of His Officers." Dec. 1, 1883, p. 767.
"Stopping the Christmas Stage." Dec. 10, 1892, p. 1188.

"The Pirates' Christmas." Dec. 16, 1893, p. 1189.
"An Unwelcome Toast." Dec. 14, 1895, p. 1175.
"Small Game Better than None." Dec. 17, 1898, p. 1217.
"How the Buccaneers Kept Christmas." Dec. 16, 1899, p. 20.
Tribute by Howard Pyle on Henry Mills Alden's 70th Birthday. Dec. 15, 1906, p. 1809.
The Landing of Carteret in New Jersey. Mural painting. Feb. 9, 1907, p. 203.

THE LADIES' HOME JOURNAL

Cover design. May 1897.

McCLURE'S MAGAZINE

Cover design. Jan. 1900.

SCRIBNER'S MAGAZINE

"Some Thanksgiving-Time Fancies." Nov. 1895, p. 535.
"Esmond and the Prince." March 1897, p. 267.

SCRIBNER'S MONTHLY

"Family Cares." April 1877, p. 833.
"Bliss." May 1877, p. 127.
"In the Park." July 1877, p. 415.
"A Quotation from *King Lear*." July 1877, p. 416.

TRUTH (NEW YORK)

Stained Glass Window, Colonial Club, New York. March 1899, p. 69.

MAGAZINE WRITINGS, BY OTHER AUTHORS, WITH ILLUSTRATIONS BY HOWARD PYLE

Note: Periodicals are listed alphabetically.

THE CENTURY MAGAZINE

"The Chevalier de Resseguier," by Thomas Bailey Aldrich. May 1893.
"Paul Jones," by Molly E. Seawell. April 1895.
"A Business Transaction," by James Jeffrey Roche. June 1895.
"The *Constitution*'s Last Fight," by James Jeffrey Roche, Sept. 1895.
"Maid Marian's Song," by Ednah Proctor Clarke. Nov. 1895.
Hugh Wynne, Free Quaker, by S. Weir Mitchell. Nov. 1896–Oct. 1897.
"The Battle of Copenhagen," by A. T. Mahan. Feb. 1897.
"Nelson at Trafalgar," by A. T. Mahan. March 1897.

COLLIER'S WEEKLY

"Poisoned Ice," by "Q" (A. T. Quiller-Couch). Dec. 10, 1898.
"Dead Men Tell No Tales," by Morgan Robertson. Dec. 17, 1899.
"Columbia Speaks," by Owen Wister. Jan. 12, 1901.
"A Sahib's War," by Rudyard Kipling. Dec. 7, 1901.
"Song of Peace," by Edwin Markham. June 14, 1902.
" 'Why Seek Ye the Living Among the Dead?' " by John Finley. April 15, 1905.

EVERYBODY'S MAGAZINE

"The First Self-Made American," by Adele Marie Shaw. June 1902.
"The Madonna of the Blackbird," by Arthur Train. Jan. 1913.

HARPER'S BAZAR

"Daisies," by Margaret E. Sangster. May 9, 1885.
"The First Thanksgiving," by Theron Brown. Dec. 5, 1891.

HARPER'S NEW MONTHLY MAGAZINE

"The Battle of Monmouth Court-House," by Benson J. Lossing. June 1878.
"Daddy Will," by Charles D. Deshler. July 1878.
"Owlet," by John Esten Cooke. July 1878.
"Manuel Menendez," by Charles Carroll. Aug. 1878.

"Ab'm: A Glimpse of Modern Dixie," by Charles D. Deshler. Sept. 1878.

"The Owl-Critic," by James T. Fields. July 1879.

"The First Mrs. Petersham," by Harriet Prescott Spofford. Aug. 1879.

"The Old National Pike," by W. H. Rideing. Nov. 1879.

"Sea-Drift from a New England Port," by Lizzie W. Champney. Dec. 1879.

"Some Pennsylvania Nooks," by Ella Rodman Church. April 1880.

"Old Catskill," by Henry Brace. May 1880.

" 'Salgama Condita,' " by Lizzie W. Champney. May 1880.

"Captain Nathan Hale," by Henry P. Johnson. June 1880.

"The Driftwood Fire," Harriet Prescott Spofford. Nov. 1880.

"Patient Mercy Jones," by James T. Fields. Jan. 1881.

"Old New York Coffee-Houses," by John Austin Stevens. March 1882.

"The Old English Seamen," by Thomas Wentworth Higginson. Jan. 1883.

"The French Voyageurs," by Thomas Wentworth Higginson. March 1883.

"An English Nation," by Thomas Wentworth Higginson. April 1883.

"The Hundred Years' War," by Thomas Wentworth Higginson. June 1883.

"The Second Generation of Englishmen in America," by Thomas Wentworth Higginson. July 1883.

"The British Yoke," by Thomas Wentworth Higginson. Aug. 1883.

"Last Days of Washington's Army at Newburgh," by J. T. Headley. Oct. 1883.

"The Dawning of Independence," by Thomas Wentworth Higginson. Oct. 1883.

"Evacuation of New York by the British, 1783," by Henry P. Johnson. Nov. 1883.

"Christmas," by George William Curtis. Dec. 1883.

"The Birth of a Nation," by Thomas Wentworth Higginson. Jan. 1884.

"Our Country's Cradle," by Thomas Wentworth Higginson. Feb. 1884.

"The Second War for Independence," by Thomas Wentworth Higginson. April 1884.

"King's College," by John McMullen. Oct. 1884.

"Toinette," by John Esten Cooke. Dec. 1884.

"Witchcraft," by Edmund C. Stedman. Dec. 1884.

"Knoxville in the Olden Time," by Edmund Kirke. June 1885.

"An Indian Journey," by Lucy C. Lillie. Nov. 1885.

"Esther Feverel," by Brander Mathews. Dec. 1885.

"The City of Cleveland," by Edmund Kirke. March 1886.

"The Gunpowder for Bunker Hill," by Ballard Smith. July 1886.

"The City of the Strait," by Edmund Kirke. Aug. 1886.

"The Southern Gateway to the Alleghanies," by Edmund Kirke. April 1887.

"The Kentucky Pioneers," by John Mason Brown. June 1887.

"Aaron Burr's Wooing," by Edmund C. Stedman. Oct. 1887.

"Canadian Voyageurs on the Saguenay," by C. H. Farnham. March 1888.

"Morgan," by Edmund C. Stedman. Dec. 1888.

"Washington's Inauguration," by John Bach McMaster. April 1889.

"Youma," by Lafcadio Hearn. Jan. and Feb. 1890.

"Old New York Taverns," by John Austin Stevens. May 1890.

"The Quaker Lady," by S. Weir Mitchell. Nov. 1890.

"Flute and Violin," by James Lane Allen. Dec. 1890.

"A Maid's Choice," by W. W. Gilchrist. Dec. 1891.

"The Little Maid at the Door," by Mary E. Wilkins. Feb. 1892.

"How the Declaration Was Received in the Old Thirteen," by Chas. D. Deshler. July 1892.

"Two Moods," by Thomas B. Aldrich. July 1892.

"Giles Corey, Yeoman," by Mary E. Wilkins. Dec. 1892.

"Monochromes," by W. D. Howells. March 1893.

"The Evolution of New York," by Thomas A. Janvier. May and June 1893.

"The Sea Robbers of New York," by Thomas A. Janvier. Nov. 1894.

"Stops of Various Quills," by Wm. D. Howells. Dec. 1894.

"New York Slave Traders," by Thomas A. Janvier. Jan. 1895.

"New York Colonial Privateers," by Thomas A. Janvier. Feb. 1895.

"Society," by W. D. Howells. March 1895.

"Pebbles," by W. D. Howells. Sept. 1895.

"In Washington's Day," by Woodrow Wilson. Jan. 1896.

"Colonel Washington," by Woodrow Wilson. March 1896.

"At Home in Virginia," by Woodrow Wilson. May 1896.

"General Washington," by Woodrow Wilson. July 1896.

"First in Peace," by Woodrow Wilson. Sept. 1896.

"The First President of the United States," by Woodrow Wilson. Nov. 1896.

"The Assembly Ball," by Sarah Beaumont Kennedy. Feb. 1897.

"Washington and the French Craze of '93," by John Bach McMaster. April 1897.

Old Chester Tales, by Margaret DeLand. April 1898–Dec. 1898.

"Old Captain," by Myles Hemenway. Dec. 1898.

"The Body to the Soul," by Ellen M. Gates. Aug. 1899.

"A Prelude," by Bliss Carmen. April 1900.

"The Yellow of the Leaf," by Bliss Carmen. Nov. 1900.

"The Pilgrimage of Truth," by Erik Bogh. Dec. 1900.

HARPER'S MONTHLY MAGAZINE

"Colonies and Nation," by Woodrow Wilson. Jan. 1901–June 1901, Aug. 1901, Oct. 1901–Dec. 1901.

"A Dream of Young Summer," by Edith M. Thomas. June 1901.

"King Custom," by Maud S. Rawson. Oct. 1901.

"Margaret of Cortona," by Edith Wharton. Nov. 1901.

"The Sea Man," by Josephine D. Daskam. Dec. 1901.

"Cap'n Goldsack," by William Sharp. July 1902.

"The Voice," by Margaret DeLand. Sept. 1902.

"The True Captain Kidd," by John D. Champlin, Jr. Dec. 1902.

"The Chanty Man," by E. Phelps Whitmarsh. Jan. 1903.

"The Castle of Content," by James Branch Cabell. Aug. 1903.

"Peire Vidal, Troubadour," by Olivia H. Dunbar. Dec. 1903.

"The Stairway of Honor," by Maud Stepney Rawson. Jan. 1904.

"The Story of Adhelmar," by James Branch Cabell. April 1904.

"The Charming of Estercel," by Grace Rhys. June 1904.

"The Sword of Ahab," by James Edmund Dunning. Aug. 1904.

"The Maid of Landévennec," by Justus Miles Forman. Sept. 1904.

"In Necessity's Mortar," by James Branch Cabell. Oct. 1904.

"Non-Combatants," by Robert W. Chambers. Nov. 1904.

"Saint Joan of Arc," by Mark Twain. Dec. 1904.

"The Gold," by Mary E. Wilkins Freeman. Dec. 1904.

"Melicent," by Warwick Deeping. Jan. 1905.

"The Great La Salle," by Henry Loomis Nelson. Feb. 1905.

"Special Messenger," by Robert W. Chambers. Feb. 1905.

"Eden Gates," by Justus Miles Forman. March 1905.

" 'An Amazing Belief,' " by Mrs. Henry Dudeney. April 1905.

"Carlotta," by Justus Miles Forman. May 1905.

"Old Immortality," by Alice Brown. May 1905.

"The Fox Brush," by James Branch Cabell. Aug. 1905.

"The Island of Enchantment," by Justus Miles Forman. Sept. and Oct. 1905.

"The Sestina," by James Branch Cabell. Jan. 1906.

"A Sense of Scarlet," by Mrs. Henry Dudeney. Feb. 1907.

"In the Second April," by James Branch Cabell. April and May, 1907.

"The Noble Family of Beaupertuys," by Stephen F. Whitman. July 1907.

"Lincoln's Last Day," by William H. Crook. Sept. 1907.

"The Cruise of the Caribbee," by Thomas V. Briggs. Dec. 1907.

"The Rat-Trap," by James Branch Cabell. Dec. 1907.

"A Sign from Heaven," by Basil King. Jan. 1908.

"Dona Victoria," by Perceval Gibbon. Feb. 1908.

"The Choices," by James Branch Cabell. March 1908.

"A Princess of Kent," by Marjorie Bowen. April 1908.

"The Scabbard," by James Branch Cabell. May 1908.

"The Minstrel," by Norman Duncan. June 1908.

"Edric and Sylvaine," by Brian Hooker. Aug. 1908.

"Manasseh," by Perceval Gibbon. Sept. 1908.

"Pennsylvania's Defiance of the United States," by Hampton L. Carson. Oct. 1908.

"The Ultimate Master," by James Branch Cabell. Nov. 1908.

"A Child at the Siege of Vicksburg," by William W. Lord, Jr. Dec. 1908.

BIBLIOGRAPHY

"Lola," by Perceval Gibbon. Jan. 1909.
"The Apple of Venus," by Marjorie Bowen. Feb. 1909.
"The Grain Ship," by Morgan Robertson. March 1909.
"The Satraps," by James Branch Cabell. April 1909.
"The Garden of Eden," by Justus M. Forman. May 1909.
"Rowand," by William Gilmore Beymer. June 1909.
"Williams, C. S. A.," by William Gilmore Beymer. Sept. 1909.
"The Castle on the Dunes," by Josephine Daskam Bacon. Sept. 1909.
"The Second Chance," by James Branch Cabell. Oct. 1909.
"Landegon," by William Gilmore Beymer. Nov. 1909.
"Young," by William Gilmore Beymer. Dec. 1909.
"Swanhild," by Brian Hooker. Jan. 1910.
"The Wrecker," by James B. Connolly. March 1910.
"The Initial Letter," by Marjorie Bowen. April 1910.
"Holy Mr. Herbert," by Marjorie Bowen. May 1910.
"The Black Night," by James Hopper. June 1910.
"Page, A. B.," by Perceval Gibbon. July 1910.
"Ysobel de Corveaux," by Brian Hooker. Aug. 1910.
"The Buccaneers," by Don C. Seitz. Jan. 1911.
"General Lee as I Knew Him," by A. R. H. Ransom. Feb. 1911.
"Man and Dog," by Laurence Housman. March 1911.
"The Soul of Mervisaunt," by James Branch Cabell. April 1911.
"Miss Van Lew," by William Gilmore Beymer. June 1911.
"Sea Tolls," by Robert Welles Ritchie. Sept. 1911.
"The Crime in Jedidiah Peeble's House," by Muriel Campbell Dyar. March 1912.

HARPER'S WEEKLY
"The First Public Reading of the Declaration of Independence," by Eugene Lawrence. July 10, 1880.
"The Christmas Tree," by Will Carleton. Dec. 24, 1881.
Exchange No Robbery, by M. Betham-Edwards. Feb. 18, 1882–March 25, 1882.
"A Modern Puritan," by Mrs. Zadel B. Gustafson. April 15, 1882.
"The Dead Stowaway," by Will Carleton. June 3, 1882.
"A Valentine to Phillis," by unknown author. Feb. 17, 1883.
"The Evacuation 1783," by Eugene Lawrence. Nov. 24, 1883.
"The Ant and the Grasshopper," from *Aesop's Fables*. Dec. 29, 1883.
"Mr. Merridew's Goldpiece," by Virginia W. Johnson. Dec. 15, 1884.
"Markham's Bays," by Kate Putnam Osgood. Feb. 28, 1885.
"The Two Cornets of Monmouth," by A. E. Watrous. Sept. 12, 1891.
The Parasite, by A. Conan Doyle. Nov. 10, 1894–Dec. 1, 1894.
"The King's Jewel," by James Edmund Dunning. Dec. 10, 1904.

HARPER'S YOUNG PEOPLE
Old Times in the Colonies, by Charles Carleton Coffin. Aug. 3, 1880; Aug. 17, 1880; Sept. 21, 1880;
    Oct. 5, 1880; Oct. 19, 1880.
The Story of the American Navy, by Benson J. Lossing. July 13, 1880; July 20, 1880; Aug. 3, 1880.
"Hours with the Octogenarians," by Benson J. Lossing. May 10, 1881.
"A Perfect Christmas," by William O. Stoddard. Dec. 20, 1881.
"Willie's Christmas," by Helen S. Conant. Dec. 12, 1882.
"The Revolt of the Holidays," by E. I. Stevenson. Dec. 18, 1883.
"Facing a Giant," by David Ker. March 11, 1884.
The Accommodating Circumstance, by Frank R. Stockton. July 15, 1884; July 22, 1884; July 29, 1884.
"The Sword of Hildebrand," by Sherwood Ryse. Dec. 16, 1884.
"The Book of Balbo," by Sherwood Ryse. Nov. 3, 1885.
"Hugo Grotius and His Book Chest," by Mrs. M. C. Pyle. March 15, 1887.

THE LADIES' HOME JOURNAL
"The Werewolf," by Eugene Field. March 1896.
"Love at Valley Forge," by Sarah King Wiley. Dec. 1896.
"The Last Years of Washington's Life," by William Perrine. Oct. 1899.

BIBLIOGRAPHY

McCLURE'S MAGAZINE
"The Man for the Hour," by James Barnes. Dec. 1899.
"At the Turn of the Glass," by Martha McCulloch Williams. Dec. 1900.
"The Chase of the Tide," by Norman Duncan. Aug. 1901.
"The Second-Class Passenger," by Perceval Gibbon. Oct. 1906.
"The Hanging of Mary Dyer," by Basil King. Nov. 1906.

THE NEW YORK LEDGER
"The Captain's Well," by John Greenleaf Whittier. Jan. 11, 1890 Supplement.

OUR CONTINENT
Under Green Apple Boughs, by Helen Campbell. Feb. 15, 1882–March 22, 1882.

ST. NICHOLAS
"How Kitty Was Lost in a Turkish Bazaar," by Sarah Keables Hunt. April 1878.
"The Story of May-Day," by Olive Thorne. May 1878.
"How Willy-Wolly Went A-Fishing," by S. C. Stone. June 1878.
"About Violins," by M. D. Ruff. Feb. 1879.
"The Origin of the Jumping-Jack," by I. L. Beman. Feb. 1879.
"How a Comet Struck the Earth," by Edward C. Kemble. June 1879.
"Gretelein and Her Queer Stove," by Rosamund Dale Owen. Sept. 1879.
Phaeton Rogers, by Rossiter Johnson. Jan. 1881 and March 1881.

SCRIBNER'S MAGAZINE
"The Siege and Commune of Paris," by E. B. Washburne. Jan. 1887 and Feb. 1887.
"Tarpeia," by Louise Imogen Guiney. Dec. 1887.
In the Valley, by Harold Frederic. Sept. 1889–July 1890.
"The Pardon of Ste. Anne d'Auray," by William P. Northrup. Dec. 1890.
"The Oak of Geismar," by Henry Van Dyke. Dec. 1891.
"Peter Rugg Ye Bostonian," by Louise Imogen Guiney. Dec. 1891.
"An Unpublished Autograph Narrative by Washington," by Henry C. Pickering. May 1893.
"January and May," by W. W. Gilchrist. Dec. 1893.
"McAndrew's Hymn," by Rudyard Kipling. Dec. 1894.
"A Forgotten Tale," by A. Conan Doyle. Jan. 1895.
"A History of the Last Quarter Century," by E. Benjamin Andrews. May 1895, July 1895, Oct. 1895.
"Undergraduate Life at Harvard," by Edward S. Martin. May 1897.
"The Birds of Cirencester," by Bret Harte. Jan. 1898.
The Story of the Revolution, by Henry Cabot Lodge. Jan. 1898–Dec. 1898.
"The United States Army," by Francis V. Greene. Sept. 1901 and Oct. 1901.
"A Story of Three States," by Alfred Mathews. April 1902 and May 1902.
"Sinbad on Burrator," by A. T. Quiller-Couch. Aug. 1902.
"The Story of a Great-Grandfather," by George Hibbard. Jan. 1903.
"The Natural Born Preacher," by Nelson Lloyd. April 1903.

SCRIBNER'S MONTHLY
"Papa Hoorn's Tulip," by R. V. C. Meyers. Jan. 1877.
"The Story of Lesken," by Anna Eichberg. June 1878.

WIDE AWAKE
"A Cycle of Children," by Elbridge S. Brooks. Dec. 1885–Oct. 1886.
"George Washington's Boyhood," by William F. Crane. July 1887.
"The Star Bearer," by Edmund Clarence Stedman. Dec. 1887.
"Inge, the Boy-King," by H. H. Boyesen. Dec. 1888.

INDEX

Italic page numbers indicate illustrations.
Except where noted, illustrations were done by Howard Pyle.

ST. LOUIS COMM. COL
AT FLORISSANT VALLEY

INVENTORY 1983